My Yellowstone Years

To the Don Murphy family,
from the J.B. Murphys,
Christmas 1997.
Let's go hiking in Yellowstone soon!

About
The
Author

DONALD C. STEWART is a Professor of English at Kansas State University where he has taught advanced courses in English literature and composition since 1968. He has written three textbooks, one a collaboration with his wife, Pat, and Paul T. Bryant of Redford University in Virginia; contributed chapters to seven scholarly books; and published several dozen articles, short stories, and nonfiction pieces. His fiction has appeared in *Four Quarters* and the *Kansas Quarterly*. His nonfiction, on such topics as fly fishing, chamber music (he is an accomplished violinist), misconceptions about Kansas, college sports, community planning, contemporary religion, and Yellowstone Park has appeared in *Fly Fisherman, The Christian Science Monitor, Parks and Recreation, Planning, Church Educator*, and *Montana: The Magazine of Western History*.

During his professional career, Professor Stewart has served as a member of the Editorial Board and the Executive Committee of the National Council of Teachers of English, as President of the Kansas Association of Teachers of English, and as Chair (President) of the Conference on College Composition and Communication. He has also been a frequent speaker at professional meetings and conventions. In 1981 the Kansas State University College of Arts and Sciences named him its Outstanding Undergraduate Teacher for that year.

As the author says in the Introduction to *My Yellowstone Years*, however, the defining experience of his life, other than his marriage and the birth of his daughters, Ellen and Mary, was a stretch of thirteen Summers, 1951–1963, during which he worked in Yellowstone Park as a dishwasher, seasonal park ranger and ranger-naturalist. When he began this experience, he was an undergraduate at the University of Kansas. By the time he concluded it, he was a husband, father, and Assistant Professor of English at the University of Illinois. "All the years of my early maturity," Stewart says, "had been profoundly influenced by Summers in America's first national park."

My Yellowstone Years is not, however, Donald Stewart's story alone. It is the story of generations of young Americans who experienced this unique rite of passage working in the great national parks of western America.

MY
YELLOWSTONE
YEARS

DONALD C. STEWART

Library of Congress Catalog Card Number 88–051698
ISBN: 0–923568–01–8

Photography by Donald and Pat Stewart
unless otherwise indicated

PUBLISHED BY

Wilderness Adventure Books
320 Garden Lane
Box 968
Fowlerville, Michigan 48836

Manufactured in the United States of America

For the young people with whom I worked in the Old Faithful Cafeteria during the summer of 1951; for my good friends and colleagues in the National Park Service from 1952-63; for the members of Jacobi's Campfire; but especially, for Pat.

When I was a child, I spake as a child,
I understood as a child, I thought as a child:
but when I became a man, I put away childish things.

I CORINTHIANS, 13:11

The woods are lovely, dark, and deep,
But I have promises to keep,
And miles to go before I sleep
And miles to go before I sleep

ROBERT FROST

ABILITY TO SEE the cultural value of wilderness boils down, in the last analysis, to a question of intellectual humility. The shallow-minded modern who has lost his rootage in the land assumes that he has already discovered what is important; it is such who prate of empires, political or economic, that will last a thousand years. It is only the scholar who appreciates that all history consists of successive excursions from a single starting-point, to which man returns again and again to organize yet another search for a durable scale of values. It is only the scholar who understands why the raw wilderness gives definition and meaning to the human enterprise.

ALDO LEOPOLD

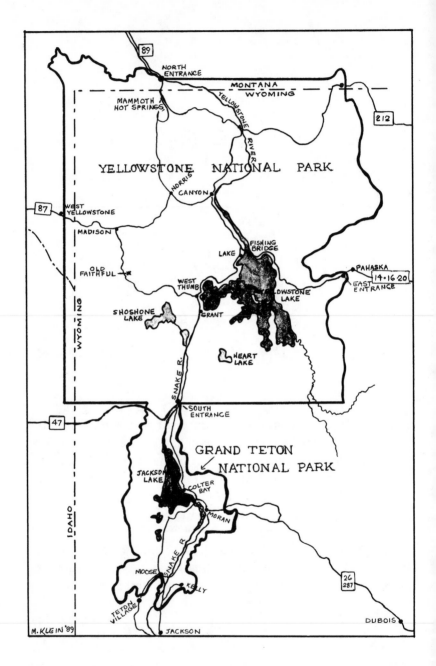

YELLOWSTONE AND GRAND TETON NATIONAL PARKS

Contents

Introduction

OTHER THAN my marriage to Pat and the birth of our children, the most important thing that ever happened to me were thirteen summers spent in Yellowstone National Park. They happened quite accidentally—even the string of thirteen was a matter of luck—but they remain today a collective event to which I return continually for strength and sanity in a world which seems to be losing both. They were my "going West," my "Oregon Trail," my reliving of the national drama of the nineteenth century frontier, the trip to the promised land.

The first year I went to Yellowstone I was just a few weeks short of twenty-one, poised emotionally for that rite of passage which finally transforms the dependent child into the independent adult. I wanted that experience badly, and by the time I returned that Fall, I had made a quantum leap in personal independence. By the time I returned from Yellowstone for the last time, in the Fall of 1963, I was a husband, father, and college professor. All the years of my early maturity had been profoundly influenced by summers in America's first national park.

MY YELLOWSTONE YEARS

That first year I was consumed with a desire to encounter the raw wilderness, a huge, unfenced, unfarmed, and largely undomesticated area. In 1951 it was not quite as much a wilderness as my romantic imagination projected, but it was a place in which "civilization" existed in islands, and outside them, even occasionally penetrating them, were real wild animals, the rightful residents of this territory. One quickly became aware of them, all of the time. The experience sharpened one's senses in ways that city life never could have.

The Yellowstone experience also gave me a sustained opportunity to get an early perspective on my life. It was all too easy, while going to college and earning a succession of degrees, to become preoccupied with assignments, term papers, examinations, requirements for a major, and learning the rules for the incessant and necessary politicking that goes with "getting ahead" in one's profession. While you were actually on the job, that kind of trivia could overwhelm you in Yellowstone, too, but relief was just ten minutes walking time away. The quiet trails of the park, in the words of the psalmist, restored my soul. Each year I went out to Yellowstone, physically and mentally tired. Each year I returned, physically and spiritually renewed.

This, then, is the story of one man's experience in Yellowstone. But it is also the story of many generations of Americans who had preceded me and who have followed me, either working for the park's concessionaires or for the National Park Service. No one, to my knowledge, has yet told the story of Yellowstone's summer "savages" and ninety day wonders. But it is a story worth telling, a slice of Americana that was very special in the lives of all who experienced it.

Part I

1

Preparations And
The First Trip Out

IN JANUARY of 1951 I went to
the Dean of Men's Office at the University of Kansas and asked
about job notices for summer work in the mountains. Behind me
lay five summers of work on the playgrounds of Kansas City,
Kansas. Five summers of oppressive heat and humidity. Five
summers of coaching increasingly intractable small boys to play
softball and of herding them, on busses, from my playground to
playgrounds far removed from ours in neighborhoods I would
never have walked comfortably in during the night. Five summers
of putting up with a Director of Recreation who was incompe-
tent, not funny (although he thought he was), and vindictive
toward me for reasons which had nothing to do with my work but
a lot to do with the political opposition which opposed his ap-
pointment. Five summers of umpiring kid baseball games during
which fanatical parents and egomaniacal coaches heaped upon
me and all of the other young umpires in the program the abuse
generated by their accumulated athletic and personal frustrations. Never again, I had said to myself at the beginning of the

previous summer, never again will I do this work. Next summer, some way, somehow, I will be in the mountains.

The Dean's secretary fished around in the materials she had and came up with a one-page announcement by the Yellowstone Park Company. They were looking for dishwashers, lodge porters, cooks' helpers, waitresses—people to do a whole range of grubby service jobs that have to be done in tourist areas during the season. But Yellowstone Park! I had been there once and although the hydrogen sulphide odor at Norris had made me sick to my stomach, I also remembered Old Faithful and the Canyon. I wasn't sure how much other scenery was there, but Yellowstone was up in the mountains, and that was where I wanted to be in the summer of 1951, so I studied that sheet carefully and opted for a dishwashing job. My logic in choosing that job at that distance wasn't bad, but it was a stupid choice. I saw only that dishwashers got $100 a month plus room and board whereas the lodge porters got only $70. Any idiot would have guessed that the lodge porters, who directed tourists to their cabins, would clean up in tips, especially if they were good, but I didn't know that and was too dumb to figure it out. A Minnesotan I met the second year out there shifted from dishwashing to lodge portering, worked double shifts when some of his co-workers wanted an extra holiday, and ended up making as much as $500 some months. In the early 1950s, $500 a month for three months just about put you through one year of school. That young man literally paid for his undergraduate education at the University of Minnesota doing that kind of work.

I didn't know all of that. I just filled out the application, indicating that I would wash dishes, and sent it off. My mother would not be enthusiastic about this venture, I knew, because she liked having my brother, sister, and me home in the summers, and my sister was getting married in 1951, but I wanted off the playground, out of Kansas City, and into the mountains then, and nothing else mattered a lot. I did consider not telling my parents but decided that would be foolish and so let them know I had applied. Mother didn't pay much attention to what I said. Apparently, she thought there was little likelihood that I would get such a job, and there was no point in telling me that and spoiling my hopes for awhile.

Then, one evening in early spring, I got a call from Mother. She didn't sound very happy. What was the matter, I inquired? Well, it seemed that I had got a contract in the mail. The Yellowstone Park Company was inviting me to come to Yellowstone to wash dishes. The contract specified that if I came and stayed as long as I said I would, which was a bit past Labor Day, they would pay my expenses both for the trip out and the trip home. Goodbye playground! Goodbye hot summer! Hello mountains! I was ecstatic and could hardly restrain my enthusiasm. But Mother was not happy at all.

"Mom? What's the matter?" I could sense impending tears.

"You'll miss your sister's wedding and your twenty-first birthday and, and. . . ."

She paused. "Suppose I don't want you to go. . .?"

"But Mom. . . ." I never finished the sentence. In every human life there comes that moment which mothers hate the most. It never really comes when children go off to college because the ties which bring them home on vacations are still there, and the loss does not seem so complete as it does when they take full-time jobs and move to distant places. Looking back, I realize that my mother was facing such a moment. She had adjusted to our going to college. Both our parents were very supportive, but this was something different. This meant a break for the whole summer, a going away which would make me independent in a way I had never been before that. You don't send your laundry home every weekend from Yellowstone Park. You do it yourself. You have to manage every detail of your life, and I had never done that fully before. Still, I was going, and Mother knew it, and I am grateful to say both she and my dad were mature people who knew that the best way to alienate a child is to attempt to frustrate every thing the child wants to do, especially when he/she is poised on that brink between childhood dependence and adult maturity.

They accepted my decision and started helping me think through what I would need for the summer. Mom suggested that I buy some crinkly crepe shirts which would not need ironing; I also got some hiking boots for days off; we read the contract carefully to see the various kinds of clothing I would need for the mountains' alternate cool nights and warm days. I don't remember all the details of planning, but I do remember that if my mother had not given me the assistance she had, I would have gone poorly prepared for my summer. I even had some practice runs with the washing machine and some lessons in which kinds of clothes to mix and which not. My only problem was that I was short two arms. I could have used extras to carry a footlocker, laundry box, suitcase, violin, and music rack. I had to take my fiddle because the teaching I was getting from Raymond Cerf at KU was inspirational, and I wanted to practice during spare hours. When those would occur I did not know, but I knew that they would be immensely enriched by Bach, Beethoven, and Brahms.

Before the end of the semester, I had one lovely exchange with a devil. I had gone to a high school basketball game to watch a friend I had grown up with play for his team, and who was selling tickets but a man I shall call Ace Gravel. He was the worst of the abusive baseball coaches I had had to endure every summer.

"Going to be back out there this summer doing battle with me, Stewart?"

"No."

"No?" He seemed genuinely disappointed. "No? Why not?"

"I'm going to work in Yellowstone Park this summer." He looked positively perplexed. The moment brought it all into focus for me. I'm going to the mountains, Gravel. No more of you, no more baloney from the Director about being "uncooperative," no more hot, humid, rotten weather, no more ornery kids starting fights among one another on the playground, no more Fourth of July nightmares, with kids throwing firecrackers at each other and nearly blowing off each other's hands. That was all behind me. I had earned this summer in the West. And I could not have picked a better summer to go. Quite by accident I was preparing to miss the worst flood to hit the Kansas River Valley and Kansas City in fifty years.

June 3, 1951. Sunday evening. Weather cloudy and a bit rainy. The date was not particularly significant for me. In four years, however, it was to become my wedding date. That Sunday evening I boarded a Burlington train at Kansas City's Union Station, listened to Mother's last minute instructions, particularly the one about sending a postcard when I got to Billings, told my brother, sister, Mom, and Dad, goodbye, and boarded the train.

It is impossible now for me to recapture the exhilaration and sadness of this watershed moment in my life. I was going more than 1,000 miles away, to a new region, to a new experience, to a new life. Instinctively, I knew the experience would change me in ways I could not anticipate, but I was as eager for it as it is possible for a young person to be. I was Adam heading for my own paradise; whether or not Eve was there didn't really matter. But I was also grateful for having been the child of Hattie and Charley Stewart. My parents, brother, sister, and I were a close family, and we had a sense of loyalty for one another that has not diminished over the years, despite the differences in our life experiences and the geographical separation we all experience. Knowing who you are and where you are from makes going into a new experience an adventure, not an ordeal.

So, I was on the train, heading north then west, and I was ready. We travelled very slowly that night. I have dim memories of the train halting, then creeping along, then halting again north of St. Joseph, Missouri, of looking out the windows once and getting faint glimpses of water on both sides of the tracks. I didn't know where we were—do not to this day know exactly where the Burlington line ran—but I had the sense that something was not quite right. The next morning we were in Nebraska, heading west at high speed because we were well behind schedule. The porter and the steward spoke cryptically about the engineer making up time; we had been slowed by high water the previous night. I barely picked up the remark, but a month later I would remember it vividly.

We were on a milk run. We stopped at every little burg and crossroads one could imagine. There are those who say how much more enjoyable train travel was than air travel today. Sorry, I don't agree. I rode the trains to Yellowstone on four separate occasions, and I remember the trips as being long and tiring. A plane gets you there. A train gets you there, too, eventually when your sitter is tired, when you have tramped up and down the length of the whole string of cars, eaten in the diner with its outrageous prices, heard the bump and rattle of the cars as they jolt along, and tried every position into which you can maneuver your body in an effort to get some sleep. You smell stale, the train smells stale, the people smell stale. Long train rides? No thanks. I'll take my own car if I want a long ride through a part of the country I want to see.

There was boredom in this first trip, but I managed to pass some time playing with one of those hand games in which you try to get the numbers in order. Unfortunately, after a few false starts, you suddenly realize that, using one system, you can create every pattern suggested on the back of the game. I also read what books I had brought, and observed the name of every station along the way. Because I had heard the porter talking about it, I developed an intense longing to reach Alliance, Nebraska. Alliance is in *western* Nebraska. Getting to Alliance meant that we might be in range so that we could see some of the Colorado mountains. At least, that is what I thought. My hunger for the high country was distorting my sense of geography.

I could not say now at what time we reached Alliance. My memory wants to tell me that it was late afternoon, but that is quite impossible. Alliance is much too far from Billings for us to have arrived there at that time. More than likely we reached Alliance in the forenoon then turned north, through a portion of South Dakota and Wyoming. The engineer was really pushing the train at this point because stopping points were much farther apart, and he was making up lost time. To this day I do not know the exact route the train took, but looking at a map, I can see that it obviously lay west of the Black Hills and east of the Big Horns.

I do remember going to supper that evening with a boy of about ten who was going to Billings to see his aunt and uncle and who needed a big brother for the trip. I entertained him with the puzzle game which he could not figure out, asked him about his school, told him I was on my way to Yellowstone, and encouraged him to join me in looking for mountains. In the evening, about an hour before sunset, we saw mountains, snowcapped, at a distance. They must have been an extension of the Big Horns, but I didn't know that then; I just knew that they looked beautiful in the evening sun, and my expectations grew by the hour. By 9:30 P.M. we were in Billings.

When I stepped out of the train at Billings, I was still in mid-voyage, and I was tired. One night's sleep on the train, and a day of train food equal one-half night's sleep and one-fourth of the normal nutrition one gets at home. And I knew I would not get another night's sleep because I had a weird layover. My connections were not the kind which are made for the comfort of people travelling from Kansas City to Yellowstone. I left the care of the Burlington line at 9:30 in this strange Montana town and had to wait in the depot until 2 A.M. for a Great Northern train heading west.

I have never been a night person. The idea of cat-napping in a strange train station, then boarding another train in the early morning hours was, to say the least, a novel experience for me. I had counted on getting some sleep in Billings, however, because I assumed that the benches in the depot would permit me to stretch out and sleep. They were that way in Kansas City. Apparently, a lot of people thought of that possibility, many of them vagrants who were not customers of the railroads. Therefore, to discourage loitering and overnighting by bums on cold nights—I don't know this but suspect it—the train depots of the north central Rockies had benches which were compartmented by arm rests. There was absolutely no way I could bend, twist, curl, or wrap myself around those things in an effort to get some sleep.

And, by this time I *was* tired. But I was semi-alert, because of my violin. Someone could have stolen my clothes, my money, my laundry bag—the whole shebang—but I would never have parted with the fiddle. It isn't a rare or valuable instrument. But it was mine. You have to be a string player to appreciate the way one becomes attached to a particular instrument.

So there I sat, surrounded by the footlocker, the laundry box, the suitcase, the violin, and almost too tired to go to sleep. And I forgot to mail the postcard to my mother. It didn't concern me a lot then because I knew I was all right, but from her point of view, I had disappeared into the vast northwest and she wanted some signal that I was findable. Unfortunately, she had to wait five days to get that signal. Ah, the things we put our mothers through.

Half on one seat, half over another, the arm of one seat pushing constantly into my back, I dropped into a semi-comatose state. One doesn't really sleep in such a situation. My adrenalin was still pumping; after all, I was in mountain country, I was still en route, and I was concerned about the violin and my connection. Could I trust the agent to wake me up?

Again the images come back fitfully. June 5, 1951, 2 A.M. The hulk of the Great Northern's westbound train rose above the Billings station. The early morning air was sharply cool. The hissing and clanking that always goes with a train at pause was interrupting the night. I boarded and entered a smoky coach filled with dreary-eyed people who, half-awake, looked at me as if to ask, "Who the hell are you, and where the hell are we stopping?" I found a seat, spread my gear around me so as not to lose track of it, and leaned back against the coach seat. At least, I could get some kind of sleep here, but it would not last too long. We were due in Livingston at 4.

The train rolled out of Billings and resumed its journey west. I had not looked at maps. I had no idea now where I was or how far Livingston was from Billings. I was totally at the mercy of the conductor. But I determined to stay awake so that I would not miss my stop and wake up in the morning half way to the Pacific

Coast. It was futile determination on my part. Two nights without sleep were catching up with me. I dozed off and remember now only the gentle tap of the conductor and the magic words, "Next stop, Livingston." Livingston! Northern gateway to Yellowstone! I was almost there.

At four o'clock on that June 5th I ended my long train ride into the west and got out into the darkness and cold of a Montana morning. I couldn't see a thing, and I had more hours to pass. I went into the station, again to endure the uncomfortable benches but tired enough to sleep in any position for a couple of hours. When I woke up, it was about six o'clock, and the sun was in the sky. I have always been happy that I woke up on a clear day then. I went out of the station and looked south. It is a moment I will never forget. There, framed against a brilliant blue sky, were some of the peaks of the Snowy Range which form the northern border of the Yellowstone plateau. It was as if nature had conspired to give substance to my most romantic memories of the high country. For a young man who had spent five consecutive summers in the heat and humidity of Kansas City, this was a liberation, a sight of paradise that I had hungered for more than I had realized. The great mountains of the West! I was too ignorant then to fully appreciate that, quite by accident, I had placed myself in the jewel of the north central Rockies: the plateau of the upper Yellowstone.

I stood there, enthralled, for several minutes, appeasing a hunger for sights that had, for five years, lingered only in my memory. Then my stomach told me that mountains or not, I had to get some breakfast. I put my stuff in a locker, then went across the street to a little diner, in this case to order not what I wanted but what I knew would be good nourishment: an egg and toast and some oatmeal. I don't remember the diner now, but I do remember the restorative power of that good breakfast. I then returned to the train station where I was to board a Greyhound bus going south to Gardiner. At that point, I had been told, park buses would pick us up. The Greyhound bus was there; I was ready, and at eight we left Livingston and headed south.

Right out of Livingston we crossed the Yellowstone River. In Livingston the Yellowstone is a big river—it is a big river in the park, too, not the small transparent stream one often associates with mountain country, but that did not lessen my exhilaration. I think it is very difficult for young people today to appreciate just how exotic "Yellowstone" was, in 1951, to me. The big jets which take us from New York to San Francisco in three to five hours, which cross the oceans in less than a day, which make trips like Kansas City to Denver merely one-hour local stops, have taken the magic out of travel in the United States. When I was growing up, our perceptions of distance were much different. Yellowstone seemed as remote from Kansas City then as Central Africa is today.

I had not been in the north central Rockies since 1946 when my family travelled to Glacier National Park, Lakes Coeur d'Alene and Pend Oreille in northern Idaho, Grand Coulee Dam in eastern Washington, and Yellowstone. Strangely, I did not remember Yellowstone, except as already noted, that well. But during the hot playground years, the memory of an absolutely clear and swift small stream somewhere up on Going-to-the-Sun Pass in Glacier fixed permanently in my mind the images by which I chose to remember the high country. As we crossed the Yellowstone at Livingston, those images were coming back with increasing vividness, and my anticipation of actually reaching the mountains intensified by the minute.

As you go south up the Yellowstone Valley from Livingston, you get the sense that Mother Nature is steadily but progressively closing the door on a precious wilderness she wants to protect. The valley narrows, the gorge at points deepens, and, in the nineteenth century, explorers like the Washburn Party of 1870 faced a rapid and considerable ascent to the Yellowstone Plateau. From Gardiner, at the North Entrance, to Mammoth, the Park Headquarters, the road rises 1,000 feet in five miles. Then one has to go up another 1,000 feet above Mammoth to reach the high ground which comprises the major portion of the Park's plateau.

In 1951 I remember only a stop at Chico Springs, an obvious tourist trap (and a harsh reminder of what private developers would have done with the Yellowstone country had they been given the opportunity to exploit it) and then the approach to Gardiner.

There is absolutely nothing remarkable about Gardiner. It is just there. In those days it was the place where commercial transportation stopped and one had to depend on that provided by the Yellowstone Park Company. Young people were coming in numbers, but we were to go many different directions. We were met by drivers of the old White buses, vehicles which looked too small to be buses and too large to be cars. They were really large touring cars. The drivers hollered out for Canyon, Roosevelt Lodge, Fishing Bridge, West Thumb, and Old Faithful. That was my bus. I was going to Old Faithful, and anticipation continued building by the moment despite the fact that I could remember none of the part of Yellowstone I was seeing, and rain was beginning to fall. The gorgeous blue morning had given way to a late spring cold mountain rainstorm. The weather was setting in; this was not going to be a passing shower. This was going to be rain for the rest of the day. That happens in Yellowstone, at any time of the summer. Sometimes, it's snow.

I was serenely untroubled by the rain, however. My gear was loaded onto the bus along with that of the others, and I had a firm grip on my violin. My window seat gave me a chance to look, and I wanted to do a lot of that. We were sixty miles from Old Faithful.

The bus ground up the hill from Gardiner, making its way slowly around the hairpin curves and one-lane bridges over the Gardiner River which came boiling down from Mammoth and higher country. The stream was white, but it was not clear. Too much of the spring runoff was still in it, but my mid-June or later, that would clear, and the Gardiner would become the river I still remember: transparent, very cold, and swift over its rocky bottom.

At Mammoth I first saw some things I remembered: the Hotel in which we had stayed in 1946; the terraces and Liberty Cap, all of which I recalled enjoying. But Mammoth has several drawbacks for a person escaping to the western mountains and hungering for wilderness: its permanent buildings, manicured lawns, and aridity—much open space, the terraces, and not too great immediate proximity to clear streams or "the forest primeval." I was happy that I would not be working in Mammoth. I would come back for some sightseeing, but it would not have satisfied my craving for adventure, the sense that I had been put down among temporary structures in the midst of the Yellowstone wilderness. That was to come later.

We left Mammoth and rose steadily toward Kingman Pass, the last big turn above the Mammoth Terraces and the gateway to the Park. One comes out of the Mammoth Area and Kingman Pass onto the Swan Lake Flats, a large expanse of open territory above Mammoth on the park plateau proper. I cannot describe perfectly how exhilarated I felt when we levelled out and began to follow the road through the Flats. It was as if we had finally closed the door on civilization and were at last intruding in a significant way on the Yellowstone wilderness. There was too much rain that day for me to see across the Flats to Electric Peak or the Gallatin Range south of it, but I could see the large expanse of sagebrush and rough grass in the meadow, the Lake itself, far away, on which I was later, on many occasions, to see nesting trumpeter swans. We were going south, deeper and deeper into God's country.

At Norris I recalled vividly the acrid hydrogen sulphide which permeates the air. The road, at that time, went right through the geyser basin, in fact separating the museum from the area in which people took most of their walks, and it presented a traffic hazard in busy seasons, but in early June there were few tourists. There was much steam and gas coming off the basin because Norris is a very hot place. It lacks, except for Steamboat some years ago, a predictable erupting large geyser, but it has hundred of steam vents, fumaroles, small hot geysers, and paint pots to interest the park visitor. I noticed that the gas did not bother me as much in 1951 as it had in 1946. Perhaps my frame of mind had something to do with that.

We continued south, through the Gibbon Canyon and, ironically, past Madison Junction which I took no note of whatsoever. It would later be the place in Yellowstone with which I would have the longest and happiest identification. There we were only sixteen miles from Old Faithful.

The road from Madison then led up the Firehole Canyon and onto another plateau which, when considered as a single unit, forms the area in which three of Yellowstone's major geyser basins are found: the Lower, Middle, and Upper Geyser Basins of the Firehole River, the latter containing most of Yellowstone's large and most famous geysers. At the southern extremity of the Upper Basin, alone among a group of extinct geyser mounds, is Old Faithful, the most famous geyser in the world. It was steaming and splashing some as we came, and people were walking away from it, so an eruption had apparently taken place. Old Faithful was familiar to me; I had remembered the geyser, the buildings around it, the Lodge on the south, the Inn on the west, and even the Cafeteria which was one of a group of buildings located on a horseshoe road leading away from the main highway between the Inn and the Lodge. The bus pulled up at the Cafeteria. I had arrived.

2

Settling In

AT THIS POINT, and for about two weeks following, the Yellowstone idyll ended. There is no way I could have been prepared for what followed, unless the company had chosen to tell me, and for very good reasons, it had not. Cafeteria employees, the men, that is, were housed in a dorm attached to the Cafeteria. It looked like an old Army barracks with small cubicles. The commissary steward was in charge of assigning us to rooms, and he led me to a little hole which had a double and a single bunk bed and was illuminated by a bare 75 watt bulb hanging from a cord in the middle of the ceiling. The two denizens of the room, high school boys who worked at the Lower Gas Station, were not there when I arrived that first day, and it is a good thing they weren't. We would have had an early fight. Let me re-create this situation.

I am full of enthusiasm for my venture to the mountain country. That enthusiasm has been steadily building all during the long ride from Livingston to Old Faithful. But now I am confronted by some rather chilling facts: literally chilling. I am to live in a small room with rough wood floors with two high school kids whose personal habits I can quickly see are not going to square with mine at all. Their beds are unmade. Dirty jeans—no, dirty is not an adequate word, nor is filthy—jeans that are so impregnated with dirt and grease that it is difficult to tell whether or not the natural cloth fibers or the grime are the dominant elements in these garments, dirty underwear, socks, bits of paper, mostly candy bar wrappers, newspapers, and bits of gravel litter the floor. My impression is that these pigs—again an unfair term because pigs are actually rather neat—these slobs have moved in sometime in early May when their school let out and have never cleaned the room from the time they entered it. It is quite literally the filthiest and most depressing place in which I have ever been told that I am going to live. Making matters worse is the rain which keeps pounding away outside, and the cold. Where is the heat for this dorm? I am told there is none. No heat? My God, it must be 40 degrees outside, and we have *no* heat?

I put down my foot locker, my suitcase, my laundry box, my violin and surveyed the mess. I will admit that for a minute or two I did think of picking up my stuff and leaving. It would have been an ignoble end to such a romantic adventure, and the tendency was strong. Even at college where I had lived in a crowded room and slept in a cold dorm, we had had heat, and my roommates did keep things reasonably well picked up. The room in Battenfeld Hall at the University of Kansas was a "living place." One could manage in it. Now I understood why the Yellowstone Park Company said we had to fulfill our contracts before they would pay our transportation both ways. If we had known what we were coming to, we wouldn't have come. And I suspect a lot of college students my age had come, taken one look and said to hell with it. Back home to comfort and a better job.

I feel sorry for such people. They never know what they miss. Although I was as depressed as anyone that day, I had learned to be somewhat flexible. A person can always adjust, my dad had said. Adjust and make the best of it. Don't start something you don't intend to finish. Hang in there. The Stewarts were not a family of quitters. I spit on the floor, right into the mess, and then said quietly to myself, "Shit." Then I went looking for the commissary steward. I was *not* going to live in that crap and I was sure as hell going to make those high school clowns who denned with me accept that fact, even if I had to beat their heads in. I got a broom and started sweeping, pan after pan full of crap—the gravel, the trash, the garbage which they had not removed. Then I did some straightening of the clothes and went to get bedding. I was making my bed and preparing mentally for battle when I heard a knock on the door. I opened it and was confronted by a tall blond fellow who looked as if he might be about my age. Some of the names which follow are made up, but the events are as true as I remember them.

"Hi, I'm Gene Goff, University of Nebraska."

"Greetings. I'm Don Stewart from KU."

"Hey! An old rock-chalk Jayhawk?"

"Something like that."

"Say, Phil (our commissary steward) put me in a hole—I just came in today, and I'm looking for another room and another roommate. Look what I found down the hall." He took me to a room two doors down. Empty, better lighted, and *clean*. It had not yet been occupied by a couple of hibernating bears. Gene went on. "Say, let's get Phil to put us in this one, what do you think?"

"I think that's a terrific idea. He put me in with a couple of high school hobos, and I've been cleaning the garbage out of the room. It's a pigsty, with apologies to pigs."

"Great! Then let's get Phil to make the change."

Phil was not as enthusiastic as we were. Like most commissary stewards, he wanted the people he supervised to be as tractable as the supplies he ordered and shelved until needed. In his world, an employee grumbling about his room assignment was like a can of soup complaining because it had been put next to the green beans. So, he struggled to invent some feeble rationalizations for the status quo. He had to save the space because others were coming in and. . . .

"Phil. We *are* the others, two others who can't stand those holes you put us in. We want this other room. Okay? You can put some single person who comes later in the rooms we vacated."

Gene was very persuasive, and Phil didn't have a good reason for denying us the room. I picked up my gear and for the first time felt that something was beginning to go right in my work situation.

Now I was hungry, and we were told that we could eat in the Cafeteria. We would go to work the next day, after Hazel, the manager, had processed our papers and got us on the payroll.

Through the rain we made a mad dash, along the concrete landing at the back of the Cafeteria and into the dining room. There we got our trays, went through the line, and joined other employees. The conversation was interesting, very interesting to me. "My God! They expect us to live all summer in those quarters? Our pigs in Iowa are better housed than that!" The speaker was a blond, round-faced girl whose color was up. "I will be on the first bus out of here tomorrow. Aaaaaaaaaaaaahgh!"

"But Sally, if you leave they don't pay your expenses out."

"So? If I stay in that filthy, grimy, cruddy room all summer, my friends will never take me back. Oh God, I can't think of one good reason now why I decided to come out here!"

Sally couldn't but I thought I could. It amused me to hear the echo of my own outrage an hour earlier. In fact, quarters were *the* topic at the tables. How many years, I thought, had the people who ran the Yellowstone Park Company conned young people into coming out, and how many years had they heard the outraged voices they were hearing in June of 1951? I suspected they were quite used to it. Still, you had to look at it from Sally's viewpoint. Why would she apply for summer work in the mountains? Two good reasons, neither of them having to do with money. One, the environment and climate would be terrific. Which is better, Iowa's humid summer heat, or Yellowstone's dry comfortably warm days and cool invigorating nights? That's no choice except for a sluggish person with no circulation. But I had the feeling that something else was included in Sally's expectations: handsome, virile young men, all of whom would be attracted to her. Is that such a bad dream? You are walking along, hand in hand, with some broad-shouldered, narrow-hipped cavalier, snow-capped mountains in the background, on their slopes the mountain forests out of which come deer to feed at dusk, and he tells you how terrific you are and, and, and . . . it's a great romantic vision. Sally had it, but at that moment she was digesting lousy quarters, cold rain outside, and the complete absence of anything like her dream man. The men she could see probably looked like the same zit-faced clowns she had left at home. Hardly something to satisfy a romantic palate. The wonderful irony in the situation was that, in time, many parts of the dream would come true. There *were* handsome young men and beautiful girls working in Yellowstone in the summer. In a recent *National Geographic* I saw a picture of a beautiful Carolina girl who could have been an identical twin to one of the girls who worked in the Haynes Picture Shop at Old Faithful the summer of 1951. Why didn't I have a job there? Anyway, the weather would get better, and we would have the kind of summer we had anticipated. The quarters we would adjust to to the point that we would forget about them, and Pat, our cook, would treat us so well that we wouldn't even have complaints about the food. The paradise was attainable, but it was only for those willing to gut it out those first few days when every aspect of our experience was so lousy.

I felt much better after getting some food, and I knew I would feel even better after a check of the area, a good hot shower, and one night's rest in a bed, not a damn train station. That reminded me that I still had not sent the postcard to Mother, and I was now two full days from home, and the card would not get there for another two anyway. It turned out to be three, and it reached home just about the time Mom was ready to use the telephone (and in those days working people only used long distance for very special occasions) to find out whether or not she still had a locatable son. My brother told me Mom was sure I had missed a connection or forgot to get off the train. Perhaps she had visions of my ending up penniless somewhere in

Idaho and not knowing what to do. Well, the card arrived and the home folks knew that I was safe in the Cafeteria. I even told them about my resolution to clean out the pigsty and my new roommate. The summer had begun.

The first thing I went looking for after I got settled was a place to practice my violin, but on the way, I stopped to attend to the great lady herself: Old Faithful Geyser. The day was raw and grey, and little pools of water stood in pockets along the asphalt sidewalk to the Lodge. Still a sizeable crowd had gathered to listen to the ranger and to watch the preliminary surges of the geyser. A column of water about five feet high leaped out of Old Faithful's orifice, causing the crowd to exclaim, but it receded after splashing water over the mound of the geyser. A pause followed, then another surge and splashing accompanied by a great deal of steam. Again the crowd gave a collective cry as expectations mounted. Five more preliminary surges followed, each accompanied by the same response. Then a column of water twenty to thirty feet high roared out of the geyser, hung there for a split second, and then was pushed high into the air as the eruption began. The column of water ascended rapidly to a height of approximately 150 feet, then just as rapidly began to drop. In four minutes it was over except for last minute surges and the volume of water pouring off the backside of Old Faithful's mound on its way to the Firehole River.

I watched Old Faithful many times that summer, I saw it erupt frequently over the thirteen years I worked in Yellowstone, and I spent my last summer there, often giving talks at the cone of the geyser and telling park visitors something about the significance of what they were seeing. I still think it is a beautiful geyser. I like Grand and Great Fountain better, but I have never lost sight of the fact, as some did, that I was specially privileged to see this marvelous natural wonder erupt hundreds of times. It is as clear in my memory today as it was when I first saw it.

After the eruption, I resumed my quest. Where could I practice? The dorm was impossible. It was too cold, and the rooms had paper thin walls. I would be hooted out of there in no time. Besides, I did not care for the idea of performing daily; I just wanted a place to keep up my scales, bowing exercises, and pieces so that I would be sharp when I went back in the Fall. The Old Faithful Lodge was warm, but the Recreation Hall attached to it was frigid. Still, it contained small closet-sized rooms behind the stage and off the large open portion of it which could serve as remote practice rooms. The first time I practiced I used one of the rooms back stage, but I was interrupted there by some of the savages—the employees' name for themselves—and eventually settled on a room at a far distant corner from the stage. Those pounding on the piano down by the stage, the basketball players rumbling back and forth in the middle of the floor, and occasional sightseers passing through could do so without being disturbed by or without disturbing me. I did have one eavesdropper: a marmot which lived under the building and came out everytime I tuned up. He tried to figure out what kind of creature caused the terrible caterwauling which disturbed his afternoon nap. When I saw the marmot, I would strike some high chords sharply, trying to imitate the marmot's bark, and each time I hit the chord the marmot would lurch forward, like a dog about to bark but stifling it at the last minute. I think I thoroughly confused the poor animal.

The first day, after I had checked out the Lodge Recreation Hall and decided I would practice there—it was too cold then; my fingers would have been numb—I went back into the area where the barber shop, first aid station, cabin registration desk, lobby, and dining room were located. It was warm. The curio shop was there, too, a glassed-in shop—you could see into or out of it on both the registration desk and dining room sides—and I wanted to check it out for something that might be useful for my sister's birthday in early July. Most of the jewelry, glassware, and other trinkets were too far beyond my pitiful income for me even to consider them. I bought some picture postcards of the area and then, as I was about to leave the shop, saw just what I was looking for: a carved wooden bear in a small crate. It cost only a dollar, and it could be mailed for three cents. Now my sister, I am sure, really didn't care a whole lot about a crummy wooden bear from Yellowstone, but I had an idea that I might have some fun with that bear. So, when I got back to the dorm, I began my first letter from Yellowstone, and after I had given most of the news, I told Mom that I had a perfect birthday present for Margaret Ann, but she wasn't to tell her so it would be a big surprise. I told her I was sending Marg a bear cub, the cutest thing you could imagine. And I gave a few instructions for feeding. Mother never really dealt well with practical jokers. In a few days I got a letter with the home news, relief that the card had come and they knew I was safe, and a short note asking if I was sure Marg would like a bear for a present. This was vintage Mother. As my brother told me later, she was saying, "What in the world is he thinking of? We don't want a bear. How would we take care of it?" Translation: doesn't that kid know enough not to go collecting wild animals? I started getting questions about what the park authorities would think. Was it permissible to capture and ship out bears? I kept reassuring her that it was (like hell: you can get a whopping fine and a jail term for poaching in the park; that was taken care of by the Lacey Act of 1894), that the bear was small and would do well on milk for awhile until it required other kinds of nutrition. And Mother was getting in a state as Marg's birthday approached. My brother kept telling her that some funny business was afoot and not to worry, but Mother was never too confident of my judgment when I was that age, so she worried. A few days after the bear arrived, I got a letter saying, "Frankly, I was relieved when the bear came today."

So, I had the bear thing going, I was beginning to get used to the idea that I could survive in the quarters given me, and I had found a place to practice. The basics were taken care of. It was time now to learn the most basic basic: my job.

I have never met anyone who thinks dishwashing is fun, but the way we did it in the Old Faithful Cafeteria was fun. Well, it became fun once Dick, our crew chief, arrived. I don't remember Dick's last name, but I remember what he looked like very well.

He weighed about 160 pounds, but he was the strongest man that size I have ever seen. It seems to me that Dick was or had been a Marine. He had arms the size of small tree limbs, and he was one of those people who are wide as a NFL linebacker at the shoulders but taper down to my size at the waist. He had little hair on top, although he was a young man, but he had dark hairy arms and legs. Dick was physical, no doubt about that. He had come back for another year apparently for one reason: everyday, when he got off work, he would go fishing with Art, the vegetable man. Dick loved to test himself against those big, smart browns in the Firehole, and that was an era in which the fishing was very good indeed.

When Dick joined Jerry, David, Blair, and me—he was late getting to the Park—he took one look at the way we were working and said, "Step aside. Lemme show you guys how to wash these goddamned dishes."

It worked this way. The girls out front would bring the dirty dishes and silver from the Cafeteria and put them on a stainless steel counter which was to the left of the dishwasher when he was loading the racks. This counter formed one of four sides of what was an incomplete rectangle which, in turn, was the dishwasher's space. Mounted above it was another counter, the purpose of which was to slide or store empty dish racks. These were wire squares with half inch dowling used as dividers inside them. The dowling created the rows in which one would put dirty dishes.

When it was time to run them, the dishwasher would coolly saunter up to his place, casually flick the electric switch which turned on a fountain of water which drained into a large basin in front of him and put a pile of dishes under it. If they were small dessert dishes, he let the water from the fountain splash on each dish as he peeled it off the pile—this washed away much garbage—then took the top dish at the twelve o'clock position and flipped it down the first row in the empty dish rack. There was just enough space between the slats in the rack to accommodate the dishes. The second dish he took at the six o'clock position and flipped it down the rack next to the first dish. By gripping them alternately at twelve then six o'clock, he could stagger them so that the bowl of the first opened downstream, the bowl of the second upstream. This kind of staggering permitted him to get more dishes on the rack than if he loaded them haphazardly. We used this method with larger bowls, plates, saucers—the whole batch of dishes. After Dick showed us how to do this, we became very good at it. Well, Jerry, David, and I did. Blair's coordination never caught up with his desire to become a bonafide dish slinger. Dick was fastest at first, but we caught up to him. And we did not destroy the crockery the way he did. When Dick was tossing dishes into the racks, chips fell like snow flakes.

Once a rack of dishes was loaded, the dishwasher pushed it into the machine and turned it on. A pulley, like the kind which pulls a car through a car wash, hauled the dirty dishes through a screen of soap and rinse water, and they came out the other end, gleaming white and so hot that the unloader could scarcely handle them. We removed them from the rack, stacked them in a wooden cart, and shoved the empty back to the dishwasher on the rack which formed a canopy over the counter which held the dirty dishes. One night, after a power failure put us behind, we did the dishes for 500 people in thirty minutes. It was, to put it smugly, a piece of cake.

We loafed around the kitchen far more than we washed dishes. In our oilskin aprons we showed up at the counter where Toots and Sonja turned out the red and green Jell-O salads, at Smitty's or Pat's work tables, Smitty being the first cook, Pat the chef, and in the back room at the commissary or the vegetable room where Art worked. It was a good job except for two things. We made only $100 per month, and we got no tips. In the second place, it was murder on hands. Ours became soft, rough, red, and chapped. The biggest problem was cuts. I once cut the fourth finger on my left hand, right where it pressed on the violin string. Until that healed, practicing was physically painful. If you don't believe that, try pressing an exposed nerve sometime.

There was one little problem in the dishwashing sector. We had to do the blankety-blank silverware. Actually, this was an easy job, too, because the little machine we used tumbled the knives, forks, and spoons, and the detergent was strong enough to dissolve practically anything but metal, but we had an insidious enemy to contend with: gum. Let me reconstruct a particular scenario: it is 8:20 P.M. and the Cafeteria closes at 8:30. All of us are anxious to finish because (1) we have dates, (2) we are anxious to prepare for tomorrow's day off, (3) we want to see a program in the lodge, (4) we are tired and want to go to bed early. The latter is the least probable, but it did occur on a few occasions which I will note. Anyway, we are finishing the last of the dishes. The man at the silverware washer gathers up a load of silver and, because he is in a hurry, does what he knows instinctively, he should never do. He tosses the dirty silverware into the machine, puts in the required amount of soap, and starts the wash cycle. In a few minutes he will have the pleasure of removing from the machine a bundle of clean, shiny, hot, and sterilized silverware. That is, he *would* have, if he had taken proper precautions and checked the silver for gum. There are people who think a plate, a fork, even a glass is the proper repository for gum they are throwing away. When it gets mixed among a batch of silverware and run through a very hot wash cycle, it melts and deposits itself as a thin grey film on *every single piece* of silverware in the batch.

On those few occasions when I opened the silverware washer and saw that grey film on everything, I cursed. Oh my, but I did curse, and even today's rather permissive standards of publication will not permit me to say what I said to myself on such occasions. So, it is now 8:30, time to close up, and the dish crew has the good news. We have to hand clean about 200 pieces of silverware. At 9:30 we finish this grubby business and run the silverware through the machine again, this time vowing to kill the next crew member who does not check for gum. Then we hurry off to repair, as well as we can, a partially ruined evening.

Dishwashing at Old Faithful was fun, but it was boring, too, because there was so little to do. Of the eight hours we spent on the job each day, probably not more than two were spent actually washing dishes. That was a good thing, in one way. When we were sick, as I was the first two weeks, or tired, as I was on one day I will note later, the job gave me a chance to recuperate while still working.

I got sick that first two weeks for a very simple reason: it rained all the time. I began to think that all it ever did was rain in Yellowstone. And we had to go out of the warm Cafeteria into that cold rain, then back into the Cafeteria, then back out. A perfect heating and cooling which set us up for the colds which everyone had. Why did we have to do so much of this? Well, we lived in that cold unheated dorm which didn't help a lot. Any trip from dorm to work or meals meant going in or out. We could take our jackets, but the dishwashers, particularly those who came on early, had certain tasks to perform which took them outside. One was the kind of job every person should have once in his/her life, just so you will appreciate a good job. You may remember that I mentioned the fountain at the right edge of the counter where we rinsed the dishes before putting them into the wire racks. That fountain washed garbage off the plates, saucers, bowls, and cups. It washed it down the drain at the center of the basin. I don't know why I assumed that it washed it out of sight. Clearly, the amount of garbage that was going down that drain would have stopped up an eight-inch sewer line in a matter of weeks. No, the people who designed that dishwashing unit were not stupid. There was a great basket under the drain. The thing was the size of a medium sized wastebasket; it was made of metal; and it was porous. Water flowed through it easily. Garbage got trapped in it. It was not easy, just after eating break-fast, to take twenty pounds of wet, dripping garbage out to the cans on the landing back of the Cafeteria and dump it into them. It made me sick at my stomach the first few times I did it. But it had to be done. Garbage pickup was early in the day, for a reason obvious to anyone familiar with Yellowstone in those days. The bears roamed freely through the campground, and occasionally they came wandering through the cabin areas and around the Cafeteria. A Yellowstone bear of that era could smell unprotected garbage half a mile away. So, the garbage went out early in the morning, and the trucks picked it up and hauled it to the landfill where the grizzlies came at night, away from the camps and away from the roads. But it was still a disgusting job. I would not want to have spent my life doing it . . . but there are people who do that kind of work everyday, and they do not get paid near what they are worth in services to the public they serve.

3

The Cafeteria Crew

SETTLED INTO my job and established in a routine, I started getting a sense of the people with whom I was working. Some remain forever on the periphery of my memory because I had so little to do with them. For example, Hazel, the manager, was ... Hazel, the manager. Hazel looked like a manager: wavy greying hair, glasses in gold wire frames, a built-in furrow in her brow. She was pleasant, but she never laughed at much. Reminded me of an elementary school principal. She signed us on, gave us our checks, and generally let the chef, Pat, run the kitchen. She and Irene, her first lieutenant, supervised what went on out front, in the Cafeteria lines, and the tables, where the "dudes" ate. I had never used that word, but I liked it. The "dudes" were everybody who came to eat in the Cafeteria, the tourists to YNP. Like employees of every place in the world which has large numbers of visitors who are not familiar with the place, we enjoyed with increasing smugness our knowledgeability and the stupidity, gullibility, and general flakiness of the dudes. People in such situations never stop to think that anywhere else *they* are the dudes. It's so nice to feel superior.

I didn't see a lot of Hazel, as I was saying, and I didn't see all that much of the girls on the serving line, except when they and the busboys hassled us about not getting dishes as fast as they thought they should, or when they weren't getting clean dishes. Dick had the standard answer to one of the girls complaining about a fork which had a piece of carrot baked in between the tines by the heat of the silverware washer. "What are they complaining about? It's an extra serving."

There were other reasons we didn't see much of the girls out front. A young man of twenty-one has many things on his mind, but they occur only sporadically, when they displace girls. It is impossible to think that any of us wouldn't look the field over to see if *our* girl might be among the group. Surely the women were doing the same thing. I saw no one that I could fall instantly and madly in love with, but I will say that over the summer I came to like several of the girls pretty well. They were a good bunch, and some of them were really cute, now that I look back on it, but not one of them was right for me. And, I certainly wasn't right for any of them. I weighed about 135 pounds, and these were spread over a 5' 11'' frame. I think I was a good conversationalist, and I had that musical ability, but no woman I have ever met has been instantly captivated by my virile masculine charm. I suppose that I belonged in the "Who? Oh, yeah, I know who you mean" category. Nothing outstanding; nothing obnoxious. I was just there, washing dishes, disappearing periodically on the geyser hill or with my violin, and generally melting into the woodwork. It was just as well. I was too green then for a real love affair.

But I did have some female company on my first day off. Both were nice girls. Correction: both were nice women, generous and friendly persons. But one was a flake. She would stand at the edge of the road, her thumb extended, and sing out the name of every passing car's state, information which she got, of course, from its license plate. Her cheering, she reasoned, would entice the driver to stop and pick us up. That particular day it was cold and rainy and we were bundled up appropriately, but because we looked like refugees from the Pogo comic strip, a number of cars passed us by. Tourists had gradually been getting the idea that most of the park hitchhikers were kids trying to get from one point to another and were safe to pick up, which was true, but they were cautious. Today they would be even more cautious. But in 1951 the country did not yet have the collection of zombies, maniacs, and unrestrained sadists who molest, torture, and kill people who offer them rides.

Well, my two companions, I'll call them Betty and Janie—they will be in their fifties or early sixties now, incredible this passage of time—kept singing out to the passing cars. Betty gave out a pitiful but resonant *Ohi-i-i-i-o* to every car from her home state, and we eventually got a ride. We were lucky that day. Our chauffeur turned out to be a first-year seasonal ranger at West Gate who was touring the park just to get a sense of it and who, obviously, wanted some company. So, he took us around the Grand Loop Road, all 143 miles of it, and I got my first good look again at the Lake, the Yellowstone Canyon, Tower Falls, and the terraces at Mammoth. It was a great beginning because it gave me a sense of the whole park and places to which I wanted to return. One of them, high on the agenda, was Mt. Washburn, which at that time was closed to vehicular traffic. To get to the top you had to walk about four miles over a decaying asphalt road used only by trucks taking supplies to the lookout. I would come back to that in late June for one of the best experiences I ever had in Yellowstone.

I said that I didn't know or remember the help out front too well. True. The kitchen was another place. Briefly, I have mentioned my companions on the dishwashing crew. It is time to do them more justice. Jerry and David were only sixteen when they came to Yellowstone. Apparently, they got out of school early in Minnesota, and west they came. They were complete contrasts. Jerry was blond, crew-cut, and puckish. He must have been a hyper-active child. I never saw a kid on the move the way he was, and he talked so fast you could hardly understand him. David was small, dark, and much slower, mentally and physically, than Jerry, but the two made a good team on the basketball court. They played together in high school, and one of the first things they did was to get me over to the Lodge Recreation Hall for a game of basketball. I was happy to oblige. I loved basketball and was in good shooting practice. We began playing, and I was having a fine time, for about five minutes until I had to quit for a moment and stop wheezing. I had thought I was in shape, but I was so winded and obviously wiped out that I was shocked. When you are not quite 21, you don't expect to discover your physical limitations so abruptly, especially when you have no bad habits such as excessive drinking and smoking. Jerry just laughed. I think he had set me up. "Man, you're not out of shape. You're just trying to play a very physical game at 7,300 feet!"

"What?"

"Altitude. You have to get used to the altitude."

Of course. I hadn't even thought of it, but the oxygen available at Kansas City's 600 feet was considerably more than Old Faithful's 7,300. As Jerry and David had reassured me, at some point in the summer, and I don't remember when it occurred, I adapted to the altitude and started playing without discomfort. My body was tuning up to the rigors of 7,300 feet.

David and Jerry were both good dishwashers. Jerry caught onto Dick's system faster than did David, and he could run the dishes through pretty fast. He was also curious, and before long he was wandering over into the chef's area, getting some pointers on being a cook's helper. Had he come back the next year, he probably would have done that or even cooked. My roommate, Gene, worked his way up from pot washer to second cook. I don't know why I wasn't more alert to the possibilities of doing something like that, but in the long run I got a much better job working for the Park Service. The money wasn't much different, but anyone who tells me that working over a hot stove beats interpretive work in uniform is just making the wind blow.

David was less ambitious than Jerry but not less mischievous. He got me into trouble with the chef once, but fortunately I had no criminal record in the Cafeteria, and the chef treated us well.

In fact, in a very nice way, he humiliated us. It was a slow afternoon, and David and I were way ahead on the dishes.

"Hey, Don, let's go get some ice cream." (Like a good Minnesotan, he put the emphasis on *ice*.)

"What are you talking about?" I was so naive in matters like this.

"The commissary steward is gone; you can just go in there and help yourself so long as Pat doesn't catch you."

"So, you're sneaking it?"

"Sure, why not? There's plenty to go around."

"David, that's *stealing*. You know, theft, robbery, etc."

I have never stolen anything in my life, and I didn't feel comfortable letting a high school kid talk me into helping myself to some illegal ice cream, but ice cream is ice cream. A stupid move, and I went with David. Pat was not far behind us.

David and I didn't have time to enjoy the first bite. The chef caught us red-handed and gave us hell. Considering the number of times he had given me permission to use the Cafeteria food to prepare a lunch for a day-off hike, I felt like a Judas. It is very disturbing to betray a trust, and I didn't do things like that. My conscience was really giving me a solid going over.

David felt bad, too, but not for any reasons of conscience. He felt bad because he had been caught. It ruined his image of himself as the wily gun runner. Well, the chef wasn't through with us. He had given us proper hell, and we deserved it. Then he did what every smart employer does. About fifteen minutes after he had caught us he came whipping by the dishwasher's area and tossed on our counter a carton of chocolate ice cream which must have had close to half a gallon left in it.

"Here's some ice cream! Now, in the future, goddammit, if you want some ice cream, just ask for it! Don't try stealing it behind my back for Christ's sake!"

David and I felt very foolish. Boy, did we feel foolish. That hurt. The chef had given us a lesson and a peace offering in one blow. I never stole anything from that date forward.

I have only skirted around the chef. Now I should do him justice because he was, despite some faults, one of the best bosses I have ever worked for. To begin, he was extremely generous. A cafeteria crew functions on its belly. We had good food, lots of it, and occasional treats which made the anticipation of meal time a regular thing. For example, we got cold watermelon when we didn't expect it; we got it one, two, even three nights in a row. On our birthdays we got cake, ice cream, candles and singing from everybody eating on that shift. How did they know when our birthdays occurred? We certainly didn't tell them. However, the commissary steward dispensed the mail each day and when a bunch of cards looking especially like greeting cards came in, I suspect he checked our personnel papers to see what the date was. I never really knew. Anyway, all of us who got the treatment enjoyed every minute of it. On a special day late in the season, the chef gave us a complete steak dinner. There was a certain irony in all this. While the dudes were eating the junk food, of which Smitty's meatloaf was certainly the junkiest, we were being handsomely fed in the back room. Perhaps it was the company's way of making up to us for low salaries.

You may think that I exaggerate about junky food and Smitty's meatloaf. Not in the least. Have you ever eaten a meatloaf that tasted like cooked dirt? That looked like cooked dirt? With some bread thrown in? That was Smitty's meatloaf. Smitty was the first cook, the man next to the chef. The joke around the Cafeteria was that Smitty swept the floor then used what he collected in the dustpan to make his meatloaf.

The rest of the Cafeteria food served to the public wasn't so bad. I remember the red and green Jell-Os prepared by Sonja and Toots, apricots in a dish with what amounted to a round pie crust over them, fair vegetables, and the breakfast menu which was pretty standard and generally well cooked: eggs, bacon, sausage, waffles, pancakes, orange juice, milk. I might add that waffles, plentifully soaked in butter and maple syrup (even the commercial kind) taste better on a cold morning in the mountains than they taste anywhere else.

Pat was generous in dispensing food to us. He was also generous with his Irish temper which fluctuated wildly between joy and depression, depending on his love life. I never knew the details and did not care to. All I observed was that on some days an uncommon racket would come from the chef's area. Pans would start dropping; I can't remember whether or not he kicked them, but I did hear one story about a knife he threw across the kitchen. On such days he was like a violent thunderstorm just about to happen. I stayed miles out of the way then. On other days, he chirped like the soundtrack of a Disney nature movie. He would whistle, bustle about the kitchen with energy and purpose, and generally spread sunshine everywhere.

I saw him blow up for other reasons only once: the day he fired Dick. The episode took me by surprise because I never saw it coming. Most of my life I have been pretty gullible about people and their behavior. Also, I have never been one to bellyache about the jobs given me or to try, by whatever devious means available, to improve my situation by any method other than deserved merit.

I had been coming to work when I was supposed to, putting in my time, then going to see the geysers or practicing my violin in my off duty hours. But Jerry and David had been watching the work schedule much more closely than I.

"Ain't you noticed how many times Dick gets the good schedule while we get the crud?"

"What's the *good* schedule?" I naively asked.

"The seven to three, straight through. You get off early. He's been takin' that shift most of the time so he can go trout fishin'."

I hadn't paid any attention to *that* fact. One set of hours wasn't much different from another as far as I was concerned, just so long as it didn't screw up my day off. But Jerry and David had complained to Pat who had started looking over Dick's shoulder.

Then came the day when Pat stormed around the kitchen in a fury. Dick muttered to himself. He seemed perplexed by all the uproar. The chef and Dick exchanged some angry words . . . and then some more words. The ones I remember best came from

Pat addressed to Dick:

"Well, are you going to work or aren't you?"

I don't remember Dick's answer, but it must have been un-satisfactory. Pat blew up, Dick was fired, and Pat said he would make out the dishwashers' schedule from that time on, which he did. I was sorry to see Dick go, but he did not seem terribly per-turbed about the whole affair. I wonder what happened to him. Never saw him again.

Pat felt bad about the whole thing. Told me that Dick really was a good kid but dammit, he wasn't doing his job the way he was supposed to and some other things of that sort. Well, life goes on. I felt as if I had watched a tornado go past. Fortunately, it never touched me.

Looking back on the incident now, however, I realize that I was out of my element in that situation. There is a peculiar insta-bility in a work force consisting of college kids on summer vaca-tion, itinerant workers who move south and north with the sea-sons, alcoholics who can hold a job only long enough to get money to buy booze, and drifters. The students who worked in the Cafeteria were a pretty good class of people, and even our itinerants that summer were sociable and generally dependable, but one drifter made me as uncomfortable as any person I have ever been around. I don't even remember his name, but I do re-member how wide and big he was. He had the arms of a steve-dore, the body of a prizefighter, and a look of satanic dissipation about him. From his conversation, I could sense the violence that lay close to the surface in this man. I have rarely been around people who I think would or could kill people in cold blood. This was one of those. His entire conversation was a tale of drunken-ness and violent sex.

"We wuz up in Bozeman, see, you been up there? Yeah? and these guys I was with stuck a couple of pigs good, we really stuck 'em. . . they were so drunk they didn't know how many of us were on 'em." He was not, I can assure you, referring to working in a packing plant. Every experience he cared to remember in-volved beating someone, or assaulting some woman—he never specifically said he had raped anyone, but if the ladies he had been around had been compliant, it must have been terror and not desire which motivated them.

I had the feeling that he moved in some sort of primordial darkness, that he belonged to an era when man was first beginning to walk upright and to assault the earth and his fellow *homo sapiens*, before he had institutions which defined such things as morality, legality, love, and compassion. And he seemed strangely attracted to me, as if his boasting would somehow make me admire what he had done and what he was. I continued to hope that he would quit, soon. And he did. But before he left us, he became an object of great interest to a number of the girls in the Cafeteria. It is impossible for me to understand the animal magnetism of such a person, but this one had it, and the women crowded around him like moths attracted to a hot light. I kept thinking to myself, "Don't they see the death and destruction lurking in this man? Do they realize what he would do to them given the slightest opportunity? Have they ever been violently assaulted sexually and actually liked the experience?" Stories did come back to me, in pieces, of parties on the Firehole River and of this man's advances to some of the girls. Evidently, some began to get the picture, but I never learned whether or not any were victims. Perhaps they were too pale for him. A man of that type eventually seeks his own kind, and the college girls, as much as they might have liked to think that they could handle passion in its rawest forms, were not really as able to deal with it as they thought they were. This dark shadow of the summer quit abruptly and moved on. I have no idea what happened to him.

Of the others I worked with that summer, one stands out because he became so visible to millions of Americans. I do not remember when this short, dark-haired, fair-skinned Irishman from Grand Island, Nebraska, first came to the Cafeteria, but he was welcome. He had a good disposition and a marvelous singing voice, and in no time the Cafeteria people responsible for putting on programs in the Lodge got him to sing. He could do the Mario Lanza songs with great style and passion, and the audiences began to fill the Lodge Recreation Hall when he sang. Once in a while our people would ask me to play my violin before Joe sang. This was a nice gesture, but it was never a good experience for me. It was too cold, my fingers were usually numb, and the crowd really wasn't interested in what I played. But Joe brought the house down. He was a star, a fact we all accepted because although enormously talented, he was such a congenial fellow. Our commissary steward was the only one who did not enjoy Joe's spectacular popularity with the dudes. Phil had had ambitions to become a singer himself, but all he had left was a wheeze. He would sit on one of the beds in my room, singing operatic arias to me and hungrily asking for reassurance that he was every bit the singer Joe was. How do you let someone like that down easy?

Years later, I accidentally tuned in a portion of Lawrence Welk's TV show. "An' now we'll hear," Mr. Welk was saying, "from Joe Feeny who is going to do a number popularized by Mario Lanza." Or Joe would a do a number popularized on the Welk show by Joe Feeny, usually some Irish love song which would melt all but the hardest classical music snob's heart.

Anyway, here was our old friend Joe Feeny singing on the TV, and while he may have wanted a different kind of stardom than that offered by Lawrence Welk, it was show biz, and Joe seemed happy in it. I doubt that he has ever been responded to more enthusiastically, however, than by the Yellowstone audiences on Cafeteria night in the Old Faithful Lodge.

4

Off-Duty Hours

ALTHOUGH WORK took up the bulk of our time, we had a day off each week, and blocks of time for recreation during the days. I never wasted these hours and some produced memorable moments. One, which I still remember vividly, occurred in late June. Our commissary steward kept telling me what a great trip the hike up Mt. Washburn was. It was really quite simple. You went past Canyon on the way over Dunraven Pass, got off at the barrier to the road up Mt. Washburn, and walked the four miles to the top. A great view, he told me. As I look back on it now, it was a crazy thing for me to do. I didn't really know where that road was; I had but one image of Mt. Washburn from my first trip around the Grand Loop Road on my first day off, and I had no transportation over there. But I got up early, packed a lunch, and stuck out my thumb on the road leading from Old Faithful to West Thumb.

I should have known it was going to be a great day. The rain of the first two weeks had stopped. The air was brisk and cold, but the sky was that gorgeous mountain blue, perfect in its clarity, depth, and purity. On that kind of day, everyone is an optimist. I was full of anticipation for the trip, excited yet apprehensive about the endeavor I was undertaking, and deliriously happy that I was doing this instead of heading for a hot playground. Before long a car stopped. The couple in it were obviously unused to picking up hitchhikers, but they had heard that most were Park employees on their days off. I put them at ease and told them where I wanted to go. They were just driving around the Park and were grateful for someone who had been there before them. We stopped at West Thumb to look at the paintpots, enjoyed the view of the Lake, stopped at Artist Point along the Yellowstone Canyon, and then proceeded up toward Dunraven Pass. I could see Mt. Washburn and the lookout, so I kept watch for a road and a barrier, and we found it. They had got me there before noon, which was remarkable considering the distance I had to travel, and I thanked them profusely, took their pictures, and wished them a happy trip around the park from that point. I then crossed the barrier and started up the broken-up asphalt road to Mt. Washburn.

In earlier years cars had been allowed to drive up Mt. Washburn, but the number of people who went up there began to drive the lookout nuts so that he could not do his job effectively. And the road broke up and was not in good repair. In 1951 we were only six years beyond World War II, and a lot of things around the country needed fixing. The road to Mt. Washburn was one of them. But I welcomed this state of affairs. It meant that only those willing to walk to reach the top of that mountain would earn the view they could get from there. This was a tame trip, but it could not be made by any fat, flabby, out-of-shape dude.

I had anxieties, however. In Yellowstone in those years, you could never completely forget, especially when you left the main roads and went into areas where few people appeared, the king of the turf: the grizzly bear. A lot of grizzlies lived around the Canyon Area, most of them because they could make regular trips to the Trout Creek Dump south of Canyon to supplement their diet. But the point was that it was always possible, when rounding one of the blind hairpin turns on the Mt. Washburn Road, to find a grizzly coming downhill. I do not know what I would have done had I run into one of them in such a situation. I always made lots of noise so that I wouldn't, but the prospect was scary. There were no trees to climb there. I would have had to rely on dumb luck and hope that the bear would decide to go some other way. I certainly would have given it all the room it wanted. Fortunately, I never confronted that problem. For some reason, the grizzlies and I never crossed paths in Yellowstone, for which I have always been grateful. They are wonderful wild creatures, but not when they are angry and making gestures which indicate that they are going to reduce you to strawberry preserves, which they can do in about fifteen seconds.

Mt. Washburn also had one other attraction: bighorn sheep, but in all the trips I made up the mountain, I never saw a single sheep. During the summer of 1980, however, when I was touring the park with my daughter, Ellen, we saw several right on the road at Dunraven Pass, and the rascals were begging food from cars. This astonished me because I had never seen anything like it in my earlier years in the Park. The only reason I can deduce is that the bear population, which used to occupy this territory, has been so reduced that the sheep now feel safe and have started panhandling just like the bears did. Panhandling bighorn sheep are a flaw in nature. It's like discovering that a star really isn't a star; it's just a big incandescent lightbulb that God stuck up in the sky for a couple of millennia.

On that June morning, however, as I worked my way to the top of the mountain, I put my anxieties down and took in the beauty of the scene that was unfolding before me. There was still snow in places along this road, and little rivulets of clear cold water were streaming from the packs. As the road rose, I could see the approaching timber line and the view from all directions. The Yellowstone Canyon to the south emerged as a great wide gash in the solid green density of the lodgepole forest. One could see the course of the river as it turned north by this great and spectacular canyon. Open meadows on surrounding mountains appeared and then the fluffy cumulus clouds which drift over the mountains in summer and produce the afternoon showers. The air became colder as I got higher, too. Mt. Washburn tops around 10,300 feet, which doesn't make it a spectacular mountain, but it dominates the territory around it so that as you reach the top you can see 100 miles in all directions. As I came to the crest of the mountain, I could see Yellowstone Lake to the south, the Gallatin Range far to the West, and the intermediate features over a large portion of the Yellowstone Plateau.

The lookout itself was a bit of a disappointment. It was perched on a huge concrete square, presumably to discourage people from bugging the lookout himself who appeared to be gone this day. No one was even in the area, and so, after taking the measure of the view in all directions and feeling that I had accomplished something I wanted to do by going up there, I left the mountain top and descended by the road coming up from the north side. But the magic of the occasion, that which I had never expected and which made this one of the finest moments I ever had in Yellowstone, suddenly opened out before me. The high mountain meadows were full of blooming wild flowers, so thick that they made a multi-colored carpet spreading out for acres.

I have never been a gardener, botanist, or general good observer of plant life. It's a defect in my character. Oh, I know about tulips and iris and marigolds and the other cultivated flowers which decorate the yards of city folk. But to notice flowers—to really *see* them the way I was seeing those flowers—was a new experience for me. The scent they gave off was the most exquisite perfume I have ever smelled. At that moment I had a sudden vision that I had arrivevd in heaven and was ready to lie down in the beautiful wild garden and contemplate eternity. That vision is with me yet: purple, yellow, rose, blue, and orange flowers in profusion, the wind only a breath carrying a sweet scent cleansed of all impurities, white clouds floating against a deep blue sky.

A few summers later I met a boy from New York City who had grown up in an inner city apartment. He was interested in the chemistry of the hot springs, and one of my colleagues was explaining it to him. He said he didn't miss grass, trees, flowers, and such stuff. He was entirely a mental creature, the kind of person who will function well in outer space because he won't miss what many of us would die without. I think my moment among the flowers would have gone completely past him. Too bad. No, perhaps that's best. I want those meadows as uncluttered when I'm old as they are now.

This mountain meadow was, for me, certainly one of the most splendidly beautiful things I have ever seen and experienced in my life. I was just 21, and I felt very good about my life and especially about that moment. The rest of the day was anticlimactic. I don't remember how I got back, but I must have been lucky again. I went clear around—to Mammoth, then south to Old Faithful, 143 miles with an eight-mile exhilarating hike tossed in in one day, all on the good right thumb. I don't recall even worrying about getting back; I just assumed that I would.

A month later I went back to Mt. Washburn. It was beautiful again, but not like the first time. You can never duplicate that first experience, especially when it sneaks up on you and you don't expect it. Then the response is all spontaneous; the moment grips you and holds you. Every time after that you seek a return to that first moment, but that is a mistake. You should seek a fresh experience.

This had happened to me once before, when I went to hear Joseph Szigeti play the Brahms Violin Concerto with the Kansas City Philharmonic. I didn't know much about Szigeti; I had heard him on the radio once, playing the Mendelssohn with the Hollywood Bowl orchestra, the summer we were in California, and I remembered his wobbly tone, uncertain pitch, and other defects. The night he played in Kansas City I told my mother, who went to the concerts with me, that I was going because the man was a violinist, but I wasn't expecting much because he wasn't good like Heifetz or Milstein who could really play.

What I didn't know was that Szigeti had on and off nights. As Raymond Cerf, my KU violin teacher said one time, "If you ask me who is the better violinist, I would say Heifetz, of course. But Szigeti is a superb musician." That night superb would not be adequate to describe what happened between Szigeti, the orchestra, and the Brahms. He was exploring depths of musical meaning that I simply had never heard, and by the end of the second movement, which ends on a sustained high F, he had everyone in that hall in a trance. I'll never know what prompted what happened next—perhaps it was just instinct or timing—but Szigeti paused only long enough for the pages to turn and then began the last movement of the concerto. If you know the Brahms, and can imagine the kind of transition that an attacca would produce from the second to the third movements, you will understand why the hair literally stood up on the back of my neck. I felt like rising and shouting BRAVO! My God!! What an effect! It was one of the most moving experiences I have ever had in a concert hall. It made me devoted to Szigeti for the rest of my life.

I heard him play the Brahms years later, and he did not play it well. I think he was ill. Anyway, it was not a good performance, and I learned again, that you really can't go back to a great experience. It steals up on you like a black cat in the night, green eyes shining, and scares the hell out of you. A good thing. Our nervous systems couldn't take charges like that very often.

So, I went looking for that magic moment again on Mt. Washburn, but it wasn't there. It never will be there. The magic moments of the rest of my life are in the future; they are the ones I can't predict, those that will come in all their energy and power when I least expect them and capture me again.

On that second trip I decided to stop in Mammoth and see Bonnie. Bonnie was the Cafeteria's dark-haired, melancholy beauty. She ran the cash register out front most of the time, but she came down with jaundice and was sent to the hospital in Mammoth to recuperate. Naturally, I expected to learn that one had to stand in line to see her because she was one of the popular kids in the Cafeteria. Bonnie was surprised to see me. No wonder. No one else had been up to see her in a week. That surprised me. One of the guys was, nominally I thought, her boyfriend. I still don't know exactly what was happening, but I have often wondered if Bonnie was beautiful and popular but not part of the in-group because she was a good Mormon girl who, when confronted with the choice of drinking and "putting out" or "sleeping around," whichever euphemism you like, decided that her values were more important than her standing in the popularity contest and thus got shunted aside by other girls who were more compliant.

Pity is that I wasn't a more desirable man. I didn't carouse around or compromise girls, and I used to wonder whether or not they appreciated that. Not that I wasn't interested in the physical things in life. At 21 *every* man is a walking biological time bomb. You *need* a woman, but I had control of that urge. My parents had given me a model. Physical lovemaking went with the privileges of marriage, so, dammit, find the right girl for the right reasons, and then enjoy the privileges of a kind of companionship which makes life a pleasure, not an endurance test. Now, if I had been a Mr. America, and many pretty girls had tried to compromise me, would I have succumbed? Hard to say. Well, I wasn't, and I didn't. (Yeah, I know the line: "What did you do for fun when you were young?" I'll tell you. I used my imagination and diversified my interests. I dated but did not seduce some very nice girls before I got married, and I'm not sorry I was square either.)

Bonnie thanked me for coming. I wonder where Bonnie is now. I hope she married a nice guy and had a large happy family. She needed the company of those who loved her.

Before forgetting, I should remember Tex. I would guess his age in 1951 at about 60. He had iron grey curly hair, was solidly built, and soft spoken. Tex was a pot washer, and he did not aspire to do more than that. He was also the shrewdest poker player in the Cafeteria. The young Turks, especially Jerry, always wanted to get Tex in their quarter max, two limit raise poker games.

Every morning after one of these card games Tex would

come by and say, "Won 'leven dollahs las' night." "Won twenty-favh dollahs las' night." And on one occasion, "They threw a new game at me las' night—low ball. Only won two dollahs."

I asked Jerry why Tex always won at poker.

"He's the perfect poker player, damn him. Hell, one time he has it, the next he doesn't. And you never know from the way he holds his cards or responds. Geez, when David gets a good hand, his face flushes, he smiles like he just inherited a quarter mil, and he can hardly wait for his turn. David with a good hand is as inconspicuous as a lighted Christmas tree in a dark hallway, but Tex could be holding a Royal Flush, and you'd think he didn't have a goddamned pair of 2's." I told Tex this once. He smiled as if to say. Right. That's just the way I do it. And he always won.

Tex had good eyes, too. Or maybe he was color blind. We were taking a short hike back of Old Faithful one evening when he stopped me, put a hand on my arm, and spoke softly.

"Lookit this new born elk."

"This what?"

"Not too loud. The mother ought to be around here somewhere."

"What are we looking for, Tex?"

"This new born elk here."

"Where?"

"Right. . . be careful, now! Don't step on him."

"I don't seeeeeee. . .geeeez!"

Right under my feet, its dappled colors melting into the patterns of sunlight and shadow filtering down into the lodgepole forest, was the elk. It never moved, instinct obviously telling it that safety lay in perfect motionlessness. I am told that such creatures also have little odor. What bear or coyote, passing within ten feet of this animal, would see it? The bear, which has atrocious eyesight, surely would not. But the sharp-eyed coyote might be a different case. Still, nature's camouflage was never more impressive to me than then.

That young elk probably prospered. Later in the summer, as I walked that trail back of Old Faithful one evening, I became aware of a tremendous stillness all around me. I couldn't see anything, but I was aware that an unnatural quiet had settled over the forest. Then I noticed a cow elk, standing across the trail some thirty yards in front of me. I was puzzled why she didn't move. Then I became aware of another sensation. Have you ever felt that many pairs of eyes you cannot see are on you? I once thought that the only people who felt this way were the animated characters in the Disney cartoons. You will remember the scenes in which the heroic dog or dwarf or cat walks down a dark alley or through a dark forest and is surrounded by black except for the pairs of eyes pasted against the black background like stars in the sky. Well, I couldn't see any black panels with eyes stuck on, but I knew that I was being *watched*. So, I stopped and checked out the territory.

The cow elk was still ahead of me. Then I saw a slight movement to my left—another elk. To my right. Damn! They were even behind me! I had walked right into a small herd of elk dispersed through the woods. Why weren't they moving on? I didn't know, but taking the Park Service's directions about confrontations with wild animals quite literally, I stopped, leaned against a tree, and said to the old lady in front of me. "After you, madam. I think I'll just rest a spell. You go right on about your business."

She gave me a soft look, but one which also said, "Good move on your part, buster. There are enough of us here to kick hell out of you." Then she waited some more. A moment or two later I heard a thump and the animals moved swiftly through the woods. To my left I caught a glimpse of several yearlings. That was the anxiety! The cows were protecting their young, and they had to make sure I wasn't a bear or another predator which could threaten them. The young ones scampered away with the adults, and they simply vanished, like an image dissolving on a TV screen.

Years later, however, I heard about one occasion when the elk were not so lucky. A group of tourists came into Madison Museum, my station, with a first-hand account of nature, "red in tooth and claw." They had been travelling the road from West Yellowstone to Madison Junction, when out of the woods in front of them came a group of elk running easily but swiftly. A black bear was in pursuit, but it was losing ground. The elk reached the Madison River, swam it quickly, raced into the large meadow on the opposite side, then paused while waiting for a yearling which lagged behind. The young elk successfully crossed the river, but it could not pick up the scent of the others, became panicked, and turned back to the river. The bear, which by this time had also crossed the river, raced along the bank and leaped out into the water onto the back of the young elk, killing it instantly. It then dragged the carcass onto dry ground. The adult elk stormed up, threatening the bear, but as they discovered the death of the young animal, they gradually retreated, and the bear came down from a tree where it had gone to escape the larger elk. Tragedy for the elk; lunchtime for the bear. In all my years in the Park I never saw a bear run down an elk, especially a black bear. The grizzlies could do it, but the blacks rarely. Well, it happens. In fact, it didn't happen often enough. Yellowstone's predators were never able to keep the numbers of elk down to a size that the range would support.

5

Yellowstone's Magnificent Geysers; The Tetons; And the End of the First Summer

THERE WAS ONE other activity which occupied me a good deal of the time that first year at Old Faithful. I became a geyser hound. That's the term we give to people who become so taken with the big geysers that they will sit for hours, even days, waiting for eruptions. Some instant converts spent most of two weeks in 1961 waiting for an eruption of Steamboat Geyser at Norris. It was on a rampage that year, spewing millions of gallons of water nearly 300 feet into the air. I had to work and missed it. I had become a geyser hound that first summer by waiting on the Giant for a whole day and waiting weeks trying to catch the Grand. Many a morning Jess, the night watchman, would come in and say to me, "Saw the old Grand this morning. Beautiful sight!" He was always seeing "the old Grand," and I was seeing nothing but pictures of it. The hunger for a sight of Grand erupting was really getting to me. But my turn eventually came.

One morning I checked with the ranger station and learned that an eruption of the Grand was expected very shortly. I took off on the boardwalk past Old Faithful, ran down the asphalt path and bridge across the Firehole River, and legged it for the Grand. I didn't really run. I walked rapidly. In the geyser basins you never run . . . unless you are a fool. A sudden cloud of steam from a hot pool fogging your glasses, a wrong turn, and you could find yourself in a pool of water whose temperature was 180 degrees Farenheit. I read a magazine account of that very thing happening to a nine-year-old boy who was walking with his parents on a ranger-guided tour of the basin. The boy fell into the pool, attempted only to rise, but must have died within seconds. His body was pulled down by convection currents. I cannot begin to conceive of the terror or the anguish of parents who had a child taken from them so suddenly, so swiftly, and so finally. It defies the imagination.

At any rate, I never ran through the hot springs area. I walked and I watched where I was going. But I was in a hurry, so when I reached the path near the Lion group and went into the woods briefly, I legged it even faster. I was perhaps 100 yards from the Grand when I saw this explosive tower of water rise above the tree tops. I arrived just as the first of several rockets, each a small eruption, was subsiding. I stayed to watch the full eruptive cycle, that time seven or eight rockets, and I was captured for life.

Anyone who has been to Yellowstone and not seen the Grand has not seen the finest natural attraction in the Park. Between eruptions it is so innocuous that you would pass it and pay little attention to it. The Grand is a fountain geyser, one which erupts in explosive bursts, so it has no geyser cone or mound such as Old Faithful has built. It is a calm pool of water with an orifice some three to four feet in diameter. As the water in Grand's chambers heats, the water level of the entire pool rises every twenty minutes. At these intervals, Turban geyser, part of the Grand complex, erupts. It throws water ten to fifteen feet into the air, then subsides, and refills. The Grand's pool drops and the buildup of pressure begins again. Various indicators have worked over the years. I know that once water begins pouring over the various small terraces leading up to Grand's pool and orifice, pressure is building and an eruption is not too far away. Eventually, this pressure builds to a critical point. Sometimes just before, sometimes just after Turban starts, one sees a great swell rise out of Grand's orifice. That is followed by a mound of water approximately three feet high. These are the first manifestations of the steam bubbles which trigger an eruption of Grand. Right after the mound there comes a terrific explosive burst which pushes a jagged wall of water about 100 feet into the air. It hangs there and looks as if it might settle, but in the split seconds which characterize an eruption of the geyser, it is suddenly overpowered and enveloped by great jets of water which reach 180-200 feet and give an eruption of Grand the appearance of a spired Gothic cathedral. Just as suddenly as it began, the rocket ceases, and there is a pause in the action. Before long, another bubble appears, another wall, and then those dazzling jets which pierce the sky above the Grand. You stay and stay and stay, thrilling to each rocket, until suddenly the activity ceases, and the pool swiftly drains. Grand will now take several hours to fill before another eruption.

I have never heard anyone who saw Grand express anything but awe. Once when I was out on geyser hill watching this remarkable geyser, a lady who was slightly ahead of her family, came around a turn in the path between rockets of the Grand and asked me what everyone was watching.

"An eruption of Grand Geyser," I told her.

"What is Grand Geyser?" she asked.

"Watch," I said. That is all I had to say. When those spectacular bursts of Grand shot into the evening air, this lady just stood

Grand Geyser

there, her jaw dropped, her eyes wide with wonder. I have never seen unfeigned awe, amazement, and incredulity rise so spontaneously in a human face.

"Why, why this geyser is much more beautiful than Old Faithful!"

"Yes, it is. People who have been here before or know about the Park's geysers know that." I didn't do anymore talking. The geyser was doing plenty for itself. I wondered to myself: had the Grand, "la belle dame sans merci," captured one more person? Those who know and love the Grand will wait a long time to see it. I talked with a lady who had spent one 33 hour vigil waiting for an eruption of Grand. There were many others. I never had to wait that long, but I have put in my time waiting there, too. The best part is that the Grand is always as good as, if not better than, the way you remembered it. It is one of the few things in this life that I have returned to again and again without disappointment. You see it erupt and you say to yourself: by God, it is just as dramatic, just as beautiful as I remember.

There are other geysers worth waiting for: Great Fountain, for example, like Grand, a fountain geyser. I once saw the steam bubbles in Great Fountain raise a huge mound of water about five or six feet out of the geyser before exploding and sending jets clawing out into the surrounding air. George Marler, the park geologist when I was there, told me the first time he saw Great Fountain, it raised a mound about 20 feet in the air before exploding. The eruption was so spectacular he concluded that Great Fountain was the park's premier attraction. But George never saw another eruption like that first one, and he studied the geysers of the Firehole Basin for nearly forty years.

Giant was spectacular in the early 1950s. I first saw it after waiting in the cold and partial rain most of a day. Like Old Faithful, it is a cone geyser, but whereas Old Faithful erupts about 12,000 gallons of water in 2-4 minutes, Giant puts out over a million in an hour long eruption. From my first year in the Park, 1951, until 1955, Giant erupted every two to five days. My wife, who had incredible luck with this geyser, was with me the first time she saw it. We were driving into the Old Faithful Area, and a number of people were gathered around the Giant, so I told her we should stop and see what was predicted. The geyser erupted in five minutes. That was the last year it has erupted with any predictable regularity. In 1956 and the years since then both Grotto and Rocket Geysers, about 100 yards from Giant, have been quite active. Marler told me he believed that a steam lock had occurred underground. The effect was to divert a considerable amount of energy to Grotto and Rocket and to take it away from Giant. The result is that Giant has not been able to erupt for nearly thirty years now. When will it again begin a period of reasonably frequent eruptions? Whenever that steam lock ceases to exist and sufficient energy reaches Giant that the water in its chambers becomes superheated, flashes into steam and propels the great column of water nearly 200 feet into the air. It is an impressive sight, but not as dramatic or spectacular as Grand.

Marler liked Splendid Geyser, one I never saw. Others worth waiting for are Riverside and Lone Star and Castle. Actually, there are many geysers, large and small, scattered among Yellowstone's seven geyser basins. Four of these, Upper, Middle, and Lower Basins on the Firehole, and Norris are easily accessible to the touring public. The other three take work: Heart Lake, which I have never seen, Shoshone, and Monument. Shoshone Geyser Basin has one large geyser, Union, but I would not recommend someone going there without good directions and company. It is seven miles by foot from Old Faithful, and it used to be in grizzly country. What the population of grizzlies in the park now is, I don't know, but I would want to be sure. Also, since these interior basins do not have well marked footpaths, people are apt to wander around in them without realizing the dangers. The crust in a geyser basin may be undermined. Go through into hot water or steam and you could get second or third degree burns in a hurry. Geyser basins are no places to play around carelessly. I remember one Explorer scout who did a bit too much exploring in this region in 1963. A team of rangers had to go get him at night and carry him back, seven miles, over a trail built for one person. It's not precipitous, just inconvenient when you are trying to carry someone on a stretcher that distance.

Since I have always been interested in geological phenomena, it was natural for me to become involved in studying the geysers, hot pools, terraces, mud pots, fumaroles, and other manifestations of volcanic activity in Yellowstone. After all, geyser basins exist in but three areas in the world: Yellowstone, Iceland, and New Zealand. In two of those areas, the hot springs are used for utilitarian purposes. Yellowstone alone preserves the geysers and hot springs as aesthetic phenomena. A nation hungry for energy and led by an idiot Secretary of the Interior (and we had one recently) might consider this a waste, but a much more tragic waste would be exploitation of these remarkable natural wonders. I used to smile to myself when tourists would come into Yellowstone raving about the beauty of the Canadian Rockies and lamenting the fact that Yellowstone was not more spectacular. What they wanted were more Canadian Rockies. But there is no place in the world which combines natural wonders, scenery (and there is spectacular and beautiful scenery in Yellowstone, starting but not stopping with the Yellowstone Canyon), and animal life the way Yellowstone does. The gift this park represented, and I will come to that later, was one of the finest things any small group of Americans ever did for their countrymen. Considering the millions they and their heirs could have made exploiting this region, we have to remark on their lack of selfishness and concern for the future. They were the intellectual children of Emerson and Thoreau.[*]

Near the end of my first summer, one of the men who worked at the Lower Gas Station at Old Faithful asked me about going hiking in the Grand Tetons. I had been there once already, just to look the place over. The experience of seeing the Grand Tetons for the first time, like coming upon the meadows of Mt. Washburn full of flowers, is the kind of moment that etches itself in memory. I wish that, once again, I were going south from Old Faithful to see the Grand Tetons for the first time! The catalyst, once more, was our commissary steward who had talked and talked about the Tetons, rhapsodizing about them. He did that about everything, however, so I decided to check his exaggera-

---

[*]There are those who do not entirely agree. Alston Chase's *Playing God in Yellowstone* offers some well documented and thoughtful reappraisals of the event. He points out, correctly, that establishment of the park benefited white men, but did a terrible disservice to numerous Indian tribes which had lived in and around the territory for years.

tions out for myself. From Old Faithful the route is pretty direct. Seventeen miles to West Thumb, then twenty-two to South Gate, passing Lewis Lake, Lewis River Falls, and the spectacularly deep Lewis Canyon along the way. You do not get a good look at the Tetons until you come out of the woods at the north end of Jackson Lake and my God, my God, my God. Before you are those great blue chunks of granite—Moran, North Teton, Grand Teton, South Teton—rising almost 7000 feet right up from Jackson Hole. If there is heaven on earth, this is it.

That first day I couldn't take my eyes off them. Neither could the people from whom I had hitched a ride. When I got to Jenny Lake which is in the heart of the Teton Park and right below Teewinot, I thought I had walked into one of our grade school primers with its idealized versions of mountain scenery. The lake is absolutely clear. It is bordered by aspen whose white trunks intensify the deep blue sky of an early Teton morning, lodgepole pines, and "many pinnacles," Teewinot, Jenny Lake's mountain. Glaciers moving down the canyons north and south of Teewinot milennia ago, dumped their debris in Jackson Hole. When they retreated, the streams coming off the glaciers and the snow pack high in the inner Tetons filled the basin between the mountain and the glacial moraine. Cottonwood Creek drains both Jenny and Leigh Lakes—they are joined by a stream called String Lake and they are the heart of the country. Jenny was Beaver Dick Leigh's Indian wife, but he lost her and the children in one savage burst of smallpox. Before the tragedy, however, they lived in paradise. It is no accident that the Rockefellers bought so much land in the area years ago, and it is fortunate that they gave it to the public as part of Grand Teton National Park.

So, point established. When in Yellowstone, see the Tetons, too. They are different from anything in Yellowstone, and they are magnificent. They are for hikers, mountain climbers, and anyone else who has the capacity to soak up the natural wonders of the West and let them bring a few moments peace and tranquillity to the mind. Before I quit my annual treks to that country, I had hiked up most of the Teton trails, exhausted myself in its back country, and come to love it with a passion.

When Jerry—I forget his last name—asked me about hiking up Indian Paintbrush Canyon in the late summer of 1951, I was ready to go. I had been only to Jenny Lake and had not penetrated the interior of the Tetons. There was one small problem. Jerry had an expensive English Hillman automobile which he did not wish to destroy by taking it through the ten miles of road construction then going on between Yellowstone's South Entrance and the Grand Teton Park. So, he proposed getting up quite early, going north to Madison, west to West Yellowstone, south to Ashton, Idaho, and on south until we could cross Teton Pass, go through Jackson and then head north to the jumping off place for Indian Paintbrush Canyon. We did that, taking our commissary steward with us as far as Ashton and arranging to meet him on our return.

This will not be a scenic tour of Indian Paintbrush Canyon because I do not remember the hike that well. I do remember, however, that we left at four and got there about 11 A.M. The round trip hike was 18 miles, and it was slow going at the top because we hit snow fields across the trails, and we did not have snow equipment. We were in no danger of falling into any crevasses, but we could have taken some jolly good slides down some long slopes. I am happy to say that we moved circumspectly and avoided those problems. At the head of the trail we looked down on Lake Solitude, the end of the Cascade Canyon Trail. I was to come back there in future years.

Jerry and I did not get back to Ashton until 11 P.M. We picked up our commissary steward and returned to Old Faithful sometime between one and two in the morning. It may have been later. All that I remember is that I had, at the most, four hours sleep after riding 500 miles and hiking 18 in the space of some 21 hours. When I went on the early morning shift, my eyes were still bloodshot, and I looked every bit as tired as I felt. Toots, our chief salad maker, took one look at me and cried out in anguish, "Oh no! Not *you*, too!"

I must explain. Toots was a very nice lady. She had watched

with mounting apprehension, the creeping decadence which had infected many of the "nice" kids in the Cafeteria. Even David and Jerry, still innocents of a sort, had finally decided to find out what getting drunk was all about. And they had found out, complete with king-sized hangovers. But Toots had faith. I was the squarest kid in the Cafeteria. Surely there was one person invulnerable to SIN. There was. I don't brag about it. Sex I would have liked. Drunkenness—forget it. That's stupid. But at that moment I was standing in the Cafeteria, leaning against one of the metal supports for our dish racks, bleary and bloodshot eyed, dark circles under my eyes. I must have looked as if I had wasted my body in the most colossal booze and sex orgy of the summer. Toots was in despair.

I went to her in my most comforting manner, knowing perfectly well what was troubling her, and realizing that when she could see me up close, not smelling of alcohol and vomit, she would understand.

"Toots, what you see here is not the consequence of excessive drink and lust; you see only the tiredest savage in Yellowstone Park. Briefly, I have ridden 500 miles in a car, hiked 18 miles up Indian Paintbrush Canyon, and come on the job with about three or four hours sleep. There is nothing wrong with me that food and sleep will not cure." How true. The incredible mending capability of youthful bodies. At three in the afternoon, I got off work. I went back to the dorm and took a two-hour nap, then got up, ate a good supper, showered, then went back to bed. There followed the longest, most refreshing, most unbroken fourteen hours of sleep that I have ever had. I did not wake up until 9 the next day, which was all right because I didn't go on until noon. I had dreamed *nothing*. I don't think I even moved during that time. But I felt so good the next day. Sore here and there, a troublesome blister in places, but general well-being through and through. That was thirty-five years ago. I have not had so restful a night's sleep at any time since then. Perhaps that is why I remember it so well.

⊠

There was one other event of significance that summer. About a week before I finished the tour of duty I had promised the Cafeteria, I was in Jerry's room (my companion on the long ride and hike) talking with him and some of his friends about work, days off, pay, and other oddments of the job. One of the men mentioned the fact that the rangers got two days off a week. *Two* days off, I said? Hmmmmm. I had spent a summer trying to go here and there on one day. Two days would be priceless. So, I wandered over to the Old Faithful District Station and inquired about the ways one got to be a ranger. The process was explained to me, and I took down the appropriate addresses. It was a quiet passing moment then, but it was a crossroads in my life, a small act which had enormous consequences for me. I could not know that then. The young people were starting to leave the Cafeteria. More than half of my companions left before I did, our last good memory the night in late August which was called "the savage Christmas."

This tradition apparently started some years earlier when the weather, always uncertain in Yellowstone as September approaches, turned cold and snowy in late August. I have twice experienced significant snows in Yellowstone in late August, once on August 17, 1960, and again on August 17–18, 1978. The latter storm brought sufficient snow and ice that traffic was held up in the passes for part of a day. The trees on the high passes were covered with snow; it was a true Christmas setting in mid-August.

Well, some savages had started the custom of celebrating a sort of summer Christmas—one last party before the summer was over—and all participated in and enjoyed it. The chef fed us handsomely on a table beautifully decorated with candles and Christmas holly.

But September came, and day by day they left: the girls out front, the dishwashers, the cooks' helpers, the porters from the Lodge, the help at the stores and at the Inn. After Labor Day, traffic into the Park dropped dramatically. We really weren't needed much longer.

I do not remember exactly when I left that year, probably between September 6 and 10, but I felt a combination of joy and tearfulness. I hated to leave what had been the best summer experience of my life, but I wanted to get home and see my parents and brother and sister again; we had never been separated for this long in our entire lives, and my sister was now married. So I finished my last day, collected my check and money for the return trip, and headed north to Gardiner, then to Livingston, back through Billings, and the long night ride through Nebraska and to Kansas City. My entire family was there, in the crowds at Union Station, to greet me, and I was so glad to see them all that I could not be demonstrative in the way I felt. It was good to be back among loved ones. Mother was especially glad to have me back, the "adventure" over. But it was not over. The spell of the mountains was in me. I knew that I would go back.

6

The Second Year:
I Become a Ranger

My SENIOR YEAR in college was not a good one. I have never done so poorly academically as I did that year, and my life was complicated by a love affair that was going nowhere, sickness, and the sense that I was soon to leave an environment that I loved.

Amplification. The girl I met while playing piano trios with my brother, a cellist. The violin and cello in such a group can be mediocre, but the pianist had better be pretty damned good or the whole ensemble will fall apart. Our pianist was damned good. She was musical, she had the technique, and she was sexy. At that stage of my life I was much attracted by this sexy and musical pianist, and she responded, to a point. But I always knew she liked someone else better, and that pained me. It was not a good situation, and it led to some emotional trauma which I could have done without. But it was my own doing, not hers.

I was out late too much of the year, got sick, mostly flu and respiratory stuff, and that sapped my energy and did not help matters. And there was always that terrible irony. I, the kid who, in grade school, thought the day school was out the most perfect day in the year, suddenly found myself wondering how I could stay in school forever. College life had agreed with me beyond all my expectations. It had variety; it had culture; it had intelligent people with whom to talk and associate. I could not leave it. I was not certified to teach. What in the hell was I going to do?

Then, just as I was trying to choose from a number of bad options, another series of events occurred which profoundly affected my future. These things have happened to me on several occasions: clusters of events which cumulatively made an incredible difference in the direction my life took. Maybe it was the luck trailing from KU's first NCAA basketball championship in March, 1952. Clyde Lovellette and his playmates had done it. We were the best in the nation. It was a very good feeling.

I had put in my application for a job teaching freshman English. Since my work in English was far from distinguished—I spent too many hours practicing and playing my violin to do the kind of reading I should have been doing—I did not expect much from the application. But then, as is usually the case around state universities, freshmen were numerous and help was short. And then I was elected to Phi Beta Kappa. And then I was selected to appear the following Fall on KU's first honors recital. Five students were selected, on the basis of their performances on weekly recitals in School of Fine Arts programs. I wasn't even aware a selection was going on. Raymond Cerf had me playing the slow movement of Lalo's *Symphonie Espagnole* that Spring, and I happened to appear on a day when I was "hot." Even more important, my accompanist, Delores Wunsch, not the lady with whom I was in love but a superb pianist in her own right, gave me the kind of support that makes a soloist sound better than he is. Whatever, there I was, picked with four others, all music majors, for the big occasion in the Fall.

So, the semester ended on a good note. I would be back in the Fall. I would have to practice over the summer—no problem because I took my violin to Yellowstone—and I had the PBK key to make me feel good about my total undergraduate performance. Years later I discovered that I had graduated in the upper five percent of my class in the College of Liberal Arts. I wonder how well I might have done if I had really studied the way I know how to now?

Even graduation itself was a beautiful occasion. Contrary to the impressions many persons from around the country have of Kansas, it is not all flat. The northeast section is bisected by numbers of rivers which produce the rolling topography so characteristic of the region. The University of Kansas sits on a long fishhook ridge above the town of Lawrence. Mt. Oread, the natives call it, and while it is not a mountain, just try to walk up 14th Street some wintry day when a good coating of ice is on the brick sidewalks. Good luck. Smarter people seek an alternate route.

When I graduated in 1952, many of the buildings on the slopes of the ridge now were not there. KU sat high above the town and a bit clear of it. At graduation time, the academic procession went down the long hill by the campanile into the stadium. I graduated on a beautiful clear June evening that Spring. The faculty lined the walk down which we moved, and they occasionally greeted a passing student. I had spread myself over many departments. I knew many of the music faculty; obviously the English faculty knew me; and I had had cordial relations with teachers in history, the natural sciences, political science, modern languages, and speech. How many I had come to know and greet informally I did not realize until I took that walk down to my B.A. I found myself nodding to the right and to the left. Many greeted me by my first name. Halfway down the line, Mr. Cerf, my favorite of all the KU people, reached out for me. "Hi, Don." That was apparently the last straw for the kid behind me.

"Jesus Christ," he said, "do you know the whole goddamned faculty?"

The only thing which hadn't materialized was a job with the National Park Service. I had applied; they had not responded, so I chose the dishwashing job again and prepared to head west when school was out.

I don't remember the trip out in 1952. The weather was bet-

ter when I arrived, and the Cafeteria crew was much changed. A
few of the old faces were back: Hazel, the commissary steward,
the chef, but most of the people of the summer of 1951 were
gone, and the excitement and sense of discovery I felt among
them was missing.

That's a sad thing, isn't it, the way you cannot go back and
recover certain portions of your past. We all know this; it is the
reason high school reunions fail so badly. You are not the persons you were in high school. The context is gone; you are gone;
all is changed. An operation so heavily dependent on temporary
help as the Yellowstone Park Company was gives one no sense of
continuity. When we go back to something, we want to find it as
we left it. The Old Faithful Cafeteria in 1952 was not the Old
Faithful Cafeteria of 1951. Rationally, I knew that, but emotionally, I hoped that it would not be so.

In such situations, one adapts to a new set of circumstances:
new people, new supervisors, new roommates, and waits for Fate
to take over. Two things happened to me that summer which I
had not anticipated. Once again, I was just plain lucky. I had
hardly settled into my 1952 summer routine at the Cafeteria
when I received an unexpected visitor. Les Gunzel, Old Faithful
District Ranger, walked into the Cafeteria looking for me. I
couldn't imagine how I had got into trouble with the rangers. I
was a good guy. Trouble wasn't his purpose. He had my application for work in the Park and wanted to know if I wanted to join
the Park Service. The idea of being a ranger gave me a shot of
adrenalin that would have set a horse's back feet kicking, and I
was ready to do it, but there was a problem: rangers had to buy
their uniforms. Even if I could get a used one, I would be out
some $65 which I didn't have. And in those days I never gave a
thought to doing what comes naturally to today's college student:
borrow it from Mom and Dad. I didn't have the money; I couldn't
do it. Disappointment. Gunzel asked me when we got paid. July
1, I told him. The chef came by after Gunzel left and asked me
when I was leaving. I told him I wasn't; I couldn't afford the uniform. I thought, from time to time, that being a ranger might be

pretty nice, but I really did like the Cafeteria job and people. Why do we lie to ourselves that way? I wouldn't say it was sour grapes. I would not allow my desire to become a ranger surface in my consciousness because I couldn't handle the disappointment of knowing I couldn't afford to join. Looking back, I realize now how skillfully I concealed from myself how much I wanted to put on the uniform and be somebody in Yellowstone. Actually, a seasonal ranger, GS-4, really isn't a lot of somebody, but he is a lot more visible and more prestigious than a cafeteria dishwasher. The principal compensation for the disappointment I felt that June was Jan Stallings, another of the really good pianists I have met in my life. She was from Smith College, an Easterner slumming in the West for a summer but keeping her fingers nimble by playing the piano in the Old Faithful Lodge. Now, a violinist who practiced there and a pianist who came in for a similar purpose, are bound to meet. I didn't have as much music as I would like to have had and did acquire later, but I had the Franck Sonata and the Vieuxtemps 4th Violin Concerto. Could Jan read the piano parts, especially to the Franck which is extremely difficult? Can rainbow trout jump?

We set Thursday afternoons, when both of us were off work, for doing some playing, and because of that, I got the preparation I needed for playing the Vieuxtemps Concerto on the honors recital the coming Fall. How I wish I had had the book of concertos I now have, the Mozart, Beethoven, Brahms Sonatas, and other music which we could have played and played and played. We had to repeat too much. But we could do a good Franck. A Czech couple used to come in and listen to us over the racket made by bouncing basketballs in the Recreation Hall. I have never played better than I did that summer.

July 1 came and with it my first check . . . and the return of Les Gunzel. Could I now pay for the uniform and was I interested in joining the Park Service? This was looking in the face of Fate twice. I had the money except for the amount needed to buy a hat and that was given to me on credit, so I swallowed hard, kissed my transportation money from the Cafeteria away, and joined the Park Service in July of 1952. It turned out to be one of the smartest things I ever did.

It would be very difficult for the moderately well-heeled college student of today to understand how joining the Park Service that summer was, for me, a bold thing to do. I had no car and so was cutting loose from my safe moorings in the Old Faithful Cafeteria. I began to wonder about such things as eating, sleeping, learning a new job. But first, I had to get a uniform. Gunzel took me to Mammoth where I entered the Chief Ranger's office and began getting processed. At that time the Park Service gave us temporary appointments. In a few years they would put us all on permanent status and furlough us for the winter. It simplified the bookkeeping. The conditions for employment were simple. We were paid a monthly salary out of which came charges for our quarters and food, *if* we ate at the government mess hall. My quarters were a bunk in the Lake Ranger Station and food at the Lake District Mess Hall. Looking over my old pay records, I note that the annual salary of a GS-4 in 1952 was $3175 per year. That first summer, after withholding, Social Security, quarters, meals, and "other" were deducted, I got home with only $324.86 of my gross of $557.04. Still it was more than I would have made in the Cafeteria.

I spent all of my Cafeteria money on a used blouse (euphemism for a very heavy uniform jacket), trousers, gray shirts, and green tie. The Park Service supplied the NPS insignia and the badge. I lacked only a hat—that was no *hat*; it was a felt *Stetson*, the Canadian mounty kind—and that I obtained on credit from an elderly lady who ran one of the last stores which were not owned by Hamilton, the Yellowstone Park Company, or Jack Haynes. I regret that I do not remember her name. I was ready to swear on a Bible that I would come back and pay the $19 I owed her for the hat. She was generous, but she said some had not been so conscientious. That really shocked me. When I first joined up, I naturally assumed that the rangers were all green and gray versions of the Canadian Mounties, men of absolutely unassailable character, strength, bravery, intelligence, etc. I had swallowed the whole stereotype. I also discovered that there were two kinds of rangers: protective and interpretive, and that among the seasonals, there was no comparison between the intelligence, education, and character of the interpretive men and those in the protective division. The protective division, the largest, maintained law and order, patrolled the roads and lakes, and rescued those in distress. Occasionally this meant taking the ropes and going down into the Yellowstone Canyon after some loony savage who lacked the good sense to stay on the trails. The seasonal protective rangers were the lowest ones on the pecking order, but invariably, some thought of themselves as the next thing to the superintendent. Take a man out of blue jeans and put a uniform on him, and he is transformed. He has power; he has respect. At least, in 1952 he did. It was a giddy feeling.

I had my uniform, such as it was, then, and I was ready to go to work, but I had one more surprise. I was not going back to Old Faithful, for good reasons. As he took me to Lake Station, one of the Assistant Chief Rangers explained their thinking.

"If you should have to enforce the law there, you would not have to deal with kids you had been working with, as would be the case if we put you back at Old Faithful. Better to start in an area where no one knows you except as a ranger." It was good thinking, and the station turned out to be a blessing. After all, how many people sack out in the cool morning of a Yellowstone summer, dress, go out and put up the flag, and have before them the main body of Yellowstone Lake, its surface just beginning to ripple in the early morning breezes? I took a picture there, the lake an indigo blue with the white caps rolling in, and sent it home, telling my folks that I had changed jobs, location, and accomplices. And what a set they were!

I suspect that few groups of permanent and seasonal rangers at one station ever differed so widely as the bunch assembled at Lake Station in 1952. I was the last to join the group. There was Tom Bithell, just graduated from Utah with his Phi Beta Kappa key and pre-med training. He was brash, bright, and gifted with

words. He had a fair complexion, curly hair, and a way of turning
on some of the girls at the Lodge. One, in particular, I believe,
would have jumped into bed with Tom had he given her the least
indication that he was interested. Whether or not he ever did, I
do not know.

Bithell was a godsend to the District Ranger, Delyle Stevens.
Steve was an old-time ranger. He liked his work when he had to
go to Fishing Bridge to kill a grizzly which was tearing up the
campground, or directing his men to stop a person coming in
South Gate when he had no pass, especially when that man was
the Canyon District Ranger with whom Steve did not get along at
all. He thought naturalists, the interpretive rangers, were a bunch
of sissies, a peculiar irony because at that time Yellowstone was
served by as fine a group of naturalists as may ever have been assembled in any of the national parks. They were intelligent, well
educated, and devoted to their work. But I did not learn that
from my first boss at Lake Station. The naturalists were objects
of our scorn and contempt.

That summer was not a good one for Steve. His wife had
died a few months earlier, and he had, as I remember, two sons
and a daughter who were not quite grown. I do not remember
them well except that they seemed like very nice people. All were
a bit reserved. The oldest son was contemplating a career in the
Park Service, and he was good help for his father. It startles me
to think that those children are in the middle years now, probably
with families and possibly even with grandchildren. I think their
mother's death touched them deeply; apparently her gentle spirit
was more of a molding influence than their father's more abra-
sive disposition.

Steve was never unkind to me. He thought I didn't amount to
very much, but I could do the work around the station that
needed doing: taking tags from fish caught in the lake for a study
the biologists were doing; giving out what information had to be
given (Steve might have thought I was too much a naturalist at
this activity); taking weather information in the morning; checking with East Gate; keeping in touch with our fire lookout, Gerry

Mernin, on Pelican Cone. I wasn't good for boat patrol or road patrol; I wasn't too hot at repairing fence in the stockade either; I sure as hell would not have been much help in trapping grizzlies. Looking back on it, I really was a fifth wheel in that station, and I discovered this fact the following year. The one job I could really have done well for Steve he had Bithell taking care of: writing the monthly reports. Still, it was a good place for me to begin rangering.

For one thing, my work schedule was much like that of Boston-bred Dan Yuhr (pronounced Yoo-ah) who was our boat patrol. I remember very little about the manner in which Dan performed his work. I do remember that he was exceptionally smooth-tongued with the mess hall cook, and this was extremely beneficial for me. Mrs. Burris knew Dan was giving her a line, but she loved it, so, if the road crew and the other rangers had had stew at 5:30, Dan and I often had T-bone steak at six. The food was something which had concerned me. How would I get it? From whom? Was it any good? Considering the amount and kind of food I got that summer, it was worth every penny.

The long and emotionally draining school year had left me thin and worn down. I was starting to recover at the Cafeteria, but the fare at Lake restored me wondrously. One gets hungry in the high country. We would be up an hour before breakfast doing various station chores so that by the time we got to the mess hall, we were ready to eat. I am not a large person, have never had a large appetite. But I do remember very well one breakfast in which I put away three plate sized pancakes with butter and syrup, a whole grapefruit, two eggs, a glass of milk and a bowl of oatmeal. There might have been some bacon in there, too. Hungry? Yes, I was, *very*, and I began to eat as if each meal were my last.

I learned something else that summer: I was a lousy poker player. Jim Russell, our road patrol from Texas; his wife; Don Bock, the seasonal who worried for all of us; Bithell, Yuhr, and I played penny ante poker on an occasion or two. I could not get good hands very often, and when I did, I was no better than

David at hiding my emotions. I needed some lessons from Tex.

So, I lost thirty or forty cents in a poker game. Who would worry about that? I did. I worried about any money I lost. This was the student you must remember who in his senior year in college used to debate whether or not to spend a quarter on an ice cream soda at the Union.

To continue with my accomplices at Lake Station in 1952. Jim Russell: small but well formed man; black curly hair; dark, smooth complexion; soft Texas accent. Jim was our road patrol, a potentially dangerous job. But he was good. He was also a worrier. He told me once that everytime he stopped somebody he had that half-conscious anxiety about whether or not the guy he stopped was just your average tourist, late for a motel reservation and cheating on the speed limit to get where he was going, or some gangster going through the park but trigger happy at the possibility that he was being stopped by some law enforcement official for a reason other than speeding. I presume that part of Jim's training, part of any road patrol's training, is either radioing in the license number of the vehicle he is stopping or at least noting it on something so that if anything happens, his backups can catch the guilty party.

Jim was also too conscientious. On one occasion he stopped a doctor who had come cautiously over Sylvan Pass, the route in from the East, and then decided to make up time when he hit Mary Bay. He had a reservation at Old Faithful and a good many miles to go to make it. So, he started pedalling his Cadillac at high speed right past Jim who was out doing his duty. He flagged this guy down and brought him to Lake Station to give him a citation. When they got there, Jim was having second thoughts. The doctor was such a nice guy. He wasn't giving Jim any static, was marvelously courteous and polite and not phony about it either, and all the time his wife, a blond bitch, was just giving him hell when he went back to the car. I couldn't hear her, but I saw her— red-faced, pointed nose, scraggly blond hair—practically going apoplectic at the time they were losing and the reservation they were going to miss if they didn't get out of there. If I had been more mature then, I would have taken Jim into the back room and told him to give the guy a swift warning ticket and send him on his way. He didn't need both the ticket and that woman to contend with. I hope he divorced her. What a rotten individual. Anyway, Jim, for reasons I still don't understand—probably the feeling that the law is the law and that everyone has to abide by it —wrote up the ticket and the doctor got $25 which may not seem like much, but $25 in 1952 would probably get you better than $100 now. I suppose the doctor had no trouble paying it; but he would have had the wife on his back all the way and for a good many months afterward, re-living in technicolor, the way her husband spoiled their vacation that summer. Yes, he should have divorced her.

Jim and his wife were the initiators of one of the most awesome experiences I ever had in Yellowstone Park. The year I had been at Old Faithful I heard numerous references to "the grizzlies." The suggestion was that the grizzlies were not something you would want to meet in the back country, and I had had some anxiety about them when I hiked the trails around Old Faithful and up Mt. Washburn. But it is one thing to have an anxiety based on an abstraction, which the grizzlies were, for me, and quite another to have that anxiety materialize into some very concrete perceptions.

The Yellowstone grizzlies were no such tangible reality for me. They were creatures of mystery, spoken of in awed tones around the stove in the Lake District Station in the evening. Then, Jim and his wife suggested one night that we go up to Trout Creek. As I remember, the Russells, Don Bock, Bithell, and I were in the party. Trout Creek in that context was the name of the landfill where concessionaires from Canyon and Fishing Bridge dumped their garbage. The dump was located in the Hayden Valley, probably less than a mile from the main road but hidden from it by several bare but prominent hills. It had been created around 1941 when the Park Service decided that the nightly feeding of bears had become too hazardous for public safety. Before 1941 garbage was dumped in a certain place and the bears would then come in. People who wanted to watch were kept behind something resembling a baseball backstop, and a mounted, armed ranger stood guard. I doubt that the ranger who drew that duty ever felt too comfortable doing it. Having large numbers of black and grizzly bears milling around in shouting distance and a skittery horse under you would not help a person's blood pressure or ulcers. Anyway, the Park Service called a halt to this insanity and created Trout and Rabbit Creek dumps. The objective was to get the grizzlies out of the campground areas— the feeding had the effect of drawing them into these places— and it worked. The grizzlies, who do not like people, discovered the secluded interior dumps and began to congregate there. The Yellowstone population used these places as supplemental feeding for their regular diet. It was, in fact, necessary supplemental feeding.

I didn't know all of this in 1952; I just knew that we were going to Trout Creek Dump and there were supposed to be some grizzlies there. We got the special key to the lock on the barrier across the road to Trout Creek and went there in the evening in Russell's car. I remember a clear evening, a bit cold, but refreshing, calming. We took the little dirt road down an incline, over two or three small hills, then crested a rise above the dump. What I saw there took my breath away. *Forty-five* grizzly bears, everything from huge males which probably weighed out around 700 or 800 pounds down to smaller sows and cubs. Our arrival startled them, and they flushed like a covey of quail. Grizzlies are nervous and skittish bears. One sow took her cubs up on the edge of the dump and sat there for several minutes watching us intently. When she decided that we were not a threat—we sat very quietly in the car—she and her cubs returned to the dump. I remember being heartsick at the sight. I use the term to convey a combination of awe, fright, and wonder. Never, all the time I had hiked the trails, had I concretely visualized what I saw before me: these magnificent bears, the silver tips of their dark brown coats shining in the fading light. They were better proportioned than the black bears, too. Whereas the blacks have a somewhat curved back and receding butt, the grizzlies have a hump at the base of their necks and great haunches. The great white claws with which they turn over rocks and fallen trees while looking for insects are also prominent. In succeeding years I have read accounts of the grizzly's prodigious strength. It is easy to believe when one is confronted by animals of such size in the late evening. We stayed until we could see no more.

Our experience that evening was a special privilege, call it a perquisite of belonging to the Park Service if you want to. Only a few of us got to go into those dumps to see those great bears. None go now. The Craighead brothers, who did an important study of the Yellowstone grizzlies in the 1960s reported in the mid-70s that the Park biologist had decided to close the dumps to get rid of what he called the "garbage bears." They argued that all of Yellowstone's grizzlies used the dumps as supplemental feeding stations and that closing them might cause the bears, now hungry, irritable, and potentially very dangerous to humans, to once again wander into camping areas and cause trouble. The dumps were closed. The bears did wander into camping areas and were shot. Speculation now is that Yellowstone's grizzly population, once estimated at about 250, is below a number sufficient to replace itself.

The case against Park Service mismanagement of the bear problem has recently been thoroughly reported and documented by Alston Chase in *Playing God in Yellowstone*. It is a sad story of bureaucratic bungling and stubbornness, and it should be of great concern to every person interested in the preservation of wildlife in our national parks. One has to ask this question: can it be that there is no sanctuary in the contiguous United States for the great white bear that once dominated the whole western half of the country? Are they no longer safe even from those whose public responsibility is to preserve them? I certainly hope not. The image of 45 grizzlies on a Yellowstone evening is vivid in my memory even today.

☐

Two days off a week. That was the single greatest boon in working for the Park Service. I had lost my Old Faithful practice places, but I had not forgotten my Old Faithful pianist, Jan Stallings. On days off I had to take care of certain chores, laundry, mostly, but I managed to get out onto the road and start hitchhiking by ten the first day off I had. That must have been a sight for tourists, a young man, in a red baseball hat, violin, rack, and music under his arm, thumbing a ride in Yellowstone Park. The people who passed me must have wondered who the weirdo was and where he was going. I can't say I was your typical savage out for a day off. Where would anyone be going with a violin? Fortunately, there was always some kind soul who was more curious than afraid, and I would get my ride to West Thumb, then to Old Faithful. Sometimes I would get a ride the whole distance, sometimes half way. I always managed to get to Old Faithful in time to find Jan and practice. I don't remember just what kind of arrangement we had. It was one of those "I'll be over sometime in the afternoon on Thursday—will you be off?" affairs. She was always there, or close by so that I never had trouble finding her. Looking back on the situation, I realize how absolutely cockeyed it was. Imagine a girl agreeing to play violin concertos and sonatas with an unpredictably arriving ranger every Thursday afternoon! It's called imposition. Good thing I was not in love with Jan. That would really have messed things up.

Why didn't I buy a car and regularize the situation? Are you kidding? Buy a car? With what? If I had it to do over, though, I would starve a couple of months, give violin lessons, and tutor failing athletes to earn enough to buy a car. It was stupid trying to get around that park without transportation. Still, I did it, for four summers, two of them from the most disadvantageous spot you can imagine: East Gate.

There were some permanent men at Lake whom I very much admired. The assistant district ranger, Bud Estey, was a very tranquil person. He was what a ranger should be. I couldn't imagine Bud getting bent out of shape in any emergency. He took them as they came and simply acted. He also had two of the cutest little girls I have ever seen. Both must now be grown beautiful women with, I hope, large and happy families. I took a picture of both Gail and Jo by the ranger station one day. Perhaps I was anticipating the day when I would become the father of two pretty little girls, which I did. They are now two pretty big girls—they wouldn't like that girl stuff either. Both are women; at 23 and 26 one definitely does not think of herself as a "girl" anymore.

And there were Tom Schoder and Bob Morey. I didn't see a lot of Schoder because he shared road patrol with Jim Russell and was therefore out of the station quite a bit. I do remember one incident, however, in which Schoder tried to rescue a man who eventually drowned. Schoder went into the Yellowstone River near Tower Falls and something went wrong. I don't remember whether a boat in which he was riding tipped over or a rope which was supposed to give him support from the bank broke, but he nearly lost his life in this effort. It was the kind of dangerous work park rangers occasionally have to do.

Morey was around the station a good bit. He was one of Steve's favorites because he could do everything: fix a fence, check out the horses, fight fires, and trap grizzlies. Bob had the physical strength, stamina, and good disposition to adapt to the variety of physical and mental chores the Park Service laid on its rangers. He later came back to Yellowstone as Lake District Ranger.

And there was one other ranger-to-be working out of our station that summer: Gerry Mernin, later Yellowstone's South District Ranger, or he was the last time I checked. An experience I had going to see Gerry formed the basis for the best short story I have yet written. Background. Gerry was our fire lookout. Today the Park Service lets fires burn, recognizing that the lodgepole forest needs an occasional fire to clean out down timber, kill insect infestations, and stimulate growth of new trees. The last time I was in the Park, summer of 1980, the southern part needed a good fire to wipe out a pine beetle infestation which was damaging a good many trees. In 1952, however, fires were fought as soon as the lookouts spotted them. It was lonely heroic work for the kids who did it, but they were very good. Yellowstone had lookouts at four points: Mt. Washburn, Mt. Holmes, Mt. Sheridan, and Pelican Cone. Washburn was accessible to the casual hiker like myself, but the other three were considerably remote. Gerry was all by himself on Pelican Cone, ten miles or more from the East Entrance Road, and he wanted some company other than the occasional deer, chipmunk, or even grizzly bear which wandered past his station on the mountain. We called him each day with weather and fire reports, and, as I remember, he gave us some information, but his main purpose was to watch—all the time—particularly after lightning storms, to see if fires were breaking out anywhere. He had the instruments for getting a read on any fire, and he had learned where all the geysers and steam vents were so that he would not call in any false alarms. The Yellowstone area presented some real problems on this score because on a cold morning there would be all kinds of white plumes in the air from the Park's thermal phenomena. But those lookouts knew their terrain. I remember a fire exploding on the ridge just above Madison Junction where I worked in 1960, and two lookouts had reports on it to the fire dispatcher in Mammoth within five to ten minutes after the fire broke out. Sheridan saw it, I believe, and Holmes, too, and they were miles and miles from our area. The dispatcher liked two reports because he could then draw the lines from each and determine a point of intersection for locating the fire. Crews, either smoke jumpers, or ground fighters, could then be dispatched more quickly and efficiently.

Well, Gerry. He kept asking one of us to come and see his space up on the mountain, and I finally said I would go. I liked interior hiking, but if I had known then what I know now, I would probably never have made the trip. Pelican Creek was grizzly heaven. I had gone to Old Faithful in the morning to play sonatas with Jan; I returned in the early afternoon and allowed about two to three hours for the ten mile hike to the top of the mountain.

"You know that trail up there, Don?" Steve just wanted to

be sure I knew the trail wasn't marked very well.

"No, but I can follow it."

"Well, keep your eyes open; it ain't too good a ways up."

I wish he had sat me down and said, "Now focus for a minute. How much do you know about back country trail markers in the Park? Oh, you know a lot? Yeah, how are they marked?"

Well, I didn't know a thing about it. I just thought I would follow the path. Stupid jerk. Steve should have spelled it out. "After awhile the path will grow very dim. At that point you must follow rectangular orange markers, about the size of 3 x 5 note cards, nailed to certain trees. It is most important that you pay attention to the point when they start up the mountain."

Well, Steve didn't give me that talk. I thought I was the great woodsman, and so I set out in light jacket and red baseball hat. I met Nat Lacy at Fishing Bridge, and he gave me a ride to Pelican Creek. Then I was on foot. Gerry later told me he could see the progress I was making coming up the creek. When I disappeared from sight, he thought I was on the mountain, but I was a lot later getting up there than I should have been. While Gerry was looking for fires—even if he had seen me he couldn't have helped—I was focussed on the trail and doing my perpetual day-dreaming. I just remember being semi-consciously irritated that the trail was getting harder and harder to follow and the problem was interrupting my reverie. From time to time I checked my location with Pelican Cone—I could see the lookout on top very clearly so was not particularly concerned.

The moment of truth came, however, when I found the trail just petering out into nothing. That was very unsettling. By then it was evening, and a light rain had begun to fall. I was perplexed because the damn trail hadn't started up the mountain, so I took my bearings again. The moment that followed was one of the longest in my life. Remember: I wasn't that experienced in the wilderness; I was really a city boy infatuated with the wilderness but not at all ready to cope with it on a serious basis. I looked up and saw *no* fire lookout. It had disappeared from the mountain in front of me. I remember my heart bouncing off my shoe tops and my system starting to go into shock. I re-grouped, and I started looking around again, very slowly. I found the lookout. It was on a mountain which was nearly behind me! I said some very choice words, directed at myself, because now I knew what Steve had only hinted at. I had been completely asleep when the trail cut across the meadow and ascended the mountain.

Well, what was I going to do? I had no faith that I could follow the path I was on back to the point in the meadow where the trail ascended Pelican Cone, and I had only about two hours of daylight left. And I was hungry. We skinny people get hypoglycaemic after five. But I had only one real choice—to go directly up the mountain. And I knew that once I began to ascend it, I would lose sight of my only reference point: the lookout. Still, it was my only choice. I just had to attack the hill and the forest and hope that there were no impassable obstacles between me and the lookout.

So, I began one of the most difficult journeys of my life. It is not easy to give up a position in which you at least have some visible reference points for a more secure but difficult to reach one, but literally or metaphorically, we all face such moments, and the best course of action is to cut loose and go for it.

I climbed over so much down timber that I could have heated the town of Manhattan for two years with it. I plowed through tough and occasionally dense undergrowth. I kept going up. Elevation was my only guide. Just keep going up the mountain, I told myself, and I kept doing that. It was very tiring work, and the more tired and hungry I got, the more I became reconciled to the fact that I would have to spend the night in the woods and try to find the lookout in the morning. I kept going up, but I started trying to remember all I knew about camping out impromptu. I was not warmly dressed, so I would need a place out of the wind and something for ground cover, something soft enough that it would make a satisfactory bed and provide some cover. Firs were the thing. They had flat flexible needles and their branches made a softer more comfortable bed than those of the lodgepole pines. I also began looking for a tree with some dense overhang to shelter me from the rain and keep me reasonably dry. So, prompted by necessity, I started looking for a usable fir. When I saw a little one upslope from me about ten or fifteen feet, I went for it with intentions of stripping it. But I never touched it. It grew beside a wide and well travelled path. By luck, and by fortitude, I had hit the trail up Pelican Cone. Two or three turns on it, and I was on top of the mountain. It was nearly dark, and Gerry said, "Hey, what took you so long coming up? I saw you coming through the meadow pretty fast some time ago."

I showed Gerry where I had been and where I had struck up the mountain. He seemed a bit awed that one could miss a well marked trail that much. "Hell, if I'd seen you up there, I'd of had the smoke jumpers out. Man, you were way off the trail!"

"I know." I did not feel any more comfortable about it when, several days later, Jack Knoll, the fire guard who lived in the Pelican Springs Cabin at the base of the mountain, asked me if I had seen that sow grizzly up in the area I had been. I had not and was grateful for it. If I had, chances are that these fingers would not now be tapping away on this computer keyboard. You have to be lucky once in awhile in this life.

Gerry fed me, then showed me the apparatus he used in spotting and reporting fires. He had two large containers for water outside the lookout because water was not readily available on top. He was much more dependent on us than I had believed.

During the night a storm came through, and Gerry was up several times plotting lightning strikes to check out in the morning. None of them produced anything, however, probably because there was so much rain accompanying the storm. I did think how much more pleasant the shelter of the lookout was than a pine and fir bed underneath some tree on the slope of the mountain, though. Another thought never entered my mind but should have. Where should one not be in a lightning storm? On the highest point, of course. I presume the lookout was grounded some way. It would not have been safe it it hadn't. But wouldn't that be some firecracker, a lightning bolt whamming into the rod by the lookout in the middle of the night? I'll take a raincheck, permanently, on such natural extravaganzas.

Gerry was very proud of the biscuits he could make for breakfast—that was the principal inducement to other seasonals to come up, but I was the only one to take him up. They were good biscuits. I enjoyed my breakfast with Gerry and then started down the mountain about nine. I was curious, of course, about the trail I had missed; I wanted to see where it left Pelican Creek and started up the Cone. The only event of note occurred when I was about halfway down the mountain. A small black bear was feeding on some insects by the side of the trail. What caught my eye was the absolute jet blackness and sheen of his coat. Along the road I had seen so many bears that were fed tourist junk food, and looked bad to awful because they were not on a healthy diet, that I had never considered what a wild well-fed bear would look like. This little creature obviously had never been near the road. He was smooth, fat, shiny . . . and scared. I stopped. The noises of the woods slowly disappeared. He looked back at me, but because bears' eyesight is very poor, I don't think he really saw anything. When I moved my arm to scratch my head, however, he knew that something live was on the trail, and that little bear tore off through the woods like a frightened rabbit. Such a beautiful little bear. Too bad people couldn't have left all of them along so that they would have had to forage for themselves. Mother Nature is a much better provider for bears than man is.

I got back to the station, answered a question or two about the trail from Steve, and went about my business. I never did tell him how badly I had screwed up getting to the top of the mountain. But I had learned one thing about myself which was very comforting. In a crisis, I did not panic; I used my head and got myself out of trouble. It was a quality which served me well many years later when the crises which came were much more severe, more sustained, and threatening not only to me but to those I loved.

◻

In the early part of the twentieth century, a man named Howard Eaton guided horseback parties through Yellowstone along a trail roughly paralleling the route of the Grand Loop Road. My first two years in Yellowstone, I was fascinated by the idea of hiking all around the Park on the Howard Eaton trail, but it had not been maintained, and more than once I had started out on it only to wind up on some other trail or at a dead end, frustrated and disappointed. This had happened to me at Old Faithful; it had happened to some extent at Lake. But I did get in one long trek on the Howard Eaton Trail which I have not forgotten.

I hiked it from Lake to Canyon, a distance of about fourteen miles, on the east side of the Yellowstone River. That is significant because it put the river, and it is a large and deep one, between me and the road and any possibility of help should I need it. I was only 22 that summer, and stupid in the way that adventuresome 22 year olds are. I was not properly dressed for the trip, in case the weather changed abruptly; I wasn't sure a trail was there; and I knew nothing about grizzlies who might come from the east side, cross the river, and go to Trout Creek dump. Fortunately, neither weather nor grizzlies gave me trouble that day, and I had no trouble keeping my bearings because there are no trees through much of that area, and the river was a constant point of reference. Fourteen miles was not a tough hike for me: four hours or thereabout without straining. But I got one very unsettling and nasty surprise.

Osprey often nest in old dead trees. Osprey do not like animals or people walking near their nests in high old dead trees. On that particular afternoon in the summer of 1952 I walked near an osprey's nest, high in an old dead tree.

I heard the noise of the bird first and then slowly began to realize that *I* was the cause of consternation for it. And it came for me, right at me. It would drop out of the sky like a rock and then flare its wings about four or five feet above me, creating a terrific WHUMP! in the air. I was afraid that if I didn't raise my arms and prepare to fight it off that it would go for my head. I did not want talon marks in my scalp. I *very much* did not want talon marks in my scalp. But I could hardly keep any sense of the direction I was going and still watch that damned bird as it circled and came back for another assault.

If you have ever seen a movie in which someone staggers along a path, terrified by an assault from birds, and noticed the awkward way this person strikes out wildly, trying to fend them off, you have a picture of what was happening to me. I couldn't get over the irony of the fact that my fears had been of grizzlies, or other big game like moose, or thin crust in hot spring areas, but I never gave a thought to getting dive bombed by an osprey. I don't remember how long the incident lasted: probably until I was sufficiently out of range of the nest that the osprey felt it had driven me off—but I was shaken and worn. I sat down, took off my boots, and cooled my feet in a beautiful small stream flowing over white rock. It was the best way I could think of composing myself. Then I went on to Canyon where I arrived without further incident, but I lost a considerable part of my appetite for the Howard Eaton Trail. Ospreys on kamikaze missions can do that to you.

Life at Lake that summer was enlivened by the apparent beauty queen and the real one. The apparent one was a telephone operator at the Lake Hotel who had a clear, soft, sexy voice with a lilt. Our imaginations were running wild. Then Dan Yuhr took her out, and he said she was not the girl her voice led one to believe. I couldn't accept that, thinking no Boston boatman had real discernment in good-looking women, anyway, so I eventually went to the hotel to see her for myself. I came, I saw, and I left—shattered. That voice? Attached to that large girl with the bad complexion? I guess she had a good disposition, but at that age, who wants a good disposition in a woman? You want a ravishingly beautiful creature. Well, *we* did. We were as chauvinistic as our culture had made us, and totally unrealistic about male-female relationships, so the telephone operator was a disappointment. Chances are that, in the long haul, she might have turned out to be a hell of a lot better bet than the real beauty queen of the area. She was a Fishing Bridge naturalist's daughter, and she was a *very* good looking woman: medium height, perfectly proportioned figure (none of that excessive bustiness which makes Hugh Hefner's *Playboy* center-folds look like Jersey cows), transparent skin, and intelligence in her eyes. She was a candidate in the area's beauty pageant, and two or three of our rangers—I remember only that Bithell was one of them—were the judges who chose her. The whole evening was, as I look back on it, rather special.

We were invited to the proceedings, and the boys had read the manual for ceremonial dress. We wore our uniforms with one change: we had white shirts instead of the working grey. They made us look very sharp indeed. The girls did what they always do in these pageants, and Bithell and his buddies picked the naturalist's daughter. Steve gave them some good-humored hell.

"Jesus Christ! Here the Park Service goes to the concessionaire's beauty pageant and picks the naturalist's daughter!" He evidently saw in this some conflict of interest or the suggestion of such, or at least the possibility that the gesture was bad politics, but I'm still with the judges. They picked the best looking girl, by quite a bit, and she did work for the concessionaire. So, wherever you are in ranger heaven, Steve, go suck an egg. The boys did the right thing. It was a good moment in the life of a woman who by now must be about 52 years old. And I heard she had been married and divorced, not the usual pattern for a Mormon girl. Well, she was a beauty.

Some very good things were happening to me that summer at Lake. I was eating and sleeping well and getting my equilibrium back. I was seeing an entirely new part of the Park and getting an entirely new perspective on it from the men with whom I worked. And I was feeling more comfortable with myself than I had at any time in my life. On those days off I just took off and went where I wanted to, just to see whatever I wanted to see. And I didn't worry about getting hung out. I remember one evening being stranded at Mammoth at five o'clock in the afternoon (Mammoth is at least 55 miles from Lake and not on a

route likely to take one directly back to Lake) and feeling absolutely calm about it. I thought I would get back; I wasn't even
worried about not getting back. I just knew, instinctively, that one
way or another, I would make it all right. Five minutes later a car
went by, then suddenly screeched to a halt. It backed up, and the
driver took a long look at me and said, "Say, aren't you the
ranger at Lake who told us where to go and what to see yesterday?"

I recognized the man and told him I was.

"Where are you headed?"

"Back to Lake."

"Get in. We're going back to the Lodge." It was a quarter of
a mile from my quarters. They spent the entire drive telling me
about the things they had been seeing, all places I had told them
to stop. Who says God doesn't look after young and foolish
rangers?

I remember only one bad moment at Lake that summer. We
were called out in the night because Steve had killed a bear in the
Fishing Bridge Campground and wanted some help loading the
animal onto a truck. So we dressed and went over there to help
lift a bloody 300 pound carcass that, with more intelligent management, could have been a healthy bear, onto the truck. I didn't
want to touch it and shied away. Steve barked at me, and I did
what I could, but I think that night he made a note of who was
and who was not dispensable. At his station he didn't need a seasonal who was squeamish. Without knowing it, I had written my
ticket to a different station. The next summer that transfer was to
cause me initial grief and anxiety, but it had some very real and
lasting compensations.

7

The Third Year:
I Am Moved to East Gate

THERE ARE FIVE entrances to Yellowstone Park: North, West, South, Northeast and East. The North Gate, which is situated at Gardiner, Montana, and just five miles below Mammoth Hot Springs, was the busiest entrance in the Park's early history because the trains came there. When the road system was completed, and Americans abandoned the trains for their automobiles, North virtually dried up and by 1953, East, South, and West were drawing heaviest traffic. Northeast, in some ways the Park's most scenic entrance, drew less travel because only hardened mountain drivers cared to tackle the Beartooth Pass between Red Lodge and the gate.

I wouldn't have cared for the barrenness of North's site or the town's bars, but it had stores and restaurants, and one could get things there. West is still virtually in the town of West Yellowstone, and it is a particularly attractive site because it has the advantages of being near the Madison River and in the wilderness, yet it is also close to the town and the resources it has. South at that time had a road crew and government mess, so the men stationed there could eat at the government provided grub station or at Flagg Ranch which was not far away on the Snake River. South was scenic. Northeast was just a mile from Silver Gate and a little farther from Cooke City, and it, too, had the advantage of being picturesque.

Then there was East Gate. The setting was beautiful, no question about that. Middle Creek ran right behind the ramshackle cabins we used for quarters, and we were surrounded by mountains. *But*, the government mess hall was four miles *up* the road toward Sylvan Pass, and we had no vehicle for going there. Pahaska Tepee, Buffalo Bill's old hunting lodge then owned by Henry Coe, was two miles out of the Park. When Steve told me he was sending me to East Gate, I felt as if I had been put out in Siberia. It was not an intelligent thing to do to a man without a car. Where in hell did he think I would get food? We had what laughingly passed for a cook shack, but there was no power at East Gate so we were dependent on Coleman lanterns and flashlights at night. What would I do for breakfast, especially when I had to open at six in the morning? And I had no alarm clock and no one to wake me up. The situation was fraught with anxieties for me, and I still wonder, occasionally, what Steve thought he was doing, even when he said, "Well now, Don, I don't want you to think we're kicking you out. John Rohn's got some green men out there and needs some help." But he was kicking me out. Why not send any of two or three other men at Lake Station to the gate? They had *cars*, transportation, Steve. They would not be in the bind I was. I still remember being driven out there, 27 miles from Fishing Bridge, over Sylvan Pass and down the mountain on a rainy afternoon which suited my frame of mind. I will admit that I was frightened, hurt at not being kept at Lake, and concerned about an unknown. I had yet to learn that in taking the tourists' money at the gate, we had to be careful not to make mistakes. If you came up short, you made up the difference out of your pocket. For one who had as slim a cash flow as I had in those years, this was not a comforting experience. Once again, I was called upon to adapt.

To those who have been in much more desperate straits, my concern must seem rather foolish. Looking back upon it now, with all the familiarity developed by thirteen summers in Yellowstone and years of providing for a family, I would not have lost a moment's sleep over the experience. But you must remember that we are talking about a 23 year old who had been away from home only the previous two summers and during the college years, and who had, even when away from home, never been cut off from various support systems which kept me fed and housed. Now I was to be thrown more completely on my own resources than ever before. I sometimes wonder if Steve didn't send me out there so that I would give up Park Service work and do something more suitable to my abilities and temperament. If so, he did me a favor, because I learned once again just how well I could adapt.

As I have said, it was drizzling, dark, and cold the day I arrived at East. The men to whom I was introduced—John Rohn, the permanent ranger in charge of the gate; Harry Nicholson, the senior seasonal; Don Guiton, a chemistry major fresh from Oberlin; and Jack Stark from Arkansas City, my state, were a very good crew.

Quarters were something else. Adapting to the cruddy dorm at Old Faithful was one thing; adapting to a one-room shack without electricity, plumbing, or lights was quite another. I was given the only cabin which had wallboard. All of us had small, half-moon-shaped wood-burning stoves, except Nicholson and Guiton, whose cabin had a pot-bellied stove. I remember almost no furniture. We had beds with coil spring frames and old mattresses. We used orange crates as storage places for our clothing. We must have had one chair, anyway. I do not remember. We also had a small porcelain wash pan, and Harry Nicholson loaned me the side mirror from his car so that I would have something to shave by. I also bought a flashlight so that I would have a supplement to my Coleman lantern. The outhouse was closest to my cabin, and I must say that, considering the nature of outhouses, one could hardly have asked for one in a more picturesque spot.

There are compensations in every situation. On those occasions when I repaired to the outhouse for my morning healthy, I would see the blue sky and trees through the cracks in the doors, and hear the water of Middle Creek rushing by.

The weather cleared the next day, and I began the serious business of adapting. I spread out my gear in the cabin and found, very quickly, that I had a problem no one else had. Since my cabin had the wall board, it attracted field mice, and 1953 was a bumper year for them. No one could remember when so many mice were around. I don't know the reasons they were, but I can tell you what they meant for me. The first week in that cabin I bought four traps to try to reduce the population. They scuttled across the floor; they ran across the rafters of the cabin; they climbed up the wallboard at night, mostly the side between the outside walls and the surface away from the interior of the room, but they would inevitably come out on the rafters, and, on one occasion, in the middle of the night, one of them fell off the wall and into my bed. I lifted the covers and scrambled around, just catching a glimpse of the mouse as it came running out from under the covers and toward the head of the bed. I swept it off onto the floor, and cursed mightily. Then I moved the bed away from the sides of the room to avoid repetitions of that incident.

The first week I killed seventeen mice without making the least dent in the population. On one evening alone, in *ten* minutes, in three traps baited with, of all things, jelly beans, I caught *four* mice. Two had been killed in one trap! Finally, I gave up because I could make no headway against this onslaught of rodents. It does seem to me, however, that the population diminished as the summer wore on. I suppose as the weather warmed up, they moved out to more natural sites. One source of help came from a weasel who moved into our area and probably wondered how she had ventured into such good hunting. I saw it once, bounding through the grass, a mouse in its jaws. Probably food for the kids. Curiously, the next summer, I did not stay in that cabin, but the resident who did had no trouble with mice. I was just lucky in 1953.

Well, shelter was thus taken care of, in a manner of speaking. There is something to be said for having your own little place, even if mouse infested. The other big problem was food. I decided to take meals at Pahaska Tepee, but getting there was a problem. Guiton offered to take us down occasionally, as did Harry or John Rohn, but I could not bring myself to be a leech or use the others' cars, so I walked that distance, when I had the time, a good many times. As it turned out, that was good preparation for one of the most physically demanding experiences of my life later in the summer.

The food at Pahaska was all right; I don't remember it with the same relish I do the food at Old Faithful or at Lake, but I survived. Breakfast was the big problem, especially when I had to open at six. I usually bought a large roll and an orange and tried to subsist on that until I could take a later meal. As I look back on it, I was undernourished a good part of the time because of the lack of a decent breakfast. And once a black bear hit the outside box we used to store food and made off with my roll and orange. I did not feel charitable toward bears that day.

We also could shower at Pahaska, in some rather shoddy but usable showers behind the main buildings. They gave us the alternative to the washpan we had at the gate.

Before long, I got into my routine. If I opened at six, I would wake up at quarter to five and build a fire in my small wood stove. How did I wake up? I can't tell you now, but I have never been a heavy sleeper, except when extraordinarily tired. Since I had no alarm clock, I simply told myself that I had to wake up at 4:45. So I would wake up then and be functioning in less than thirty seconds. I think I could still do it today.

Anyway, I would get up, partially dress, build the fire, and dip some cold water out of Middle Creek. I then heated this water on top of my wood stove and used it to shave. The shaving, dressing, and eating of my roll and orange took about an hour, at which point I would walk the hundred yards or so to the gate and prepare to open. Sometimes I would wake up our resident moose who might be bedded down in some soft comfortable place not too far from the path we took. I didn't mind doing this in the morning. I was much more nervous about doing it late at night when I closed alone and walked back to the cabin, my flashlight my only illumination and means of telling me whether or not the moose was ready to come charging or whether he would stay where he was. Moose are very large and, at times, unpredictable animals.

So, getting up and going to and from the Gate was frequently an adventure. Gate duty itself was also an adventure. When I went to open up, I would go into the little station which had windows both east and west and doors on the north and south sides. The north side also had a sliding window where the man on gate duty perched to sell permits and give tourists their maps, trash-bags, and other stuffers. To keep from losing any money at that job, I developed a little routine. I would greet each driver as he drove up and inform him that the permit to enter the park was $3.00. Few if any ever complained about it, but most wanted to ask 100 questions about places to go, what to see, where to eat, etc. I put off these questions until I had made the financial transaction. Then I would answer their questions, in some detail if there was no line, very briefly if we were stacked up, as we occasionally were in mid-July. Sometimes the lines would extend halfway to Pahaska Tepee. When it got really bad, we opened two gates and sent the people on to Fishing Bridge Museum to ask questions about getting around. The naturalists there had the time and inclination to do that for them anyway.

Some very funny and wonderful things happened to me during the hours I sat in the hot spot on the gate. One morning in the middle of the summer, 1953, I had my permits ready to sell, a pile of maps and trashbags close by, and was ready to raise the flag and open the gate. It was approximately 5:55 A.M., the sky was absolutely blue, and there was no wind. The muffled surge of Middle Creek could be heard in the background. On both sides of the gate, extending at least 2000 feet above me, were mountains whose sides were covered with lodgepole pines, spruce, and fir, the latter two mostly down near the creek. I hooked the flag to the rope and began to raise it.

A group of young women, in the first car in line, leaped out into the cool mountain air, and began singing, "Oh, say can you see, by dawn's early light. . . ." That is what a beautiful blue morning in the mountains at the gate of America's oldest and most famous national park will do to you. These were American citizens saying, "Thank you, America, for being the country you are, especially in these great parks where one can come for spiritual refreshment." I did not feel that this was an expression of phony or superficial patriotism; it was patriotism, healthy, exuberant, optimistic. It 1983 we needed to take our former Secretary of the Interior, Mr. James Watt, and plant him in the position I was in years ago, day after day, morning after morning, until he got it. He did not understand the aesthetics of wilderness. Unfortunately, there are a lot of people in the surrounding states who do not understand that either. Yellowstone, to them, is a giant economic plum: the magnet which draws all those tourist dollars into their communities. It is that, but it is other more important things as well.

A lot of interesting people came to the gate that summer. I remember the slightly heavy-set dark-haired woman with a distinct Eastern accent wiping her brow, looking as if she had just come out of shock, and asking me in desperate tones, "Oh Mistah Rangah, how do we get out of 'eah witout going through any moah mountains? Please?" Most Easterners, I discovered, had a very imperfect sense of what the Rocky Mountain West was all about. They did not study maps with the loving care I always did, and even if they did, they did not know what they were interpreting. After all, what would terms like "Shell Canyon" or "Ten Sleep Pass" mean to a dude who had never seen anything steeper than the second deck of Yankee Stadium or those little bumps in the East which are called mountains? Another problem was the advent of power steering which caused people to oversteer their cars.

Easterners would come through South Dakota, marvelling at how long one could stay in the same state and see so few people and then approach the Black Hills. These are real mountains, right? I mean, these are the real stuff of western mountain lore. And they would drive through the Black Hills—remember, we are talking about the days *before* interstate highways—and feel pretty comfortable about the whole experience. The route was not precipitous, the mountains not all that high—so, what's the big deal about western mountains? That frame of mind would persist past Devil's Tower, Gillette, Sheridan, and the ascent of the eastern side of the Big Horns. But no matter which way they came down, Ten Sleep on U.S. 16 or Shell Canyon on U.S. 14, there was that west side. Oh my, especially with Shell Canyon, was there ever that west side! The drop was about 5,000 feet in ten to fifteen miles. And Shell Canyon had narrow roads, no guardrails, hairpin turns—the kind in which you meet yourself coming back—and straight dropoffs of 3,000 feet or so. This was the real stuff, mountain driving of the first order, and here came these unprepared dudes with cars that caused them to over steer when they met traffic and think that they were heading for the edge and oblivion, steep descents to brake, and no experience with gearing down so as to let the engine hold back the car and keep the brakes from overheating. When they got to Greybull, then through the Black Canyon by the Shoshone Reservoir near Cody, and finally to Yellowstone's East Gate, the joy of the summer trip was over. They just wanted a nice safe flat road *somewhere* to safety. Trouble was that right ahead of them was the seven-mile ascent to Sylvan Pass, not as hairy an experience as the Big Horns, but something to make the heart skip a beat or two. I told them about it but reassured them that they would be on the inside and that once in the Park they would have little such driving. And I advised them to go out West or South Entrances, either of which were not difficult and led to "safety" without much hazardous driving.

There was another "interesting" section of the road leading to Yellowstone's East Gate in those days: that stretch of road from Cody through Black Canyon, right past the Buffalo Bill Dam which created Shoshone Lake. It was the steepest grade on any U.S. highway, about 14 percent, and it was so narrow that two cars could not pass in places. There were occasional pullouts so that cars coming up could get out of the way of those coming down, and most people negotiated that stretch of road all right, but I remember one occasion that caused some difficulty. I never saw it, but it was as clear in my mind's eye as the picture of the Tetons in front of me now.

The driver of a huge flatbed truck on which was a relatively small steam shovel had just come through the gate, and we were giving him a special pass. He was bringing this equipment into the park for some construction work, and we had certain procedures for vehicles of that kind. Before I could get his information, however, I had to let him erupt. @#$%☺^&*())_+_)(*&^%$ #@%^&*()_+_)(*(#$%&()^&*#@#$%^&*())(&&^%$#@☺@# $%^&*(☺)(&^ %^&*()!!! That, symbolically, was the substance of his first remarks. I do not repeat them literally because, even in these permissive times, his language was shocking. In high school locker rooms, I had never heard anything to equal it.

Here was the problem. He had come to the bottom of the grade by the Buffalo Bill Dam. The authorities there knew a problem when they saw one. Hold it, they had said. Hold it, podner, we got to do something different with that rig you're pullin'. First, they measured it to make sure he could get through several small tunnels on the route. He would just clear them. Step number two was to send a car to the top of the incline, stop all traffic coming down, and give a red flag to the last car down the road. That would signal those at the bottom that the way was clear and the truck driver now had the highway all to himself. The grade was so steep that he would have to go through several gears to get his rig rolling up the hill.

The red flag came down and the truck started up. Unbeknownst to him, however, a woman in a large car had decided that the barrier at the top was intended for everyone but herself. She went around it, ignoring the yells from the man at the top, and started down the road. Halfway up the incline, our truck driver, concentrating all his energies on grinding up the steep hill, suddenly found himself face to face with a big car which had no goddamnèd business on that hill and which was driven by a woman who looked as startled as he and who then leaned out of her car and said, "Would you please back up?"

No, I am not going to tell you what the driver said to her. Let your imagination do it. The lady may have blushed and then begun to feel real terror because the driver informed her that he was coming ahead; he would have to go through all his gears again, in an extremely difficult and dangerous situation, and he didn't give a *bleep* if he pushed her and her *bleeping* car off into the canyon. She had no choice but to reverse and back up the hill down which she had so blithely come, the ever menacing presence of this large diesel truck and enraged driver right before her. The driver had still not cooled down, fifty miles later, at East Gate. But he was beginning to see a flicker of humor in the situation, even to suggesting that it was likely that he had caused that lady to soil her underwear. I doubt that the driver of the car ever found anything at all funny in her experience that afternoon.

8

America Comes
To East Gate

GUITON, I BELIEVE, or pos-
sibly John Rohn, was responsible for one of the niftiest devices
we had at East Gate. At a time when cars were ceasing to have
license plates front and back and drivers could never remember
their license numbers, you could lose a lot of time waiting for a
driver to jump out, check the plate, and give you the number. We
put this on the permit to designate that the permit was for that
particular vehicle. John or Don rigged up the mirror and posi-
tioned it so that when a car drove up to our window, we had a
perfect view of its rear license plate. The driver would sit there,
waiting for us to make change and hand him some stuff, at which
time he would look at the permit and suddenly, in considerable
surprise, say, "Say, that's my license number! You got a list of
people coming in today? How'd you get that?"

"Extra-sensory perception."

"What?"

"Mirrors. We do it with a mirror."

"Yeah." Now he's looking back. "Oh, yeah. . . hey, that's

pretty slick."

"Saves a lot of time."

They always looked as if we had just shown them how to do a magic trick.

I waited especially for the Kansas plates. You see, we have athletic rivalries in Kansas. Just like those in Iowa, Oklahoma, Michigan, Ohio, Texas, and California. In Kansas the key battle is basketball supremacy, and KU vs. K-State in most years, is a choice ticket. I have been on both sides of the fence now, having been a student at KU and a faculty member at K-State, but it still surprises me how intensely this rivalry is felt. There are some people at K-State who would rather spend a day cleaning a cow barn than lose to KU. Snob Hill, they call it, and KU responds with derogatory remarks about "Silo Tech."

When the Riley County cars came through (Manhattan and K-State are in Riley County), I could never resist sending them off with "Every man a Jayhawk." That would always get a rise. You see, a slogan at K-State, whose mascot is Willie the Wildcat, is "Every man a Wildcat." KU's mascot, of course is the mythological Jayhawk, so telling a K-Stater "Every man a Jayhawk" is the near equivalent of saying something like "your sister is a ___." I never said it until they were pulling away and couldn't turn back. Such foolishness is long past now. I like the K-State kids and people very much. They are my friends, my colleagues, and my students. They have provided me with some of the happiest associations of my life, and I am most content to spend the rest of my days in Manhattan. But in 1953 I was a green young ranger who couldn't even remember being in Manhattan. The thought never occurred to me that Riley County would be my home for the last half of my life.

There were other counties, too. Wyandotte County contains Kansas City and Johnson County is adjacent. I had to say something when they went through. As I did to people from Douglas County where Lawrence and KU are located. One Douglas County car did surprise me. I was working the window that afternoon, and there were no cars right at it, but one was coming toward the gate. I leaned out and saw that it was from Douglas County and had started, mentally, to prepare my little greeting for the folks from Lawrence when the realization hit me that the grinning figure driving the car was my Uncle George, a farmer who, as far as I could remember, had never taken a vacation because he could not leave the farm. Talk about double take! I whipped back out the window as they drew up, and you can imagine the unrestrained glee of my uncle and aunt plus that of my four younger cousins who were also in the car. Boy, they had surprised cousin Don! Caught me on the gate just the way they wanted to. I can still see the merriment in my uncle's eyes. They were on a well deserved and much anticipated holiday, and I would be off the next two days and available, of course, and most willing, to take them around the park to see the sights. Which I did.

How can I tell young readers today what such a holiday meant to this farm family in 1953? The kids who regularly ski in Colorado, hop airplanes from New York to Atlanta for a Friday evening, surf in Hawaii, or sun on the beaches of the Riviera or the Virgin Islands can have no concept of the exuberance felt by a family whose recreation until then had probably been the half day trip to Kansas City to see relatives on Thanksgiving or Christmas, or a Saturday at the movies. Yellowstone was more than 1,000 miles from their home. It was a tough three-day drive, and it was expensive. It was their trip to Tibet. In those two days they saw geysers, mud-pots, mountains, canyons, clear streams and rivers, and wildlife. It was enough to draw my uncle back for hunting in the Bighorns, my cousin Betty for work in the Tetons, and my cousin Ed to a career in the Forest Service. Before they left, my uncle told Ed and Bob to split some kindling for those of us at the gate. You should have seen those teenage boys take that wood pile apart. I never saw the chips fly so. My colleagues at the station wished we had had them around longer. They split enough wood to keep us going for well over a week, and there were several using that woodpile.

One of the most amusing yet pleasant experiences I ever had

on the gate involved a happy New Yorker wandering in the Great West for the first time. He drove up to my window on a July morning, totally exuberant.

"Good morning! So happy at last to be at the Yellowstone Park. All my life I've wanted to come to the Yellowstone Park! And I'm here!"

Naturally, I was pleased at this kind of greeting. Who can be surly or indifferent to a guy with that much enthusiasm?

"Well, I'm delighted that you're so happy to be here. Welcome to Yellowstone. I hope I don't dampen your enthusiasm by telling you that you must buy a three-dollar permit to get in."

"Oh, no! Don't mind a bit! Nothing's too good for the Yellowstone."

So I took his money, made change, then handed him the map and trashbag we gave to all incoming visitors. He just sat there, smiling. I waited for him to drive on. Finally, he broke the impasse:

"Well, where do I park the car?"

"I'm sorry. What did you say?"

"Where do I park the car?"

"Oh." *What does he want? Restrooms? Must be.*

"Well, you can pull over to the right side there. We have dry toilets on the side of the hill."

My New Yorker laughed uproariously. "Oh no. We don't need the johns. We took care of that down the road. We want to park the car to see the sights."

"What sights did you have in mind?"

"Well, the Old Faithful."

"Old Faithful is 65 miles from here."

My New Yorker's enthusiasm began to vanish. He stared at me incredulously. "But. . . *but I thought Old Faithful was in the Park!*"

At this point I began to sense the nature of his problem.

"Tell me. I see you're from New York. New York City, maybe?"

"Yes."

"Did you, just by chance, think of Yellowstone as something like Central Park?"

He was beginning to understand now.

"Yeah, I suppose I did."

"Well, that's the problem. See, Central Park has about 5000 acres. Yellowstone has two and one-quarter *million* acres."

The numbers were beginning to freak out the kids in the back seat.

"Let me put it this way. Yellowstone Park is just a little smaller than the state of Connecticut."

The kids were now rolling in wide-eyed amazement and disbelief. "A park as big as Connecticut? Wow! As big as Connecticut?? WOW!!!"

I showed them the map, indicated various areas and mileages, and principal things to look for along the way. Their momentary disappointment turned into unrestrained joy. They had discovered the ultimate bonanza. A park as big as Connecticut! I am sure no travellers to "the Yellowstone" ever enjoyed their experience more than this family from the Big Apple which found that their definition of park was far from adequate to deal with great western parks. We call that a learning experience.

We had other kinds of visitors, too. One I have not forgotten but would like to. He was a pushy type who cons his way through life. His timing suggested that. In 1954 we had gone on all-night shifts. Instead of the good old 6 A.M. to 10 P.M. and close up the park, we had to stay open round the clock. I am not a night person, and I did not like the thought of a shift which kept me on from 4 until midnight, or worse yet, that unbelievably boring experience from midnight until 8 the next morning. The individual I remember showed up one night when I was on the swing shift. It must have been around 9:30. He was a small, clean shaven, very professional looking man in a trimly cut grey suit, and he greeted me in a manner which suggested that I should have been out welcoming him with bands and loudspeakers.

"Hi! How's everything this evening?"

"Pretty slow. You're the first person through in an hour."

"Kinda dull, then, huh? Too bad. The boys at Rocky Mountain and Glacier are complaining, too."

Name dropping. I'm supposed to be impressed? What's his game?

I waited. He waited. Finally, I said, "I suppose you know it's three dollars for the permit."

He looked positively hurt, as if I had just spit on him.

"You're not going to charge *me*, are you?"

"Why shouldn't I?"

He looked away in feigned disbelief, then back at me, the green seasonal who obviously knew little about the parks and the people who went through.

"Why, why, the boys at Rocky Mountain and Glacier and Grand Canyon just see me coming and wave me through."

You con artist. You fake. What the hell do I care what the "boys" at those other parks do. What's he trying to pull? And all for a lousy three bucks.

"Well, this is not Rocky Mountain or Glacier or Grand Canyon. This is Yellowstone. I have no authorization to let anybody through without paying the fee."

And I'm not going to, by God.

He handed me a notebook. "Why, I have credentials from thirteen western governors. Here, I'll show them to you." He spread open a notebook containing diploma-like documents which looked as if they had been mass produced.

"Very pretty."

"I'm well known in high places out here."

"So?"

"So? So? Why my good young man. . ."

This is going to go on all night. Hmm. Let's try the basics.

"Your credentials are very pretty and very impressive. But do you have a letter from the Superintendent of Yellowstone Park saying that you should be given a gate pass?"

Look at this son of a bitch squirm. Of course he doesn't have that letter. What's he trying to pull, and for a lousy three bucks? I still can't believe anybody's that cheap. Must be some sort of a game with him. Con the young rangers.

"No, I don't seem to have that, but the Superintendent would be mighty unhappy if you didn't give me a gate pass."

"Oh, you know him, too, as well as the thirteen governors?"

The hell you do.

"Yes, yes, the Superintendent and I are great friends. I'm telling you. . . say, what's your rank and how long have been on this gate?"

Oh, so now we get the "I'm-going-over-your-head routine so that the big boss will really get you." It's always the second-raters who try that number.

"My rank and length of service on this gate aren't that important, but if you're wondering, no, this is not my first year in the Park or working for the Park Service. I am not green, if that's the angle you're going to take."

Boy, that set him back a bit. I should have enriched the story with a the-Superintendent's-my-uncle-lie, but that might get me in trouble. What next?

"I suppose you're really going to insist on this, then?"

"Yes."

"Even at the risk of alienating the Superintendent?"

That does it. I'll call his bluff.

"Why don't I settle the problem? I'll call the Superintendent and take care of the matter."

Before he could say anything else, I went to the station telephone and rang up the Superintendent. He was not pleased to get a late evening call from a seasonal at East Gate, but he said, in a tired, annoyed voice, "No, I never heard of the guy, but give him a gate pass and get rid of him."

I didn't want to do that, just yet.

"What did he say?"

"He said he never heard of you."

"He's forgot."

In a pig's eye.

"I suppose if I go on you'll have me stopped and make a test case of this?"

"Yes."

And so it went on, for forty-five minutes. I was determined to hold the guy as long as possible. I suspect now that he may have been running through the parks at will for years by coming after closing hours, pulling out the exit gate which was not locked, and going through that. Our all-nights shifts really spoiled that routine. Or he may have been an ego in search of fulfillment. He had credentials from thirteen western governors—just how he got them I do not know, but they can't have been very important. I finally gave him his gate pass, with the Superintendent's words, and suggested that if he came our way again, he'd better be prepared to pay unless he had a letter. My boss gave me hell the next day for not going through channels, but I wasn't sorry. Bureaucratic red tape has always annoyed me.

One other night visitor could have caused me a lot of problems, but I had a flash of ESP that evening and saved myself some embarrassment. When we went on the midnight shift, we all took a lunch, something to read, and anything else we might enjoy doing to while away the hours, particularly from about 2:30–4:00 A.M. The pattern was this. I would relieve the 4–12 man and then organize my permits in case anyone came through. The late hours were a good time to collect our materials. We stuffed bear danger leaflets, trashbags, and the park map into single units and put these in a large box. A man working uninterruptedly in the early morning hours could do enough of these to last the entire next day. I usually finished this work about 2:30 A.M. and then had to find something else to do.

On a particular evening I remember well, I finished early, about 2 A.M., and then debated my next move. You see, while my colleagues took a book to read, a radio to listen to, or a pillow to doze on, I had a different way of passing my time in the gate. I practiced my violin. As I think of it, that fiddle has been in some strange places at some strange times with me, but never in a stranger place or stranger time than the East Gate to Yellowstone Park at three o'clock in the morning. This particular evening, I was ready, even eager to practice, but I waited. Perhaps someone would come, and I might get into trouble if I were caught fiddling on government time. Considering what is done on government time these days, I think I was a minor offender, at the most.

At 2:30 I had a visitor. He was a sober-faced man driving what appeared to be his wife and possibly family into the park. He asked for no fanfare and initiated none on his own. He merely thrust his employees' pass out the car window for me to read. It was plainly printed, and it said, in dark bold letters: OTTO BROWN, CHIEF RANGER.

"Thank you, Mr. Brown."

"You're welcome. Good night." And he drove on toward Sylvan Pass. Interesting, isn't it, how one guy with "credentials from thirteen governors" tries to con his way in, but the Chief Ranger of the Park says nothing and merely presents his pass? Otto had told everyone to carry those and to pull no rank on the gates. He was a man who took his job seriously but never inflated his own importance. In 1956 I was to have the pleasure of working with his son during the summer; it was one of my good Yellowstone experiences.

One other important visitor came through East Gate during the summer of 1954. She was from St. Joseph, Missouri, and she had come to Yellowstone for the first time with her sister, her brother-in-law, and her brother. The vacation was a good break for her because, although only 22 then, she already had a Master's degree in English, from the University of Colorado—a degree she had earned in nine intense months—and she needed some respite from a year of hard academic work and physical exhaustion. Her brother-in-law drove to the window, paid his three dollars, received his map and trashbag, and drove on into the park. I was not on the window then; I was sitting in the station next to the man who was and supplying him with maps and trashbags. I might have been talking with him. I might have been gazing out the window and thinking of other things. No matter. I did not know the people from St. Joseph and probably would have said nothing to them had I been on the window. They were from Missouri, after all, and I was more tuned to Kansans. It is not likely that the young woman in the back seat of the car with her brother paid any more attention to the rangers on duty at the gate than we did to them. There would have been no reason to because, like most tourists, they were eager to get on into the Park and see its natural wonders. But this woman, who passed within ten feet of me that summer day in 1954, was no ordinary person. In June of 1955 she came back to Yellowstone . . . as my wife.

9

Middle Creek

I HAVE ALWAYS thought that the two summers I spent on East Gate were less significant than my other Yellowstone experiences, but the more I reflect on them, I realize how crucial they were to me in a number of ways. Those two summers, 1953 and 1954, tested me in unpredictable ways. As I have said, going to the gate in 1953 was not my idea of rangering, especially after one summer at Lake Station. But the rain of early June passed, and East Gate is in an extraordinarily beautiful setting. I have seen few sights more lovely than early morning on a clear day at East. There were mountains, on both sides of the gate, a mixture of conifers—spruce, fir, and pine—and Middle Creek.

It is impossible to think of East Gate without Middle Creek. If there is a trout stream in heaven, it surely must be a copy of Middle Creek. Occasionally big trout are caught there, early in the season, but for the most part it belongs to small and numerous cutthroat trout. They collect in the pools which exist sometimes fifty, sometimes one hundred yards apart in the stream. During the 1950s Middle Creek was so clear, so cold, and so clean, that we drank the water out of it. The snows which fed it collected in small rivulets above Sylvan Pass and formed a stream, about the width of a city residential street, which had cut its way over a rocky bed between the mountains near the gate. In mid-summer, when the sediment of the Spring thaw had cleared out, the water was literally crystal clear and very cold. The principal current shifted from side to side of the stream bed, pausing at intervals in small pools before speeding up again over a steeper grade. Where the water was fast it was not deep, and not attractive to the fly fishermen. In the pools, however, another situation prevailed.

There is a story about Middle Creek and me, a dream which persisted for ten years before I laid it to rest. I will tell you how this happened. My first summer at East I was told that Middle Creek had fish, and in 1953, far from the geyser basins, the lake, the canyon, and the commercial areas with their teeming life, I had to devise my own off duty recreation. Part of that, as I have already indicated, was practicing my violin. But there, right behind my cabin was Middle Creek. On my twenty-third birthday, I rode into Cody with Jack Frost, a partially crippled cowboy who worked at Pahaska Tepee, and decided to buy myself a birthday present. As a matter of fact, I was feeling a bit sorry for myself. The mail had not brought me any cards—they were to come a day late—and my birthday had always been a special occasion. So, because it was a beautiful day, this June 24th, and because it was one of my days off, I was going to do *something*.

In Cody Jack let me off to do what I wanted to do and told me where and when to meet him for the return trip. I was off to the nearest tackle shop. Looking back, I suspect that the owner of that shop, an old time resident of Cody, must have had the disposition of a poker player to contain his amusement at how green I was. I didn't know a thing about fly fishing. Because of that he sold me a stiff three piece rod, a reel, a level line, and two wooly worms. His advice: "Go fishing up in the meadahs; that's where the best fishing on Middle Creek is." I suppose it was, but what that tired old man didn't tell me would have filled a fly fisherman's notebook. In the first place, the rod was too stiff for really accurate casting. Jack Horner, about whom I will have much more to say later, was the only person I ever saw who could handle it with skill. But that's like saying the Itzak Perlman can make a good many different kinds of violins sound beautiful. The level line was of very little use in casting. I learned later that most fly fishermen used a double tapered line which was much easier to control. The worst omission was the lack of any mention of leader! Leader is a basic component of any fly fishing line. But I did not know this. I went back, tied the wooly worm onto the end of my line and expected fish to hit it. Why any self-respecting trout would hit at a bug clearly attached to a line is beyond me, but one or two did in the course of two years. Later I learned how to build the beautiful tapered leaders which give the fly fisherman close to ten feet of fine rainbow-tinted plastic from the end of the line to the fly. When that floats in the water, a fish has a much more difficult time picking it up, especially those which reflect light the way water does. In slightly rough water, a leader is almost impossible to see.

Well, I tried. I fished and fished and fished both summers. The whole package had cost me $10 in the summer of 1953. I suppose that was a bargain of sorts. But I caught only two fish that I remember those years, and I spent hours on the stream. The time wasn't wasted, however. One who has not sat beside a jewelled trout stream in the mountains can never know the tranquillity in such an experience. I remember one evening in the summer of 1954 when I had finished my tour of duty for the week. I had, because of the scheduling we were on with all night shifts, nearly two and one half days of free time. I could go down to Pahaska for supper when I felt like it. So, I put on my leisure time clothing and went fishing along the creek. I remember sitting there, my shoes off and my pants rolled up to my knees, in the refreshing cool of early evening, listening to the water surge by, looking up at the spruce, fir, and pine nearby and behind them the rising mountains at the gate, and finally at the deep blue of the early evening sky and feeling absolutely relaxed. All of the tension in my body simply drained away and left me in a state of pure healthful equilibrium. If there is life after death, let it be, for me, such a place, on such an evening. It was one of the best moments of my entire life.

I must leap ahead here, to complete the Middle Creek story. When I was married in 1955, I was transferred to another division and another station, far away from East Gate. There I learned to fly fish, in three hard years of practicing and failing and practicing and failing again until I bought a Walton Powell rod from my tutor. In the summer of 1958, my skills at last honed and my equipment superb, I began to catch fish, even big ones, so routinely that expected to do it. And from that time until we left Yellowstone in 1963, I kept thinking that I should go back to Middle Creek and try my luck again, to vindicate myself. But I never went back.

For ten years, in the hot summers of Illinois and Kansas, I would dream of Middle Creek. At times I would be standing there, back at last to test my skills with increased knowledge and better equipment, but I would wake up and feel a terrible longing and frustration. I cannot recall the number of times that dream recurred. It was maddening, especially to have it, so clear and so intense, and then to wake up to the stifling summer heat of the low country and realize that it was all just a mirage. But in 1973, for a few days, I returned to Yellowstone, and in my final day in the Park I went back to Middle Creek. It had rained that morning at Old Faithful where I was staying, and I almost decided not to go. But the temptation was too strong.

I drove across the Park and over Sylvan Pass to this memory of my youth and at last, on a partly cloudy but rapidly clearing afternoon, found myself, in boots, with my good rod and a desire to find out just how good a fisherman I was, standing once again in Middle Creek. I could remember the experience of twenty years previous when, barefooted, I would wade out to a caught fly. The cold water would nearly send me into shock. But I had boots this time, a fly fisherman's vest, a good hat, and a good rod. I began casting, remembering Jack Horner's instructions for reading water in this kind of stream, and soon began to catch fish. I caught them so fast that I bent down the barbs on my hooks so that I could release them without touching them. One park visitor, futilely trying to catch something for supper asked for help. I caught two fish in five minutes and sent him on his way. In one pool I caught six in fifteen minutes, releasing all of them. Before the afternoon was over, I had caught over forty fish, all of which I had returned to the water except for the two I gave to the man mentioned earlier, and sat down, once again, in pure joy. I remember taking off my boots, cooling my feet in the water, and recapturing that evening years earlier. But even then, in my moment of vindication, I could not completely recapture the mood of the earlier experience. But I had proved that I could take fish in Middle Creek at will. And I never dreamed about it again. The man had come back and vindicated the boy of twenty years earlier.

The years I worked at East Gate, Middle Creek was beaver and moose country. In 1953 we had a resident beaver who wasn't terribly afraid to show himself. He was collecting overtime chewing down lodgepole pines and damning up one section of the creek, and I once caught him at work when I was between him and the stream. He didn't like that. I can still see him awkwardly lumbering from the tree he was working on and dashing madly for the water. In the pond he had created, however, he was a very different animal. The clumsy creature of the land was a picture of artistic grace in the water. He would swim around his pool, eyeing me saucily and saying, in effect, "Try to come in here after me."

This particular beaver had a sense of humor. Harry Nicholson had a casting rod and was trying to catch some fish in the pond one afternoon. The fish were there, and Harry had the right equipment to catch them, so long as he was permitted to use it. But the beaver wasn't a fisherman and thought he would annoy the hell out of Harry. He swam around his pool, slapping his tail on the water and creating so much disturbance that the fish probably went to the bottom for the afternoon. Harry was really hacked off. "That damned beaver! Scaring every fish in the pool! And that son of a bitch knows just what he's doing!"

The beaver was entertaining. The moose were another item. Moose are very LARGE. Adults weigh in around 1,400 pounds, and are very tall. The males did not worry me a lot in early summer because they were still in velvet and hence easily spooked. In the Fall, when the rutting season is on, you must give a bull moose lots of territory. He will go for anything then. In summer the more dangerous ones are the cows with young calves. I never had a problem with them during the two summers I worked at East, but I had a big problem the day of my fishing triumph at Middle Creek.

Before going fishing that day, I had gone up the road to take pictures of the meadows. I had all I wanted and was walking up the side of a hill toward the highway where I hoped to catch a ride back to the gate. Ahead of me a porcupine scuttled along, intent on whatever business he had in mind. I had no long range lens on my camera, but I tried to get close enough to get a picture. Unfortunately, the pork heard me coming and trundled away into the deep shade.

My attention was quickly diverted, anyway. Less than fifty yards ahead, in deep shadow which I hadn't penetrated because of my sunglasses, a cow moose stood up abruptly, her body tense and her ears forward. Beside her was a calf at full alert. I knew trouble was coming in a hurry, so I retreated down the hill just behind three trees which grew closely together. I was determined to keep those trees between me and the moose no matter which direction she took. I felt I could negotiate around them in tighter turns than she could. I had just stepped behind them when she came roaring down the hill. A moose coming directly at you looks approximately 20 feet tall. She pulled up just the other side of the trees, no more than five feet from me, blowing hard through her nostrils, then circled back to her calf. I was sweating buckets, and I am not a sweating person. For several minutes, she stood back by her calf, just watching me and flicking her ears. I wonder if she thought at first that I was a bear. Moose's eyesight is very poor.

When she got close, she would have discovered that I was one of the two-legged pests along the creek.

I waited behind my trees, seeing precious minutes tick away. She eventually moved to my right, away from me, then stopped to see what I would do. I calculated the distance to the next clump of trees and decided I could make it even if she came after me again. So, I went for them, away from her. Wild animals respond best to those who do not crowd them. She disappeared into the woods and I went for the road, still shaking but grateful that all I had had was a scare. A moose's footprint in your skull could be very bad for your health. And to think that I had to come back to Yellowstone to experience something that had never happened to me during the years when I was there daily!

So, I did entertain myself, with fly rod, with book, and with violin, and I have no memories of being bored at East Gate, just memories of pleasant unhurried evenings when I felt good about myself and about the world around me. Now I make more money, have established myself in my profession, and have many demands on my "precious" time. I would willingly go back to those peaceful summer days of 1953 and '54. The only thing I really missed was female companionship, and the time was not quite fulfilled for that.

10

East Gate Colleagues
And Friends

THERE WERE, of course, more than water, trees, animals, and tourists at East Gate. There were people, my colleagues and the small circle of our acquaintances at Pahaska Tepee where we took our meals, showered, and enjoyed whatever social life was available to us.

As I have said, the crew in 1953 consisted of John Rohn, the permanent ranger in charge of the station, Harry Nicholson, senior seasonal, Don Guiton, Jack, and others I cannot remember. George Butchko was with us in '53 or '54, I don't remember which now. The '54 crew is not as clear in my mind. Guiton was back, but Rohn was gone, replaced by a man whose name escapes me. Our senior seasonal was Cecil Kirkis, a unique blend of character and competence. I do not remember the others.

Since this is not a work of fiction, I feel no obligation to develop full character portraits of all these men. Instead, let me color them with those incidents which stamp them in my memory, thirty-five years and hundreds of experiences away from the summers of 1953 and '54. Jack Stark and I were not a lot alike except that to others we must have come off as Kansas dull. Jack was from Ark City, and he was going into Forest or Park Service work. I liked his parents; they visited us that first summer, and I saw them, once, a year later when they came to a concert some of us from KU were doing in Ark City. Essentially, however, Jack and I had the nasal twang of the rural Kansan, and we didn't do anything that called attention to us. We were, mostly, there.

Harry Nicholson was a bit different. Harry had red, closely cropped hair, and he fussed at us like an old grandmother. He was meticulous in his personal habits, and he had a quick if occasionally bitter wit. There were reasons for that. He was a very nervous man, a time bomb always ticking and near explosion. This was caused by a built-in anxiety. Mid-way through the summer he told me about his father, an alcoholic who beat his mother and terrified him and his brothers and sisters. His mother eventually divorced Harry's father and re-married a man who Harry said was an angel. The terrible anxieties of early childhood were replaced by affection, stability, and responsibility in the home, but the scars of the early years obviously had left their mark.

Guiton was smooth. And smart. And cultured. Picture a fairly tall, slender, sandy-haired chemistry major from Oberlin College whipping up and down the park road in his Ford and radiating "cool." I liked Guiton as much as any man I worked with in the Park Service. He never made big problems out of little ones; he learned rapidly and thus kept his perspective on the work he was doing. He was uncommonly generous with his car, lending it to us to go to Pahaska or taking us there when we had short lunch hours or were in a hurry. And he was absolutely dependable on the job. Curiously, Guiton never followed up his chemistry major. He liked Park Service work and made a career of it, although not perhaps where he would most have liked to be. The last time I heard from him he was in Fort Oglethorpe, Georgia, married, with a family, and rangering. I really never thought he would settle down all that much. The last time I saw him, after he left Yellowstone, he was working the Badlands in South

Dakota, cool as ever, quick witted and tearing out the local girls' hearts. I don't know how the lady he eventually married ever corralled him.

Two things in particular I remember about Guiton. When we made change on the gate, we would say, in giving back seven dollars out of ten, "And two is five and five is ten." About the second time I did that, all that cruddy training in English usage started coming back on me, and I thought, "five and five *is* ten? No, *are* ten—plural subject." It's a stupid point of agreement, but I did what my ear told me to. Interestingly, after I started saying "Five and five are ten," no one on the gate changed from his "five and five is ten" except Guiton. He picked it up quick as a flash, said, "Of course. Five and five *are* ten" and put it into his little speech which he always delivered in Tiffany style. "And here are your trashbag, map, and permit, also good for Grand Teton National Park to the south." He should have been a naturalist.

Guiton also took a bunch of us on the one really good trip I had at East Gate. We went to Cody and someone suggested, after looking at a map, that we might try "that road going straight north." It led through the Sunlight Basin and eventually connected to the Northeast Entrance Road. It did, that is, after we did some educated guessing at unmarked forks, and went over some hair raising narrow road, especially at "Dead Indian Pass." Many years later I learned that we had passed through a portion of the east side of the Park where Chief Joseph and the Nez Perce, fleeing the army, had slipped through a trap the army had set and escaped into Montana. That was my only trip along the spectacular east side of Yellowstone. Not many people get a good long view at the eastern slopes of the Absaroka Range which makes up a large portion of Yellowstone's eastern boundary. It is harsh but starkly beautiful country.

Then there was John Rohn, our permanent ranger supervisor in 1953. After thirteen years as a savage, in Yellowstone during the summers, the Everglades in the winter, John had turned ranger, and not all the old time rangers were happy about it. He was not, as I was, square, and this bothered the starchier do-it-by-the-book-and-don't-make-waves types in the Park Service. But John was extremely smart, and he was one of the most engaging practical jokers I have ever known. During the time he was a student at the University of Nebraska, he saw an opportunity to cause the kind of chaos only Rohn could create. When paying his fees at the university, he told me—and they were only about seventy or eighty dollars a semester then—he had noticed the orderliness of the university's cashier. She had her money box with neat pigeon holes for every denomination of bill and coin—except one.

In those days, the people who lived in the towns bordering Yellowstone, particularly the Montanans in West Yellowstone, would balk at taking paper money. They liked silver, and they still carried pouches for their silver dollars. From them John had no trouble accumulating a large number of silver dollars before he left the Park. At fee paying time, he presented the compulsively orderly cashier with about seventy silver dollars for which she had no place whatsoever. Utter frustration. Could he write a check? Did he have paper money? Would he come back tomorrow with a bank draft? Mostly, would he go away and quit harrassing her with his unruly stack of silver dollars. John naturally insisted on paying with the silver dollars which must have driven that cashier nuts. You know the kind of person, one with a place for everything and every person. Clutter, of any kind, unscrews their nerve endings. Think of the clutter created by those rowdy uncorralled silver dollars. I'll bet she wanted to run a hot steam iron over John's fingers for about ten minutes.

Rohn was also a quick man with a quip, and Guiton told me of one of his best. The employees in lodges outside the Park picked the tradition of having an August Christmas from Yellowstone's savages, and the kids at Pahaska Tepee celebrated it each year. In 1953 one tourist was totally put out by the whole ridiculous idea.

"I never heard of such a silly thing," she said. "Christmas in August! I dislike, very much, all this celebrating and holly and mistletoe at the wrong time of year. It's offensive! It violates one's whole sense of the rightness of certain seasons and occasions. Besides, Christmas is my birthday!"

John lifted his eyebrows ever so slightly and said to her, in a soft voice, "I thought Christmas was somebody's else's birthday, too." He and Guiton left the restaurant and a tourist in a state one can only imagine.

All in all, I liked John Rohn very much. He was flexible, he was witty, and he made life at East Gate very comfortable for all of us that summer. We did our work well, and we did it with a minimum of hassle.

Although we did not have a great deal of social life at East Gate, I do remember four girls, two from 1953 and two from 1954, that I have always wondered about. In 1953, hands down, the stellar attraction of Pahaska Tepee was a nurse named Orpha. She and her friend, Jeanie, were getting their education at American University in Washington, D.C. I do not know how they got the jobs at Pahaska, and I really know nothing about what has happened to them since. I once talked Orpha into going to a dance at Canyon, but she insisted that Jeanie had to go, too, so I got Jack Stark to accompany her. It was not much of an evening for any of us. Looking back on the incident, I would have to say that it was first-rate comedy. I had no car but had talked Orpha into letting me drive hers to Canyon. At that point in my life, I am sure she was a much better driver than I. Jack and Jeanie were miserable because neither wanted to go on this silly double date, and I didn't really want to go to Canyon. I would have much preferred to go somewhere and neck with Orpha. But that was impossible because I scarcely knew her, and she certainly must have had some interesting thoughts about me. So, we went and came back on what clearly was one of the worst double dates of my life.

Orpha was an interesting person, and I regret now not having had a car and MONEY so that I could take her to the show in Cody, say, and just visit some. She was a fairly tall woman, blond, and well filled out. And she was, without trying in the least to be so, very sexy. She may have suspected that, however, and thus used her professionalism as a defense against the predatory males she had to combat. Never could say that I knew the real Orpha—her family, the influences which had shaped her character, the causes for her aspirations, the reasons behind her peculiar guardedness around men. And I think she was worth getting to know. We would never have attracted one another sufficiently to get involved in a heavy love affair, but I think we might have had some good times that summer talking about interesting things. Never know. She should have grandchildren by now, if she married. Otherwise, she is probably directing some large nursing staff in an eastern hospital.

In 1954 Pahaska had a cute girl from New Hampshire (she said it right—Nyew Hampsha) named Nancy. Guiton dated her; I remember working the gate one night and it seemed that every half hour Guiton and Nancy came through. They would go up to Sylvan Lake on the pass and come back down. Then back through the gate and up to the pass again. Damn! Why didn't I have a car and Guiton's polish? My wife has frequently reminded me that I have the *savoir faire* of an Arkansas hillbilly. Caused by aborted social growth in junior and high school. Why can't we live our lives over, just once, so that we don't do the stupid things we did when we were young?

Nancy was cute and distant, but toward the end of the summer of 1954 I began visiting with a very pleasant low keyed girl named Sandy. She had been the gas station boy's girlfriend all summer, I was told. But he left for home early, and Sandy was temporarily unattached. Nothing ever happened between us. I don't think I ever even held her hand. But she was a very nice girl to talk with, and she was quite pretty. I stopped to see her on the way home that year. I was to meet my parents in Rapid City, so I took some time in Cody, where Sandy lived, to visit. Had I gone back to East Gate in 1955, we might have become better acquainted. I remember stopping there, briefly, on my way into the Park that year and introducing my new wife to the lady who ran the laundry there. Sandy walked by and started to greet me warmly but then backed away as she realized that the lady with me was not my sister. Well, I hope she married well and has many charming grandchildren. Perhaps she took up a career, too, but I thought that less likely than in Orpha's case.

These girls were nice to know. They crossed my life, as I crossed theirs, very briefly and inconsequentially, but one always wonders what happens to those faint memories of a time over thirty years ago. I wish them all well and hope that their lives have been happy and productive.

On one occasion I did participate in bringing a little culture to the East Gate-Pahaska crowd. One of the boys at the gas station was much taken with my violin playing. Apparently, he had never heard anyone who could play very well at all, and he would come to my cabin and listen with genuine interest. I can say that because I have know few people who could sit through much unaccompanied Bach without getting restless. On my behalf, he arranged an informal concert at Pahaska. I played a movement from one of the Handel Sonatas with his brother who was a fair pianist, and then we played many many popular violin pieces, the kind one finds in *Violin Pieces the Whole World Loves*. Those assembled to listen seemed to enjoy themselves considerably, and I felt it was an evening well spent.

A few nights later, I received two unexpected guests at my cabin at the gate. They were Ted and Helen Ogsden, he a retired park ranger, she an author of children's books . . . and a pianist. I later heard stories about moving Helen's piano into the permanent ranger's quarters at East Gate when Ted had been stationed there. They now lived down the Shoshone Valley, in a very picturesque place, about half way to Cody. She wanted to know if I would like to play sonatas? Well, of course I would. I gave her piano parts to those I had, particularly Mozart, and we arranged a time when he would pick me up and take me to dinner and an evening of chamber music at their home. I believe I went there twice that summer and enjoyed myself thoroughly. Mrs. Ogsden was a good player, and she enjoyed the opportunity of making music with someone who could play more than Twinkle Twinkle Little Star. On another occasion they took me into Cody to hear a young pianist play; he was from Cody but was studying at Eastman, and he was very good.

The Ogsdens also were full of Yellowstone lore. He had been disappointed in not being appointed Chief Ranger of the Park, and he had spent some time in Death Valley. He did not like one of the Park's superintendents of the early 30s, but he had unlimited admiration for Horace Albright, one of Yellowstone's early and truly great chief administrators. The music, dinner, and conversations with the Ogsdens provided me with some of the best moments I had while stationed at East Gate. A violin I already knew then and have since been reminded, again and again, is a special ticket to some very rare and meaningful experiences and personal associations.

11

The End of the East Gate Era

THE STORY of my East Gate years would not be complete without a sketch of Roger Phelps and the story of my trip home in 1954, a fiasco of a minor order. Roger was a missionary's son, had spent time in India, and was going to school at Bob Jones University in the Carolinas. I met him and his brother the summer of 1952 before I left the Old Faithful Cafeteria to become a ranger. Like me, Roger had little time for drunken parties. He wanted to *see* the great western wilderness on foot, and we had some fine hikes together. One was to Shoshone Lake near Old Faithful, but the most memorable were a long trip we took in the Grand Tetons and one up Electric Peak on Yellowstone's north border. I tell these stories so that the mothers of boys who go to national parks can realize how truly scatter-brained and fearless their prodigies are when turned loose.

Roger thought in Cecil B. DeMillian terms when he planned a hike. He was working at Fishing Bridge in 1953, but he could find no one there to take on an adventure which he had set his heart on. I was available and willing, so one evening in mid-July of 1953, Roger came to the Gate and picked me up—he had bought a wretched car which wheezed its way up Sylvan Pass and coughed and sputtered all the way to Jenny Lake in the Tetons which we reached about midnight. You must understand that the distance from East Gate to Jenny Lake is approximately 110 miles—that's a conservative estimate—over roads which have a 45 MPH speed limit.

Naturally, the Jenny Lake Campground had long been filled, so Roger and I parked the car and put our sleeping bags under some trees on a small ridge near the lake. They were totally inadequate bags. Mine had insufficient down on top and nothing underneath, and I was so green about the use of sleeping bags and camping out that I knew nothing about the need for ground cover or for insulating layers underneath me which were equal to those above. I should have stayed with Boy Scouting and learned some basic things about camping when I was young. The result was that I hardly slept. I was cold, uncomfortable on the hard ground, and anxious about the next day's trip.

We arose at five o'clock and found a grill where we could cook breakfast. Roger was insistent on the need for hearty breakfasts before long hikes. He was absolutely right, but he fried the eggs in too much grease, and it gave me a severe stomach ache. By eight we had finished our breakfast, cleaned up the grill we had used, and got our gear ready for the hike. We were to go halfway around Jenny Lake and take the Cascade Canyon Trail. The early morning walk around Jenny Lake was a beautiful two-and-a-half mile trip, through aspen which were gorgeous against the clear blue sky of the morning. We covered this ground rapidly, passed Hidden Falls on the way, and then got to hiking in earnest. I was fussing about one thing and another, mostly because I was anxious about what I was getting into and because my stomach was hurting from the grease. Two things cured me quickly. Roger turned around and said sharply, "Don, I wish you would stop complaining about everything." I hadn't even realized that I was being such a bastard. That shut me up, and once I had got rid of some of the grease, I began to feel very good indeed.

In another hour and a half we passed the fork to Lake Solitude and headed for The Wall, a huge limestone ridge deep in the heart of the Tetons. When we reached the summit of our trail, we stood at 10,600 feet, looking out into Alaska Basin, a large interior snowfield streaked with unmelted snow and surrounded by spectacular scenery. I particularly remember one rock formation, mostly west and somewhat to the north of us, which looked like a giant battleship carved out of red rock.

We were now on the Alaska Basin Trail and in some very interesting work. The trail would disappear under a large field of snow, and we would have to hunt around to find where it came out, but our sense of direction was good, and we made steady progress, across the snow fields and eventually back to a connection between the Skyline Ridge Trail and the one coming out of Alaska Basin. Late in the afternoon we were back at 10,600 and beginning our descent to the head of Death Canyon, our route out of the mountains. By six o'clock we had covered twenty-six miles, and I told Roger that if we had no more ridges to climb over, we would be all right. I was tiring fast.

Unfortunately, as everyone who has hiked the Death Canyon Trail knows, it is bisected by the Phelps Moraine, a strange conjunction of names since I was hiking with Roger Phelps. I did not think I could get my legs to work going up those three switchbacks—I have never been more tired in my life—but I did and we descended, it being nearly dark by now. When we came out in the settled area at Moose, it was close to nine-o'clock, and we had hiked thirty-two miles that day. The Teton rangers told me, in subsequent years, that ours was at least a two-day trip.

At Moose we were still in trouble. We were five miles from the car with no way of getting back to Jenny Lake. We tried hitchhiking, but no one was about to pick up a couple of seedy looking bums like Roger and me. At eleven we went to a cottage and knocked on the door. Fortunately, we caught the naturalist coming back from a program at Jenny Lake, and he gave us a ride back there. I don't know the man's name, but I certainly owe him something. We could have been a couple of lying thugs instead of the nice guys we were. But were we tired! We did sleep that night, despite the discomforts, but we had to be up by five to get started back to our jobs. We ate breakfast at Flagg Ranch and chugged on. Roger's car broke down between Thumb and Lake Junction, and I eventually had to hitchhike the rest of the way to East Gate. I had called so that Jack Stark would cover my duty shift.

Imagine! Two short nights, thirty-two miles of tough hiking, and two hundred fifty miles of difficult driving, and I had to shave, get on my uniform, and get to work. I don't know how I functioned except that I was twenty-three, and at twenty-three you can do things you wouldn't dream of at fifty. If I had a chance to go back and do it again, I certainly wouldn't do it the way Roger and I did. I would like to take that trip once more—with better boots, better food, and more rest. I could do it. I have been jogging or water running for twenty-three years now, and I did hike fourteen miles in the Tetons in five and one-half hours when I was fifty . . . with a bone spur in my left heel, too. I had wanted to take my oldest daughter to Lake Solitude. The long years of conditioning did pay off. But recovery would be nothing like it was then.

That big hike wasn't enough for Roger, however. Later in the summer he was planning another extravaganza. It turned out to be the scariest one I've ever taken, and I would not repeat it.

Electric Peak on Yellowstone's north border gets its name because of the lightning which frequently strikes it in storms. Foolishly, we took the advice of a naturalist and decided to attack it from the north boundary of the Park. His reasoning was that while we would have to climb an extra 2,000 feet—there was another route to Electric Peak from the Swan Lake Flats, but it required more overland hiking before one got to the mountain— the total distance would be shorter.

We camped out in the grassy meadows below it before our "assault" on the mountain the next day. Two ironies in our situation occurred to me only years later when I knew more about the

Park. Roger had commented how comfortable he felt hiking through the high grass of Yellowstone where one didn't have to worry about poisonous snakes. Subsequently, I learned that the north boundary was rattlesnake heaven. We were very lucky indeed not to have had one in our sleeping bags. In the second place, we were in an area frequented by grizzly bears. We missed both snake and bear, and I wonder at the good angels who must have shaken their heads at our bumbling in those years.

The hike was a disaster. It started well enough because we had the mountain clearly in front of us and had no trouble with our bearings. But gaining those extra 2,000 feet of elevation, I am sure, was much more tiring at the altitude than the few extra miles we would have had to walk overland from above Mammoth. Nonetheless, intrepid Hillarys that we were, we went hard at Electric Peak. We made good time and well before noon stood at a point which required a crucial decision from us. I remember looking up at a huge cirque, the center of which was full of debris. Roger said the best way to get to the top would be to take the straight route through the cirque. I thought circling around and following the ridge of the cirque would be a better plan. I was right; Roger was wrong, but Roger insisted that we shouldn't separate, and I let him talk me into his route.

In the mountains the first thing you learn is that what you see at a distance is much tougher to confront when you get close to it than you think it is going to be. The air is much clearer and you see farther, but you make judgments about the size and difficulty of terrain in front of you based on sea level perceptions. Translation: the debris in the center of the cirque turned out to be loose scree, and some of the boulders were very big. As the going got steeper and steeper, our task became more and more impossible. At one point I kicked loose a boulder which caught Roger in the ankle and produced a gash which bled profusely for a time. But we persisted. We were on that stuff for seven hours, and it was dangerous. Worst of all, when we did reach the top, we found a cleft in the mountain which separated us from the cairn in which one wrote his or her name. We had no time to go back down and come back up to the cairn. Roger was bitterly disappointed. I just wanted to get down and off the loose debris.

We eventually did that and hurried down into the timber and back to the car. As we walked on and on, I became hungrier and hungrier. Our lunch was used up; our water was gone. All I could think of was how good a hot fudge sundae would taste. The longer we walked, the more powerful that image fixed itself in my mind. We got back to Mammoth about half an hour before the store closed, and I got my hot fudge sundae together with lots of cold water. I cannot tell you how good both tasted.

Roger was determined to put his mark on the top of that mountain, however, so he talked someone else into going back the next week and taking the route we should have taken when we went up. So Roger's name is there atop Electric Peak; mine is not. If I ever think I have energy enough to do that hike again, I'll take the upper route, and, for certain, I'll walk around the edge of the cirque.

Roger and I took one other hike that summer, into another remote portion of the park, but it was not a spectacular hike in any way. It is noteworthy in just one respect. At one point Roger thought he had found a better way to go than the route I was taking. We shouldn't divide, he said. I agreed and assured him that I was going to continue in the route I was taking, and I hoped he would come along. He did. Roger was a bit stubborn, but he was not unreasonable, and he was basically a very nice person. I remember him at this distance of years for those two memorable hikes deep into the heart of Yellowstone/Teton country.

The summer of 1954 closed the first "Yellowstone" period for me. All in all, it was a very strange summer, from beginning to end. In the first place, the Park Service, instead of hiring people as it had in the past, had put everyone on the civil service register. I took the test and, as far as I know, did very well, but because I was not a natural science major, lacked certain educational requirements which would have put me farther up. The result was that they did not get down to my name until mid-summer. Thus, as the summer of 1954 began, I did not have my Yellowstone job back, and I was uncertain what would happen. I needed work so, temporarily, I returned to something I knew how to do: playground duty, but in Lawrence, not Kansas City. I wasn't at all enthusiastic about it, but it paid money, and that I needed.

I was enjoying another benefit that summer. Since I apparently wasn't going west, Mr. Cerf, my violin teacher, had asked me to take care of his house while he and his family were in New England and then in Europe. It was a nice house, and I had the use of a car and a three-speed bicycle, a novelty to me in those days. My only chore, because a cleaning woman took care of the house, was to feed and care for Spotty, the family dog.

This could have been a very fine situation for me, except for two things. I was dying to be back in the mountains. In the evenings I would occasionally ride past the cedars on the campus and their odor would suggest the conifers of the high country, and I would be heartsick. My body was in Lawrence, but my heart and mind were in Yellowstone. Then, too, 1954 turned out to be a son-of-a-bitch for weather. The heat came: temperatures over 100 day after day. It was brutal; it was enervating. Early in the morning, at six o'clock, I would occasionally play what I now laughingly refer to as tennis with Jim White, a fellow graduate student in English who enjoyed the ride in the convertible, but not the heat and humidity. The Cerf's home was not equipped with air conditioning—few were then—so the heat permeated the house, and I could hardly sleep. One night, during a thunderstorm, Spotty kept trying to get in bed with me. I eventually went to a top bunk to get some relief from his (her—Spotty was a female, but Mr. Cerf said they called her a he) persistent pawing of me, but sleep is hard to get when you sweat without moving, and the air is still and close.

Mr. Cerf had taken about three days to orient me to those things which needed doing around the house, and he had also given me a lesson in cuisine. He was a very intelligent and very subtle man. We were having a steak dinner the night before he left, and I had asked him to cook my T-bone well done. That is sacrilege, of course. Cooking a T-bone well done is the equivalent of reducing Bach to hard rock, but I was unsophisticated in those days. As we were eating, Mr. Cerf said to me, very casually, "I often think it unfortunate that so many people deny themselves the pleasure of eating rare meat."

Well, I was one of his good violin students, and I thought of myself as something better than totally stupid, so I said, sure, I'd try a piece of rare steak. He generously offered it. I took a bite and have never eaten a well done steak since then.

He also did one other uncommonly generous thing for me. Quite coincidentally the previous Spring, the same day that I had my violin lesson, I had received a letter from my brother who was stationed in Trieste. In the letter my brother told me he had been going to the Munich PX on off duty time and had discovered that he could get me a Leica there for half what it cost in the states. I had lamented to Mr. Cerf that I did not have the money at that time but would have it (because of increased teaching the coming Fall) after my brother was back from Europe. I saw it simply as a piece of bad luck, an unfortunate juxtaposition of events. Mr. Cerf had said, "Well, I can loan you the money to buy the camera." He was wealthy and could afford to do that, but you must remember that students of my generation would no more have thought of imposing on their teachers in that way than we would have thought of robbing their homes. It was something that just was not done, an impropriety of the first order. So, when he offered to lend me the money for the camera, I was so taken aback that I was temporarily speechless, something that those familiar with my garrulousness will find hard to believe. I was so embarrassed by the whole incident that I wouldn't even mention the matter, even the last day before he left for Europe. But Mr. Cerf was a man of his word and one conspicuously attentive to details. He wrote me the check that last day, and I sent my brother the money. When Bob came back from Europe, he had a IIIf Leica with a 1.5 Summarit lens, a piece of machinery so fine that, after a tune-up a few years ago, it works like new. I will never part with that camera although it lacks some of the sophisticated equipment on today's machines. It took hundreds of Yellowstone pictures which I treasure.

Mr. Cerf has been dead for several years now, but I wonder if he ever realized the full extent of his impact on my life. There is never a time when I play my violin or hold that camera that I do not call his image to mind, hear his words of restrained but genuine encouragement, and remember his personal generosity to me, a callow youth, too young to fully appreciate what he was doing for me. I count on the fingers of one hand the great teachers I have had. Mr. Cerf was among the select of that select group.

In June of 1954, then, he left for the East, and I had the house, the car, the playground, and that oppressive heat. To most people, it would have been a good deal. Hell, it was a good deal. It was very generous of him, and I was living, temporarily, in a style to which I would never be accustomed, but I was married to Yellowstone and could not forget her.

In early July, just after the Fourth, I got a note on the playground to call Ruben Hart, one of Yellowstone's assistant chief rangers. Could I report for duty at East Gate soon? Could I? God, what a lightning bolt! So unexpected! Such joyous news! A part of the summer could still be salvaged. I talked on the telephone with Mr. Cerf who had not yet left New England, and he said it would be all right if I got Jim Smolko, a very fine pianist, music graduate student, to take care of the house for the rest of the summer. That solved a big problem. I was given permission to terminate on the playground, and I left for Kansas City as fast as I could go. I was headed for paradise again.

The rest of the summer I have already described, except for the absolute joy I experienced in being back "home" where I really belonged in the summer. East Gate was no longer unfamiliar. The schedules had been changed, the personnel were different, but the duty, Middle Creek, Pahaska, and the entire interior of the park were my summer experience again. I felt as if I had never left, and the earlier portion of the summer dissolved into a mist, heat and all. I was in a crummy cabin again, without mice, sleeping under army blankets, using Coleman lanterns and an outdoor biffy, and loving every minute of it.

But the summer ended, peculiarly, as it had begun. Instead of taking the train back, I was to go out through Cody, travel across Wyoming by bus, and meet my parents in Rapid City, South Dakota. They were coming up from Kansas City and were planning on going as far as the Black Hills. We got our dates set, agreed to meet at the Post Office there, and started coordinating the effort. I had planned my money very closely and carefully. I saved enough for bus fare, food, and an overnight in Rapid City. There were no margins.

Unfortunately, my dad, whose memory I would not defame for a minute because he was one of the most good-dispositioned and loving people I have ever known, had one flaw in his character. He loved to travel, which meant mostly covering a lot of ground and seeing a lot of the country, and his idea of getting the car ready for a long trip was to get the gas tank full and the oil changed. It rarely occurred to him to check the radiator, the hoses, the brakes, points and plugs, tires, and all other working parts of a car which never give trouble in ten to twenty-mile hops around a city but which give out at the first opportunity on a trip which extends over several hundred miles. This time the radiator overheated, they took an extra day to find someone competent who could fix it, and I almost spent a night in a Rapid City park.

When they finally made it, I was glad to see them, troublesome car and all, and we had a pleasant trip through the Black Hills, Mt. Rushmore, and the parks in the vicinity. It was a strange ending, however, to a summer which had had considerable variety, but it had in no way prepared me for the year to come. That, in many respects, was the most eventful year of my life.

Interlude

LET US PAUSE a moment before a year in which my life changed so radically and so permanently that I almost fear to wonder what it would have been like if things had turned out differently. A combination of experiences that year literally transformed me into a different person from the one I was becoming, and, I would have to say, for the better. As usual, with men, a woman was behind the change.

It is September, 1954. My friend, Jalal Besharat, which is as close as I can come to remembering the spelling of his name—a small, highly sensitive Iranian student, frustrated at not getting into medical school, terribly disappointed in love by a local girl who used him to buy her expensive presents and apparently accept an engagement which she never intended to honor—is telling me that I should marry, that once I leave college I will never again have the opportunity to meet so many attractive, desirable girls and thus find a suitable marriage partner.

Two things about Jalal's remarks strike me: first, he should not be giving me advice about love affairs since his has turned out so badly. Besides, I am now recovered from the difficult affair which ended, on my part anyway, in the winter of 1952–53. Second, I do not understand Jalal's sense of urgency. I have no intention of leaving KU soon, which is a big problem that I don't recognize. I should have finished my M.A. by now, but I have been held up by a major professor who has gone slightly batty and who will not let me limit my subject in a reasonable manner. If I cannot get free of him, I will have to write a doctoral dissertation for my master's degree, and that will take forever. But that doesn't worry me—now, as I think back to that moment, I should have worried a lot—I was *drifting*, literally coasting from academic year to academic year, teaching freshman English, nominally working on my stalled thesis, and thinking only of the next summer when I would return to Yellowstone.

So, although personally and professionally, I am like a ship becalmed, I cannot understand the urgency in Jalal's tone, but I will humor him a bit. "Jalal, I grant the point you're making about the opportunity to meet suitable marriage partners on a college campus, but I can't just walk up to a good-looking girl and say, 'My, you are very pretty—want to get married?' Courtship doesn't work that way. These things happen gradually; they develop from friendships which ripen into love. I don't know any girls that I would want to become permanently involved with at this time. In fact, I am about as far from getting married as it is possible to be."

Thirty minutes later the Head of the English Department introduced another graduate student and me to a slender auburn-haired young woman in a blue dress, Miss Patricia Pettepier, who was joining our staff that fall. She nodded coolly and departed. I said to the other graduate student, as we went up the stairs of Old Fraser at KU, "Boy, is that a cold fish!" He agreed. I went to my office then headed for the Union where I was to help with registration. I did not know that I had just met my wife.

In the Union there was a considerable hubbub, the kind that always goes with the registration hassle. The Director of Freshman Composition, Albert Kitzhaber, had put me at a table taking cards. Miss Pettepier and I were working together. In half an hour I discovered that she was not a cold fish at all. She was very pretty; she had a good wit and cheerful disposition (her father would never admit this—always referred to Patsy's buzzsaw disposition, but he teased her a lot); and she had *direction.*

"Are you just starting graduate work?" (My opener; I was going to impress the lady.)

"No. I have an M.A. from the University of Colorado."

"Oh?" *Damn! She looks awfully young to have a Master's Degree.*

"When did you get it?"

"Last spring."

"Oh, so you've been at Colorado for a couple of years or so?"

"No. I didn't teach composition. I had some jobs and a scholarship. I finished in nine months."

"Nine months?" *Now, I'm really sweating. How can you get a degree in nine months? Cheap, that's how.* "Uh, what kind of requirements do they have there?"

"Twenty-four hours. And comprehensive exams and a thesis."

"How much of a thesis?"

"Mine was about 140 pages."

"You worked pretty fast."

"I don't mess around."

She certainly didn't mess around. Nine months to get a degree that I had been diddling with for over two years.

We talked some more and some more, and I began to like this lady very much. At lunch break, when I went off duty, Mr. Kitzhaber took me aside and asked me if I would teach some extra sections the first week. They had hired a very bright and pretty girl from Chicago, but she would not arrive the first week and someone was needed to take her classes. He suggested that doing the extra teaching might ingratiate me with this new person and lead to better things. I told him thanks, I would do it, but not for any advantage with the new teacher coming in. "I'm already taken."

"Oh, Miss Pettepier?"

I didn't think my interest in the lady had been that obvious. Months later, when we announced our engagement, Kitzhaber said, "Don, you're a man of your word."

That first day I had nothing to go on, however. All I could do was be devious and try to figure out some way of courting this new phenomenon. I had one advantage over my would-be competitors. In 401 Fraser, one of the large bullpens for teaching assistants, I had shared a huge double desk with a graduate student who had not come back that Fall. So, there was a vacancy on the opposite side of my desk. When new people came into the office looking for places, I directed them to other desks in the room. When Miss Pettepier came in, I suggested that the space opposite me was vacant. Thus, without her suspecting anything, I put Pat in a place where visiting between us would be frequent and natural. And, as she later told me, she decided from listening to me work with students that I wasn't a total jerk.

The rest of the story of our courtship is for us, not for public consumption, but it was purposeful and swift. There were some landmark events during that year, however, and as I look back on them now, I realize how truly remarkable they were. First, once we decided to marry, Pat told me that KU was no place to get a Ph.D. She had much more savvy in the professional world than I had, and she had some very positive ideas about good schools. At the top of her list was the University of Wisconsin which had an outstanding English Department. These were the days of Helen White, Ruth Wallerstein, Ricardo Quintana, Madelaine Doran, Merritt Hughes, Mark Eccles, Frederick Hoffman, Paul Wiley, Harry Clark. . . . The department was full of people who were distinguished in their fields, nationally and internationally. She let me know that (1) I should finish the degree immediately and (2) get accepted at Wisconsin. The first task seemed hopeless; the bind I was in with my major professor was a Gordian knot. But he had a breakdown at mid-term, and suddenly, his students had to be transferred to other professors. I wasted no time in getting direction from Annette McCormick who observed that I had done an awful lot of work and who helped me to finish the project in two months. I regret to say that I did not distinguish myself on the exam, but I passed and got through. Also, miracle of miracles, I got a teaching assistantship at Wisconsin. We both did, Pat before me, but she still thinks they came at the same time. Perhaps. Anyway, we spoke to our department head about a problem; married couples could not both have assistantships. We wrote to Merritt Hughes, then serving his turn in a rotating chairmanship at Wisconsin, explaining that we had applied separately but were now going to be married and wondered if both were still to get the assistantships. Mr. Hughes replied that we both would be able to do this the first year since we were appointed as single individuals, but that after the first year another arrangement would have to be made.

Now, there was only one problem left: the summer in Yellowstone. I wanted to return, but I could hardly go back to East Gate with Pat. I wrote to Otto Brown, and he told me that they planned to assign me to East Gate again; perhaps my wife would be able to stay at one of the units at Fishing Bridge! Twenty-seven miles away! Insanity. The Chief Ranger was really a pretty nice guy, but he had forgotten a lot of things about newly married couples. What in the world could Pat do that far from me, without a car, alone in that big park? Did he have any idea of how frightened she might be at such an arrangement? At how costly the back and forthing would be for us? It was insane. I would have to give up the summers in Yellowstone.

A few weeks later, as Pat and I were walking across the campus, I ran into Wayne Replogle, a football coach and Yellowstone ranger-naturalist for more than twenty years.

"Hi, Stew! Goin' back to Yellowstone this summer?"

"No, Rep. Can't. I'm getting married and Otto Brown says I'm to be put back at East Gate. Can't do that with my wife."

"Why don't you call Dave Condon to see if he has a place for you? Tell him I told you to call."

Dave Condon was Yellowstone's Chief Naturalist. I did not know, however, that he probably liked Replogle better than any seasonal in his division. But it was worth a try. I went to our office and called Dave. He was pleasant and attentive when I told him Replogle had asked me to call. However, I was two or three minutes into the conversation until something I said caused Condon to stop and say, "Wait just a minute. You've been out here already?"

"Yes sir. I worked one year as a savage at Old Faithful and three years in the protective division, one at Lake and two at East Gate."

"I didn't realize that at first. Well, I had a declination just yesterday. If Otto Brown will release you, we can use you. I'll go talk to Otto."

Pat, who was inferring as much as she could from my conversation with Dave Condon, said softly, "What's happening?"

I was clenching my fists in jubilation. "Honey, unbelievable luck. Condon says he has a place for me in the Naturalist Division. Yoweee!"

"What's so good about that?"

"I get to talk to people. I get to interpret the Park to them. I do not just take their money at the gate and send them on. The best part is that we'll get better quarters. Those rickety old cabins at East Gate—no way we could live in something like that."

"You'll get better quarters, then, in the Naturalist Division?"

"Oh sure. The naturalists live *in* the Park, not along the fringes. A lot of them are stationed at the big places—Old Faithful, Canyon, Mammoth, Fishing Bridge. They have electric lights and running water . . . that is, these areas do."

"Hmm. Have you seen the naturalists' quarters in these places?"

"Well, not exactly. But I know they're better than the things we lived in at East Gate. Nothing can be that bad."

"Okay, if you say so."

"Well, you said you liked the outdoors."

"Yes, I do."

"Honey, this *is* the outdoors, the *great* outdoors. You'll love it." I knew *I'd* love it. How could she help not loving it? How could anyone help not loving it? Lots of ways, and I suspect that Pat knew some of them right then, but she said nothing. I was her intended, and like Ruth, she was prepared to go "whither I went."

That is why I was, at that moment, seeing skyrockets. I was flying. Actually, it was a perfectly easy thing for Dave Condon to do. When he went to see Otto Brown, he would check the reports on my previous work. I was pretty sure they were good.

In a week I received a letter from Brown telling me that I had been released to the Naturalist Division. It was the beginning, for us, of five golden summers.

Part II

12

Quarters

In 1952, when I had first become associated with it, the National Park Service referred to the living units of its summer personnel as "quarters." With good reason. Whereas the homes from which most of us came were solid structures of wood or brick, with carpets on the floors, pictures on the walls, electric lights, modern plumbing, and insulation, the Park Service's "quarters"—particularly those in which I had spent my summers at East Gate—offered nothing but partial shelter from the elements, a bed, a stove, and some rude furniture. The main stations, Old Faithful, Mammoth, Lake, and Canyon, had some accommodations which bordered on the respectable, but many of the Park Service's "quarters" were isolated units. When grouped, they formed little wilderness shanty towns. It took considerable fortitude and a real effort of the imagination to convert "quarters" to "summer homes." But veteran seasonals were people who, through the years, had successfully made that effort.

By 1955 I was beginning to feel like a veteran, and it did not occur to me that I should feel uneasy about bringing my bride of one week to summer "quarters" in Yellowstone Park. After all, I was no longer at East Gate, and I was now a naturalist. You have to understand that in my mind that was one hell of a promotion although the rank and salary were the same: GS-4 at $3175 per year.

At that time Yellowstone had approximately 140 protective division men but only 37 naturalists. The gate men were, in the pecking order, the lowest animals in the herd. Did they patrol the roads bringing desperate speeders in and delivering them to the almighty U.S. Commissioner for sentencing? No. Did they patrol the lakes? No. Did they protect park visitors from dangerous bears, moose, buffalo, and elk? No. Did they go into the Yellowstone Canyon to rescue savages who knew how to get themselves into trouble but not out of it? No. Did they clean up after some of the horrendous wrecks which occurred on Park roads? No. The gate men were ticket takers. In joining the Naturalist Division, however, I had jumped in my mind from a peon's position to one far superior to that of the macho protective rangers who did the police work, most of whom had little ability to interpret the Park to visitors.

At that time Yellowstone was served by what may have been one of the finest corps of seasonal naturalists ever to work in any park. Years later, in my tenth summer in Yellowstone, I was still in the *bottom* third in seniority among the naturalists. How can one forget Bud Lystrup, Sam Beal, Wayne Replogle, Arthur Nash, Lowell Biddulph, Ted Parkinson, Frank Rentchler, Bill Lewis, Clarence Allemon, Joe Murphy and many others who eventually logged fifteen, twenty, twenty-five, and in a few cases, forty summers in Yellowstone! The value of these men was inestimable. They were educated. Almost all had M.A. degrees and six had Ph.D.'s in such fields as Geology, History, Speech, and Zoology. They were articulate. They were refined. They had also spent their time in some of Yellowstone's most primitive quarters, never complaining and doing a job which a few citizens were perceptive enough to see was the best return that Americans ever got on their tax dollars. For example, I remember times when a visitor would say to me, "Say, ranger, I was checking out those terraces at Mammoth today, and they don't look the same as they used to. I remember one spring which I couldn't find but...."

"Just a second. I'll call Clarence Allemon and see what I can find out."

I would call Clarence, ask the question, and he would say, "Oh yeah. Well, that spring shifted its location about eight years ago. If he was here in '49, he would have seen it where he remembers." Clarence would go on to tell us where the spring was currently located.

What about an old road just across the Gibbon River at my station, Madison? Bud Lystrup: "Oh, that road was an old logging road. You see, back in the thirties some crews were permitted to cut wood for the hotels and concessionaires, but that practice was stopped."

Even I got a chance to draw on my knowledge of a recent past. I remember a dark, rather chunky gentleman coming into the museum in 1962, a bemused smile on his face, telling me he had just had an argument with his wife.

"I could of sworn we camped here in '57, but I remember driving in front of the museum, then taking a road alongside the river there up into the camp which was back of this building."

"What does your wife say?"

"She says I can't keep my campgrounds straight, that I just confused this one with another one somewhere, but dadburn, I'd swear this is the same place but it sure don't look the same."

"Well, I hope your wife won't get sore, but you win the argument. Come here, and I'll show you the barely visible remains of what you remember correctly." And I took him out of the building, down to the old Y fork in the road from West Entrance, over to the road leading into the old campground, and back into a portion of the old camp. He was obviously tickled, not just because he would win an argument with his wife, but because he *had* remembered his experience accurately.

That is important to people. They come to an area, have a

quality experience there, and go away with pleasant memories. They want to come back to that experience, and when some physical features are changed, they begin to question whether or not they ever had that experience. A veteran of the area can reassure them.

The last time I visited Old Faithful I sauntered up to the outdoor window of the Visitor Center, quite new, quite handsome, quite stylish, and asked the young seasonal on duty where the amphitheater was.

"The what?"

"The amphitheater behind the museum where they give talks."

"No, no. You're mistaken. We give talks in the auditorium in the building here."

"Well, didn't they used to have a museum and amphitheater?"

"I don't really think so. Perhaps you're thinking of another park." *He's telling me this, I who worked in that museum and gave many good talks in that old amphitheater.*

"Well, where's the campground?" *The one I used to walk through, the one that sow grizzly and her cubs invaded in 1963 and turned into a dangerous carnival.*

"There's no campground at Old Faithful. Sure you're not thinking of Yosemite?"

"No. I've never been to Yosemite. Hmm."

He dutifully hauled out his map and showed me all the places where there *were* campgrounds. Apparently, no one ever told him about the campground that used to be at Old Faithful.

In the 1950s Replogle could have told you anything you wanted to know about Canyon; at Fishing Bridge it was Biddulph; Bud Lystrup, Ted Parkinson, or Sam Beal knew the Old Faithful Area like their hometown neighborhoods.

My point is that, in 1955, I had good reason for feeling that I had been promoted to a much better job. I didn't have to worry about losing my paycheck in four mistakes. I didn't have to walk two miles to Pahaska for food. And, I was joining a veteran and accomplished group of naturalists. The greatest blessing for me, personally, was that, for the first time, I had a companion in Yellowstone. It was a heady feeling.

Our station, Madison Junction, a tranquil intersection on the Grand Loop Road, sixteen miles north of Old Faithful and fourteen miles east of the West Entrance, had no store, no gasoline stations, no motels. It consisted of a campground, a museum, and a government road camp. What it had did not particularly impress Pat. What it lacked caught her attention with all the subtlety of a cold bucket of creek water in the face. Our little cottage in the road camp had two rooms and a path, and not a very well worn path at that because the Park Service had just that winter built the outhouse accompanying the cabin. Previous tenants had had to use facilities in the campground a quarter of a mile away. Contemplate that fact for a moment. Can you imagine the misery of saying to yourself, "I know I have to go to the bathroom. The bathroom is 440 yards away. Will I make it in time?" We at least had the luxury of a nearby privy.

Our little grey cabin was simply furnished. It contained a wood burning stove, a cupboard, a table, some folding chairs, and a bed. The interior was "functionally finished." It consisted of the superstructure of the cabin—one by tens nailed to two by fours—wood floors, and a wornout piece of linoleum. I thought it a pretty respectable accommodation since it was much superior to the cabins I had lived in at East Gate. However, Pat did not recognize our good fortune as readily as I did. She had never lived in anything but houses. And she realized immediately, which I did not, that while I was at the museum a quarter of a mile down the hill, over the Gibbon River Bridge, and a field away, she would be alone. . . in a strange place, among strange people, among real wild animals which roamed freely through the area.

My mistake, you see, was in misinterpreting Pat's remark that she liked the outdoors. She *meant* she liked the city park's tennis courts, swimming pools, picnic areas, etc. Liking the outdoors meant something quite different to me. I had wanted to get

Don and Pat at home, Summer 1955

as free of civilization as I could get in modern America. Yellowstone Park, despite its few commercial areas, offered thousands of acres of woods, meadows, mountains, and streams which were no man's property, were bisected by no fences, and were inhabited by the wild creatures who found their homes there. It was not the 'outdoors' that my wife had bargained for, however. Our good friend, Arlene Jacobi, once said to me, "You had a nerve, bringing a bride of one week to that place!" I certainly did. But it took me many years to appreciate that fact. Besides, what does a twenty-five-year-old *man* know about the needs of women? Some apparently know a lot. I was not one of them.

In my own defense, I should point out that my wife is an unusual woman. She is very pretty; she knows how to dress and conduct herself elegantly when the occasion demands it; but she is, by her own admission, a "guy" in her response to the kinds of things that turn on many women of her generation. She does not particularly like wedding or baby showers, hen parties, or country club night life. Nor is she the hard professional woman of recent times, one determined to prove that she can compete successfully in a man's world, even to the point, metaphorically, of walking with hobnailed boots over the bodies of obstructive chauvinists. My wife is an individual. She comes from no pattern, and I do not think I was altogether wrong in bringing her to Yellowstone. She never developed the affection for the place that I did, but she could adapt to the rigors of life there which was something a good many women in her situation would not have been able to do.

One of them was assimilating the fact that she would be living the summer in that dirty little old cabin. There were puzzling things about it. For example, the interior paint job was uneven. Queer bare spots appeared at regular intervals along certain portions of the wall. And the floor had strange wooden plugs in it. Weeks later, after Mrs. Taggart, the mess hall cook, told us our cottage had once been a public restroom at Mammoth Hot Springs, we were able to decipher these strange unpainted spots. Here had been a sink, there the faucets, here a toilet. Surprisingly missing were the folk art and poetry which one so commonly finds in public restrooms. Perhaps the painters had covered it. The cottage did have air conditioning at night—quarter-inch cracks between the boards comprising the walls. The cracks allowed generous amounts of the cool night air to flow freely through. In late August and early September that air was between thirty and thirty-five degrees.

Setting up housekeeping in our rustic little domicile was a simple process. Since there were no inconveniences like dressers, closets, chests of drawers, and sundry other impediments of civilized living, we lived out of our suitcases and one big foot locker. We did put up a bar for hanging essential things—my uniform, a couple of battered raincoats, and some assorted jackets. We swept the floor, removing an enormous amount of dirt, but unfortunately the floor was not cleanable. So much dust blew in—so much had blown in for several years—that the floor was a perpetual motion dust and dirt producer. In fact, I had the distinct impression that every time I swept up one dustpanful I had loosened two. If I swept up those two, I loosened four. This geometric progression between the amount of dust I loosened and removed posed a problem, but we settled it by accepting a thin even layer of dust on our floor.

The linoleum presented a different challenge. Since we had had no experience with wornout linoleum (we were to have much more in future years), we labored under the illusion that sufficient S.O.S. and elbow grease would wash away the dirt and reveal the original pattern in all its pristine brilliance. Not so. Our linoleum never resembled anything but a washed out working woman over forty who is too tired to try to look pretty anymore.

The rest of our cleaning was routine. We removed a filthy and moth-eaten oilcloth from the table, swept the cobwebs from the ceiling and cupboard, removed the mouse droppings (they were everywhere—the mice must have used this old biffy as a winter patrol cabin), and washed the two windows. The next problem was the mattress. It was dirty and, like the floor, had collected an unremovable amount of dust. Mrs. did not want to sleep on it. She was appalled at the idea of putting her clean sheets on it. So, we took it out and beat it to death. Then, we beat it some more—and still some more. In subsequent years we came equipped with plastic mattress covers. They gave us a more secure feeling about keeping out dust and other people's bedbugs.

Once we had finished the cleaning, brought in our suitcases, and made the bed, we were ready to develop a domestic routine of eating, sleeping, cleaning, and working. In our somewhat primitive environment, however, these processes were much more complicated than they are in civilization. For example, how does one cook without electricity or natural gas? We had two alternatives: firing up the wood stove, which meant getting up at least two hours before I went to work and then putting up with the enormous and suffocating heat the thing put out on warm days, or buying a portable Coleman stove. We chose the latter. My wife later learned to cook on the wood stove—in fact, she baked birthday cookies for me on a canister lid on top of a hot burner—but for the everyday business of cooking meals for two, the Coleman was much more practical. Cooking on the wood stove was a novelty. Special treats—rolls, pies, cakes, or roasts we had only when bad weather and shopping days coincided. For example, if cold rain or light snow started up on the day I was off work, we would drive to West Yellowstone, buy our groceries, among which might be a nice ham, come back to Madison Junction, and pop it into the oven which we had fired up to keep us warm. After awhile the sweet aroma of baked ham mingling with the sharp clean smell of burning pine would permeate our cabin.

Lack of electricity also meant lack of refrigeration (a problem we only partially solved in the next few years by bringing along an ice chest) and with that a lack of any means of preserving meat, fresh milk, ice cream, frozen juices and vegetables —commonplace items on the city dweller's table but delicacies for us. That first summer we ate so much meat and vegetables from cans that we have never been kindly disposed to them since. Pat improvised a method of at least cooling butter, meat, and leftovers. She filled our water bucket with cold tap water and put the perishables in plastic containers which floated in the bucket. In subsequent years, when we had small portable iceboxes, we were able to buy small amounts of fresh meat and refrigerable items. But ice never kept ice cream. That we had only when we went to eating places at the large interior centers (Old Faithful, for example) or were outside the Park on trips. The ice chests were also a nuisance. Half of their available space was taken up by the ice which always melted too soon, frequently dumping our fresh meat into the water. Water-soaked hamburger, I can tell you, is pretty wretched stuff.

Our lack of electricity caused other frustrations. We had to depend upon government issued Coleman lanterns for light. Some of these were excellent. Others gave off heavy and asphyxiating fumes. But we made them do. I read and practiced my violin by them, Pat sewed and knitted by them, and they guided us on our ten o'clock walk to the sub-station behind the cottage each night. Ironing was also a problem. Flat irons were available the first summer, but they were inefficient. Then Viola Nash, wife of the supervisory naturalist at Norris where I worked one day each week, showed us her gasoline-burning iron and recommended it as the best solution to the ironing problem. We did some shopping during the winter of 1955-56 and found one in a

Madison, Wisconsin, antique shop; the dealer even had the pump which accompanied it. We eventually got ours working, and it did a respectable job. But it wasn't ironing with an electric steam iron by any means.

Washing clothes was impossible. Small stuff we could do by hand, but heavier clothing or large batches required machine washing which we took to West Yellowstone. We dried it at home on our outdoor clothes lines, hopeful that some playful bear would not see it until it was ready to bring in. We had more than one experience with a silly bear grabbing my undershirts, letting go, and watching them spring back into the air because of the tension in the clothesline. To the bear, this was similar to the game a cat plays with a string. It would continue to pounce upon its fleeing victim, my undershirt, until the garment looked like a Civil War battle flag that had been on Cemetery Ridge at Gettysburg.

Ultimately, we triumphed over the drawbacks of our situation and developed a routine of life. Since I had to be at work by 7:30, we usually got up at 6:30. At 6:30 the mountain air is cool, cool, cool. Nighttime temperatures, even in July, the warmest month, often hover around freezing. Ventilated as it was, our cabin had the same temperature as that outdoors. When the alarm shattered our repose, we had first to wake up, then gather resolve not only to throw off the heavy weight of blankets, but to dress in cold freshened clothes. I could tolerate it, but Pat hates being cold. That made getting up each day a new effort of pure will for her. I then chopped wood and built a fire in the stove while Pat started breakfast on the Coleman. Next, I heated a pan of water for shaving. Setting my little pan of hot water beneath the mirror on the wall (in our circumstances no one, not even Snow White, would have been fairest of all at 6:45 A.M.), I would lather up and start harvesting the stubble on my face.

For young married couples, the experience of developing a familiar domestic routine is, while the novelty lasts, one of the new pleasures of the first month. My wife would stand behind me, mimicking the various ways I contorted my face to get under

Don, resplendent in faded jacket, 1955

my chin and behind my jawbones. She especially liked to pooch up her lips the way I did to avoid soaping them, but she forgot that she did not have good depth perception looking into a mirror. I knew this and took advantage of it. One morning when "brown eyes" was having a particularly delightful time imitating me, I swiftly popped my shaving brush, dripping with lather, over my left shoulder. Before Pat realized that the brush was coming, she had a big swatch of shaving soap across her pretty face. I thought it was much funnier than she did, but she forgave me before I left for work.

Breakfast consisted of hot cereal, eggs and bacon, or pancakes. The fare was quite respectable, as a matter of fact. We didn't like coffee so we had cocoa which, at first, since we could not keep milk, we made from a powdered mix and water. But watered down cocoa tastes like chocolate flavored water. Before long, however, we discovered powdered milk. As a straight milk substitute it was awful, but added to our watery chocolate preparation, it provided a breakfast drink which was both nutritious and palatable.

After breakfast I went off to work, resplendent in my faded jacket and trousers, glittering badge, and Park Service insignia. Pat stayed in the cottage presuming to busy herself with keeping house. But how does a new bride, bursting with energy to set up housekeeping in her new home, busy herself in a remodeled biffy? We had but two rooms to clean. We had only two windows which required curtains. We couldn't afford rugs and wouldn't have bought them if we could have because of the daily accumulation of dirt on the floors. We had no tables to polish or dust either. But the bed had to be made and the dishes washed. The first job was merely a matter of reshifting the load of blankets; the latter required ingenuity because we had no sink or running water. Because we had to haul, heat, use, and heave our water, we learned to appreciate what modern plumbing must have meant to our grandparents. Much waste water from various pans and buckets found its way out our door after we had washed clothes, dishes, or ourselves. Fortunately, although we often pitched this waste water hurriedly, we never baptised a person coming over to visit us.

As the weeks went by, we grew accustomed to our little cabin; I might even say that we grew fond of it. At least, one can look back now and feel that way. We had realized that there were two ways of regarding our "quarters." A travel agent, for example, would have described it as "a rustic cabin nestled among the pines at the foot of National Park Mountain." Could anything be more desirable to a city man crying for relief from the tension, speed, and impersonality of urban life? However, there was another way to describe it. One of my colleagues, a man who valued urban comforts both in the city *and* in the wilderness, said he would absolutely refuse to live in "that dirty little old biffy." And he did refuse the year the Park Service asked him to. (He held out and got a trailer.) But he had missed a rite of passage in the Yellowstone experience which the veteran seasonals felt made you one of the group.

Actually, cooking on a wood stove, carrying water, and reading by lamplight were things most of our grandmothers and grandfathers did when they were young. Compared to the places in which most of the world's population has lived in the past six thousand years, our little cabin in the mountains was a most respectable accommodation. But so much has the modern American been spoiled by his technology that young people regard stereos, television, microwave ovens, and automatic everything elses as necessities of life.

From this distance in time, I tend to look back on our two summers in the little cottage with considerable nostalgia. After all, I was newly married to a very special person, and I was doing the kind of work I liked best in the place I liked best in the entire United States. What were a few inconveniences to someone so fortunate? Very little, to *me*. I was happy at work, still playing my violin, though not as frequently, for an audience which didn't complain, and learning to fly fish, at last.

My mother and sister, however, wondered if Pat's enthusiasm for the experience was the same as mine. That, of course, is a rhetorical question. Pat put up with the situation with the patience of Griselda . . . except for those rare occasions when she had to let me know that life in Yellowstone, however exhilarating it may have been for me, was something less than that for her. Illustration: I have just come home from my work day at the museum. Today I have given four speeches on the history of Yellowstone Park, supplied approximately 500 tourists with everything from directions to the water fountain and the bathroom to complete three-day sightseeing itineraries of the Park. I am in a holiday mood because in one more day, I will have another two days off. That means half a day in West Yellowstone to do laundry and grocery shopping and a day and a half to go fishing! Already, I am mentally on the Gibbon, the Gallatin, or the Firehole, casting for rainbow or big browns and loving every minute of it. I am feeling very mellow.

"So, how was your day?" There is a slight edge in Pat's voice which I do not at first detect.

"Great! I have served the National Park Service and the people of America in a manner to which they have no right to be accustomed, and now, after the day at Norris tomorrow, I will have two days off which are mine. Mine!"

"Which means?"

"Which means that after we do the errands Wednesday,
I—we are going fishing. I am going to catch a big fat brown trout this time if it kills me."

"Terrific . . . sounds like a wonderful way to spend your days off."

"Yeah, it does. . . what did you say?"

"I said that going fishing on your days off sounds peachy keen. Just my idea of a real good time."

I notice that she is grimly frying some hamburger on our Coleman camp stove. "Your enthusiasm is overpowering. Am I missing something?"

"Not at all. Why wouldn't I look forward to going fishing? The fact that we went fishing the last week, and the week before that, and the week before that makes no difference. Besides, I love sitting on the bank watching you casting, getting tangled up in your line, cursing and swearing at it, and then stewing because you lost a fish. It's really lot's of fun."

"I do all that?"

"No, sometimes you just complain because nothing is feeding or rising and you can't catch anything. Then you just mope."

"Hey, take it easy. I'm tired. Working in that museum all day takes a lot out of you."

"Sitting in this cabin, trying to think of something you haven't done four or five or six times already takes a lot out of you, too, buster."

"You are keen tonight, my lady, very keen."

"Don't do that."

"What?"

"Shakespeare. I'm not in the mood."

"What are you in the mood for?"

"You really want to know? Really?"

"Yes. Really."

"I'd like a day off where people do normal summer things."

"Such as?"

"Go to the city park and play tennis or ball or swim. I want to see people having family picnics on park benches while their dogs and little kids chase each other through the trees and picnic tables. Then I'd like to walk down a city street and look in some shop windows, not to buy anything, just to look, secure in the knowledge that some damn bear is not going to pop around the corner of a building. I'd like to get a hamburger and a milkshake from a drive-in, along with a glass of iced tea. I'd even like to eat something someone else had cooked for a change, especially someone who didn't have to juggle pans on a two-burner Coleman stove. . . . And don't give me that 'you-have-wounded-the-heart-that-loved-you' look. I guess it's time you found out that I wasn't the sweet little thing you thought I was when you married me."

Until then, things have been going downhill rapidly, but that last crack breaks me up. Pat is ingenuous, even in her anger. Now I'm laughing, and she doesn't know what to do.

"So, what's so funny?"

"You are funny, you French pepper pot. You're bubbling away like the Punch Bowl Spring in the Black Sand Basin. How long has this been building up?"

"Don't ask."

"Okay. But I do see your point. I should have seen it sooner. So, let's go to Bozeman tomorrow. How's that?"

"No. I don't want to."

"But you just said you did! Idaho Falls, maybe?"

"No, no, no, no, *no!* Oh, you men are so dumb! Don't you see? I *did* want to go to Bozeman, but now I've acted like a bitch and practically extorted *my* holiday, and I don't want to go because *you* didn't think of it first. I just don't understand . . . your father is so considerate of your mother. How can you be his son?"

"Dad never made carbon copies. Tell you what. Let's go to Bozeman, and I'll sulk all the way. Then I can feel put upon the same way. . . no, no! Don't throw the skillet!"

In mock anger she messes up my hair and gives me a gentle kick in the rear, but then I grab her for some delayed kiss and make up. We will go to Bozeman Wednesday, and she will enjoy

The trailer, 1957

the day back in civilization. But I will gradually forget how much such occasions mean to her until a birthday in another summer reminds me once again that the Yellowstone experience has anxieties and frustrations for her that never occur to me.

In 1957 we were promoted to better accommodations—in some respects. Although I became the senior seasonal at Madison, another man with a large family was appointed to the cottage behind the museum, the area's most desirable "quarters." For consolation, we were given a small trailer complete with butane stove, oil heater, and plumbing! Frankly, I preferred the wood stove to that oil heater, but one couldn't knock an indoor bathroom. Ours did have a drawback. It was approximately three feet square. As I think of it now, I believe that some NFL linemen simply could not have got into that room. At first I didn't mind; Pat did. However, now I trace my desire for bathrooms the size of living rooms to that cubby hole.

The trailer was very compact. It had lots of cabinets, closets, and other nooks and crannies for storing things. The trouble was that the living room was also the dining room and the kitchen. When we had friends over, we warned them to take the positions they found most comfortable when they entered. Two people were a crowd. Six were a sardine can. I suppose that is the reason we took so many trips around the area that year. One can bear a seven foot ceiling and an eight by six living room so long.

Happily, life in Yellowstone was such that one did not need canned recreation. For example, the bears were always coming through the road camp looking for food. More than once we heard them rear up and slap their paws against the side of our trailer. If frustrated, they would pass by and jerk an undershirt off the clothesline. One bear paid the price for that nonsense. I ran him up a tree and pelted him with rocks, he bellowing all the while that the whole thing was just a big mistake; he was only having fun.

Another road bear who wandered into our area was not so lucky. He was incredibly scrawny, the victim of the poor nutrition in the trash people fed him along the road. He was very disease ridden, too. At any rate, he wandered through our area one day when the Fish and Wildlife boys who had a trailer there had been particularly careless with their garbage. They had been instructed to wrap it up and give it to the camp caretakers each day. They didn't always do this, and the scrawny little bear passing their trailer smelled fish entrails which he couldn't resist. Pat, who watched the whole show, said he worked his way under the trailer gradually, nonplussed at first by a wheel off the ground which spun around and around everytime he put his paw on it and tried to use it for leverage. Eventually, however, he worked around the troublesome wheel and began peeling siding off the trailer. It was an awesome sight, the speed with which the bear was ripping that trailer apart. The West District Ranger was called and he came over, finding what he did not want to find: a spoiled and now dangerous bear which could not be controlled by any conventional means. The bear was driven away from the trailer into the woods and shot. The risks in not doing that were too great, particularly if the bear wandered back to the main road and was tantalized by some tourist who would not have known that it was at flash point. The Fish and Wildlife boys returned to find the consequences of their carelessness. They now had an extremely well ventilated trailer.

Smaller wildlife were not so dangerous. Chipmunks played all around us, and we fed them. The pine squirrels wanted their cut, too. Another small mammal, however, gave us our biggest thrill in the trailer. Early in the summer a field mouse had crawled under the conical top of the trailer's smoke stack and fallen down the pipe. Naturally, it started scrambling around inside the stove which was cold because we did not keep it going at night. (We were neurotic about possible asphyxiation.) The mouse scrambled futilely up the chimney pipe and up the sides of the burner. I'm very squeamish about picking up mice, and my wife didn't like the idea either, so the next morning we asked our neighbor, Larry Wanlass, if he would come to the rescue. He did, with heavy work gloves so the mouse couldn't bite him. After the mouse we got very nervous about animals falling down our stove pipe. With good reason.

Near the end of the summer we were awakened one night by a wild scurrying on the roof of our trailer. "Good God," said Pat, "that foolish squirrel is playing around up there. What if—?" Well, any fool knows what if. Once you've had a mouse in your oil heater, you expect everything else up there to come down it, too. Sure enough, the silly squirrel came down the pipe. Now we were in a fix! How could we get *that* beastie out without getting all bit up? By this time there was quite a thumping around inside the oil heater. Pat was afraid it would climb out the inside opening into our trailer, so she got up, peeked inside with the flashlight, started at the beady eyes staring back at her, and then placed a number of very heavy books over the hinged opening to the chamber of the burner. The squirrel battled those books some, but he finally gave up. Then he tried the pipe to the outside. But that was too ridiculous. Or was it? In less than a minute our visitor had gone up the pipe and was free on the roof again. He thumped across it then leaped off the trailer at the corner where a large coil of electric wires hung. They made a terrible racket against the metal side of the trailer, but we gave a long sigh of relief and went back to bed.

Now we thought the squirrel had a grain of sense. He didn't. The next night he was back on the roof thumping around country barn dance style. And, sure enough, back down the pipe he came. This was becoming absurd. More familiar the second time, our intruder spent less time in the burner. Then up the pipe he went again, across the roof and off, rattling those electric wires.

The next day our naivete was exposed when we told Roy Armstrong, a former permanent employee, about our troublesome night visitor. He laughed considerably about our calling it a "squirrel."

"Don't you know squirrels aren't nocturnal? When's the last time you saw a squirrel at night?"

That stopped us. We *hadn't* seen any squirrels at night. But what, then, did we have? Roy told us. "The only animal can shinny up a pipe like that is a pine marten. He just hunches his back and snakes right up it."

I was so intrigued by the idea that I got a ladder, climbed to the roof of the trailer, and looked at the inside of the pipe. On opposite sides of it were long wide breaks in the solid carbon deposits. If Roy was right, and he surely was, we had in our neighborhood the dirtiest pine marten in Yellowstone Park. The realization that a marten, not a squirrel, had invaded us that first night set us speculating about the excitement it could have caused us if it had gotten out of the oil burner into the trailer. A marten is a large weasel. It is also a fearless little creature, one of the toughest fighters and most relentless hunters of the mountain forests. When cornered, it does not hesitate to fight with every ounce in its fierce little body. We had a special problem, then. How could we keep that persistent marten out of our quarters? I hit upon a perfect plan. We had a used gallon oil can which just fit over the stove pipe on our roof. That night, when the oil burner was cold, I went out and placed the oil can over the outlet. Later our marten was back—and stymied. He thumped around up there for quite awhile then left. We felt pretty smug.

The next night he came again, thumped again, and—yes—came back down the pipe into the burner. Minutes later he shinnied up and took off. I was beside myself. "How in hell," I said to Pat, "do you suppose that animal got the oil can off the smoke stack? It was a pretty tight fit. I'm glad we're going home tomorrow. A few more nights of that creature would bug me for good."

The next morning I couldn't get the burner started. I put match after match in it. Finally, after a long struggle, I got it going fitfully. Then the tar around the pipe where it went through the roof started melting. I couldn't believe what I thought. When I went out, there was the oil can in place *over* the smokestack! That crazy marten had gone under the can, down the pipe, up the pipe, and under the can and hadn't tipped it over!

The following year the Park Service showered upon us its benevolence and blessing. We got the cottage. Now the cottage was also a winter patrol cabin with a stockade full of wood near it. There was, also, a handy chopping block, so we never lacked for kindling. It had a kitchen, living room, bedroom and a bathroom with a *tub!* When a cold rainy day came, we fired up the wood stove which had a water jacket which circulated and heated water in our hot water tank. For the first time in our Yellowstone experience, we could have hot baths in our quarters. The cottage had other advantages. It had wall board which insulated it. It had, in addition to the cook stove in the kitchen, a pot-bellied wood stove in the main room. There is nothing so comfortable as heating up a wood stove, then popping a big log in to smolder all night. We slept in divine comfort that summer.

The cottage had two carryovers from our previous quarters —mice and a pine marten. The mice were all over at first. We trapped them but were making little progress until the marten moved in upstairs. One night we heard a wild chase above us— the skittering feet of a mouse and the swift and purposeful jumps of the marten. Then a loud *eeeeeeeeeeeee.* After that, quiet. I think every mouse in our cottage packed its bags right then. We saw none the rest of the summer.

Aside from its obvious physical advantages—more room, better insulation, plumbing, etc.—the cottage had certain intangible advantages that made it one of the most pleasant places in which my wife and I have ever lived. It was only fifty yards from the museum where I worked. After three summers of living in the comparative isolation of the road camp, Pat now had the precious advantage of company in the campground and proximity to me in the museum. I do not mean to suggest that my wife was a meddler. Even at such close range, she never thought of intruding while I was on duty and responsible to the public. She simply enjoyed the satisfaction of seeing her husband working close to home. For Pat it was an intuitively comfortable thing. For me, too. I enjoyed looking out from time to time and seeing her relaxing in the sun.

We had frequent visitors to our cottage, both two and four-legged. Since it was so directly visible behind the museum, and the public restroom was partially out of sight and farther to the right as one went out the back door, people in need took one look at our cottage and made an obvious assumption. Despite directional signs PUBLIC RESTROOM →, I would see people stride boldly out the back doors of the museum toward the cottage. The closer they got, however, the more they began to falter. Either they would see the sign Pat had put up on the cottage THIS IS NOT A PUBLIC RESTROOM or they would begin to notice the absence of necessary signs on the doors or they would see our kitchen curtains. Few had ever encountered curtained restrooms, so that would give them a start. As their uncertainty melted into a sense of reality that, indeed, the cottage was not the restroom, they would stop and look about in the most pitiful way. Many would at last see the restroom to the right of the museum. Others, whom desperation had made bold, would knock and ask for directions. A third type of individual, however, would never break stride. He would come boldly up the path, see the obvious indications that the cottage was the wrong building, and, too proud to ask for directions, go right on past it up into the campground. These people usually ended up at the central campground restroom, angry that it was so far from the museum and confused because directions to it were so poorly marked.

Our most memorable restroom rover was a chubby slightly cross-eyed lady from New Jersey. She came in a large bus party which we first saw as it milled about behind the museum. We were sitting outside the cottage with some friends and telling them about our cottage's double identity when this lady began marching boldly up the path toward us. We watched expectantly. Some fifteen feet from the cottage she saw Pat's sign, stopped, smiled, and spoke.

"Lotta people think this is the restroom, huh?"

"Yes."

"Well, there *is* one around here somewhere, ain't there?"

"Yes, it's behind you—that way (all of us pointing the direction of the right building)."

"Oh yeah, I see it. Hey!" Here she began gesticulating wildly and trying to whistle between her lips. The whistle was coming in fits and starts, however; she sounded like a high school trumpet player warming up. There followed more aborted whistles and a frantic waving and pointing in the direction of the restroom.

"That's my signal to my friend, see. There she is. She waits for me to go in and find it and then I signal her how to get there. I keep tellin' her that where I come from in Jersey, you gotta speak up about them things. Hey! Pffft! Over there! Pffft!" Eventually, the friend got the message—virtually everyone else in the bus party had by this time—and trundled off in the right direction. Our visitor thanked us and departed. Our friends, who had restrained themselves miraculously up to then, exploded with laughter.

Our four-legged company gave us moments of pleasure, too. We fed the chipmunks peanuts, so several of the little scamps were all over us when we sat outside. I still remember the half ticklish, half creepy feeling of a chipmunk crawling over my feet under the chair. One brazen little chip used to run up my chopping block, right to the top of the block of wood I was cutting, demanding something to eat. It would stand up on its back feet

One brazen little chip

straining at me for a peanut. More than once I found myself, ax poised in the air, about to slice that little chipmunk in two. It never seemed aware of the danger of being accidentally split with the wood. We fed the ground squirrels, too. One used to chase the chipmunks off, but he became wary after he crawled into a bag of peanuts one afternoon then stood up, the bag over him. That little squirrel turned into a whirling dervish as he fought his way out of the bag which had trapped him.

In our driveway back of the cottage we had the baseball diamond. I should say, the wiffle ball diamond. Pat and I played a lot, using the house as a backstop. I soon developed a wide fat curve, a breaking pitch that came in on the hands, a rising fast ball, and a sinker. Pat had most trouble with the rising fast ball, but she could murder that big curve that broke down and away. I could see her change the arc of her swing to match the break in the ball. Time after time I'd throw it, just because I liked to look at it, and she'd butcher it. I never could break the habit; it was such a pretty pitch, and no one else could hit it consistently, but she lived on it.

My best moments as a wiffle ball pitcher (if one can't be a big leaguer, wiffle ball is the next best thing; it's so much fun to make a ball do what those big league pitchers do with baseballs) came the summer John and Faye Scandrett, friends from Madison, Wisconsin, visited us. John is a good athlete: good at tennis, ping-pong, football—how many sports? I don't know. Anyway, John was a challenge, my own Mickey Mantle. He could hit the curve, the fast ball, and the change, but I had one pitch that really baffled him. The particular ball I was using at that time, when held with the air holes down and spun off my index and middle fingers, would float in like a nothing pitch then suddenly dip about three or four inches right when it got to home plate. We were playing two outs per person, and I struck John out on six straight pitches throwing that thing. I didn't even throw it fast, probably about half- to three-quarter speed. He couldn't figure out what the hell was happening. He'd watch the ball come in, very carefully, and then swing, not even trying to kill it, just meeting it. From his angle of vision, however, he couldn't see that little dip it took just as he brought the bat to the ball. Best pitch I ever developed. It was fun to throw, on those cool evenings in the Park when we had eaten supper, done the dishes, and gone outside just to pass the time of day and have some fun. I wish those moments could have lasted forever.

I suppose there are many who will pity us, certainly my wife, for the primitive living to which we were subjected during the summers from 1955–60, but they should not do that. Primitive living reveals what you don't need—what you can invent for yourself. For example, the modern urban dweller has, for recreation, television (in living and sometimes livid color on more channels than he can possible watch), movies, sports extravaganzas, travel, bars with a tremendous variety of exotic entertainment, skiing, tennis, team sports, and so on. We had reading, knitting, playing games like cribbage, Monopoly, checkers and chess, wiffle ball, observing wild life, and talking. And I continued to practice my violin, but it no longer filled the emotional need it had in the previous years when I was alone. Our recreations, while less varied and colorful than those of the modern hooked on electronic games, were inexpensive, creative, healthful, and deeply satisfying. If there is anything young married couples need to do, it is get better acquainted. Pat and I talked and talked and talked. Those years were crucial to us in later ones when we were under the stresses of making money, raising children, and advancing in the job. And we were *safe*. We did not, of course, go out into the dark without a flashlight or feeling a bit queasy because bears did roam around at night, as did the elk in our area. and smaller game. But wild animals are dangerous only when surprised. I would trust myself among them far more than among the nocturnal animals of the urban jungle.

No, on balance, it was a simple life, but it was a happy one, full of daily surprises and interesting things, and comfortable for the companionship we shared. Pat and I feel only pity for those who have never experienced the richness of such an existence.

13

The Building, The Men, The Work

AMERICA IS FULL of ugly buildings. One has only to think of the great undistinguished masses of cement and brick that clutter the centers of our great cities or the rows of box-like houses in their suburbs to realize how little value we have placed on the expression of beauty through building. But there are exceptions, for example Madison Museum in Yellowstone Park. Built to commemorate one of the most important events in the history of American conservation, it also became a small monument to the intelligence and taste of a fine architect.

The event. Although some information about the Yellowstone plateau had trickled out from 1807 until 1870, the general public was not well informed about it. Then, in August and September of 1870, a group of Montanans, led by their Attorney General, Henry Washburn, explored the territory at the headwaters of the Yellowstone and Madison Rivers. Reading Nathaniel Pitt Langford's account of the expedition, one gets the feeling that they were curious but generally skeptical about the many strange and apparently fantastic rumors which had circulated about the upper Yellowstone country. However, by the time they had seen Tower Falls (they missed the terraces at Mammoth), the Yellowstone Canyon, Yellowstone Lake, and the magnificent geyser basins along the Firehole River, their skepticism had changed to absolute astonishment. "These wonders are so different from anything we have ever seen—they are so various, so extensive—that the feeling in my mind from the moment they began to appear until we left them has been one of intense surprise and of incredulity."[1]

On the nineteenth of September, as they sat around their campfire at the confluence of the two rivers which formed the Madison, they debated the future of the region. All were aware of its enormous commercial possibilities so they speculated at first on how they should divide the area fairly. Happily for us, Cornelius Hedges, a Helena lawyer, turned the discussion completely around by suggesting that the entire area not be exploited for private gain, that it be set aside and administered, either by the territory of Montana or the federal government, as a public park or pleasuring ground for the benefit and enjoyment of the people.

As one reflects upon the rampant materialism of the time, Hedges' suggestion, although it was not completely original with him, has to rank as one of the most unselfish acts in American history. And, fortunately, it came at time and a place when those material interests most in support of the park idea, the railroads, were checked at what became the Park's north and west entrances. A further advantage in the situation was that Congress did not really know much about the place, and, since no appro-

---

[1]Nathaniel Pitt Langford, *The Discovery of Yellowstone Park: Journal of the Washburn Expedition to the Yellowstone and Firehole Rivers in the Year 1870* (Lincoln: University of Nebraska Press, 1972), p. 118.

priations were requested to manage it, it could be created without controversy. Thus, idealism and luck joined hands to produce an American treasure.

Through the efforts of the Washburn group and the Hayden Geological Survey which followed them in 1871, a bill creating Yellowstone Park was passed by Congress in 1871 and signed by President Grant in March, 1872. Thus Yellowstone became the first of America's national parks, and Madison Junction became a national shrine.[2]

The building. Madison Museum was built in 1928 with funds donated by the Laura Spelman Rockefeller Foundation. The architect, Herb Maier, built it with great chunks of native rhyolite and sections of lodgepole pines which dominate the Yellowstone forests. When completed, this green-roofed building of rock and wood blended perfectly into the lodgepole forest growing on a gentle slope overlooking the site of the historic campsite of 1870.

Madison Museum as I knew it consisted of two rooms. One was square with an uneven floor made from huge pieces of rhyolite mortared together. The second room, at one time the naturalist's quarters, was rectangular with a wood floor. The superstructure of the main room consisted of large lodgepole pines set in A-frames. All of the visible supporting timbers were varnished, but they had lost none of their ruggedness; the knots on them and great knarled bumps produced by mistletoe were retained.

---

[2]Californians always argue this point, saying that Yosemite was the first national park. Not so. In 1864 Congress passed a bill, signed by Lincoln, in which the Yosemite Valley and the Mariposa Tree Grove were granted to the state of California as a public park. In 1890, under pressure from John Muir, Robert Underwood Johnson of *Century Magazine* and others, Congress set aside, as a national park, forested and mountainous lands surrounding the Yosemite Valley. The anomaly of a national park enclosing a state park, and the administrative problems which such a situation engendered were resolved in 1906 when Congress accepted the recession of the state grant by the California legislature and formally created Yosemite *National* Park.

The interior was taken up by display cases showing pictures of early trappers and explorers, copies of important documents, Indian relics, a saddle used by Langford on the 1870 expedition, maps, some old guns—the famous Henry repeating rifle, a Colt, and some muzzle loading pistols—and a bicycle ridden through the Park in 1888 by Billy Owen. Gun fanciers were, of course, attracted to the pistols and rifles—we had several offers for them —and children from farms or ranches were fascinated by Mr. Langford's antique saddle. The bicycle, one of those with the enormous front wheel and tiny back one, was our conversation piece. "What kind of bike is *this*?" "How do you get on it?" (Most children tried.) "I'll bet he walked it more than he rode it." Considering the condition of Yellowstone roads at the time Owen took his trip, I think this was probably true. The museum's finest assets, however, were two windows, one of them transparent, the other translucent.

On the west side of the stone-floored room was a very large picture window which gave one a full view of the Madison Valley and the site of the historic campsite of 1870. That window was also a window to the world because every summer Yellowstone is visited by people from virtually every state in the union and from many foreign countries. Day after day, summer after summer, black, yellow, and white citizens of every nation moved leisurely up the asphalt path from the old parking lot (it has since been obliterated), stopped briefly by the large boulder with the plaque commemorating Stephen Mather, first Director of the National Park Service, then proceeded up the steps into the building. They came because Yellowstone's fame is, has been for some time, international. Just how famous this great park is and has been was brought home to me, forcefully, while I was preparing to teach Joseph Conrad's *Nostromo*, a novel about a fictional South American republic, racked by revolution, corruption, and greed. A character in the book, a Frenchman, Martin Decoud, is drawn into the affairs of the country reluctantly; had it not been for a woman he loved, he would have left. "His plan had been to return (to France) by way of the United States through

California, visit the Yellowstone Park, see Chicago, etc." If you do not find it intriguing that a Pole who became a great writer in English but who never visited the United States, should create a fictional Frenchman involved in an imaginary South American republic but who thinks of visiting Yellowstone Park, and this is a book published in 1904, then you and I have different perceptions of "intriguery." Yellowstone had been a park only 32 years when those lines were written, but such was its fame already, that people in far away places were anxious to see it. And they came to see it then and have been coming ever since.

Also visible through the large picture-window were some of the year-around residents of the museum. A tribe of playful squirrels lived in the attic of the wood-floored wing. Early in the summer the new babies would scuffle around as they grew and became more and more exploratory. Sooner or later, the boldest would come out of a hole just above and to the right of the picture window, frightened yet exhilarated by the sudden expansion of their world. Then they would discover the window. They peered in at us as if we were fish in a bowl, strange unsquirrely creatures trapped in a pen which did not allow us the freedom they enjoyed. Later, they would scamper over the rocks in front of the window learning the dexterity necessary for a pine squirrel's survival in a hostile environment.

Eventually, when the parent decided the youngsters should begin to shift for themselves, she became as aggressive in sending them off as she had been protective earlier. One little fellow I particularly remember was reluctant to go out and fend for himself. He kept returning and his mama kept chasing him out. I was nearly run down one day as the old squirrel chased her recalcitrant offspring pell-mell around the glass display cases of the museum. Chipmunks also scampered over the rock foundation outside the picture window. They did not mix with the squirrels, but there did not seem to be too great hostility between the two. Both were busily engaged in the necessary and endless process of gathering food against the long cold winter which comes early in the mountains.

Madison Museum, 1955 (Don left, Jan Rencher right)

Squirrels and chipmunks both disappeared when our periodic weasel returned to his lair beneath one of the museum's large foundation stones. He hunted young ground squirrels, mice, chipmunks, and presumably the young pine squirrels. He was an absolutely fearless little animal. More than once I stared at him through the picture window, and he stared back unflinchingly. He never caused me any trouble, and I returned the favor, but I am sure he would never have tolerated my interfering with his obtaining a choice dinner.

There was comedy and excitement to be seen through this great window, too. Until 1961 the road ran in front of the museum. It came from the West Entrance and split right at the junction where directional signs pointed the proper ways only to Norris or Old Faithful. A traffic tangle always occurred there because many people had not taken time to study their park maps and were indecisive about how to get where they were going. Approaching the junction sign, they would wander back and forth, anxiously looking for road numbers or trying to figure out which way to go to get to Canyon or Fishing Bridge. Often, cars behind, driven by people familiar with the Park, would honk continuously, adding to the confusion and erratic driving of the already baffled drivers ahead of them.

When one of the buffalo appeared, or when the elk herd wandered into the meadow, however, people forgot all rules for driving. They would wander into wrong lanes, stop their cars in the middle of the road, or jam the parking lot exits, and rush forth to obtain prize pictures. None were so brash as one tall red-headed fellow who wheeled his open sports car into a vacant place in the parking lot near where a buffalo was grazing. With the grace of a gazelle (he certainly had no more intelligence than one), he leaped from his car, vaulted over the wooden railing on both sides of the road, and strode boldly into the meadow to take the bison's picture. I began to get very nervous when I noticed this idiot proceeding far past the line where most of the tourists had gathered to watch the animal. The man walked to within twenty feet of the buffalo and took a beautiful side shot. While doing this, he paid no attention to the fact that the buffalo was changing *his* position from sideways to head-on. As the visitor lined up another spectacular picture, however, he finally became aware that the buffalo, hitherto undisturbed by the large numbers of people watching him, had found one to single out for special attention. On the porch of the museum now, I called out to tell this man to get the hell out of that meadow. He did not hear me, and seconds later the buffalo charged. There was a horrified sucking in of air from the crowd. Fortunately, the man had presence of mind enough to run in a weaving pattern, and the buffalo did not pursue him too far. The old bull, satisfied he had driven off a troublesome mosquito, went back to his grazing. His tormentor sauntered through the meadow, crossed the road, faking a silly smile of indifference for all to observe, and returned to his car. It was twenty-five minutes, however, before he got in and drove off. The onlookers were the real beneficiaries, though. They had found out that those broadsides which said "Wild Animals Are Dangerous; Stay in Your Car and Observe Them from a Safe Distance" were really telling the truth.

The most beautiful sight I ever saw through that window,

aside from countless blue mornings, blazing red orange sunsets, and the majesty and imperturbable grandeur of the Madison Valley, were five bull elk in the Madison River at once. The herd, which circled through that area, had come out of the timber near the road, crossed it, and was moving to the meadows along the river. Because this was not mating season, the females and males travelled separately. These five bulls were all mature with well developed sets of antlers. They are all in the river yet, put there forever by a color slide Pat took as they enjoyed the cool and tranquil waters of the stream.

The museum's other beautiful window, on the south wall, was not so large as the picture window, but it was the premiere attraction of our building. In 1930 Jack Haynes, the park photographer, took several shots of men dressed in the costumes of 1870 as they gathered around a campfire near the confluence of the Gibbon and Firehole Rivers. In the background were their horses, tents, and the lodgepole pines. After studying several black and white negatives, Mr. Haynes selected the one he thought best and then enlarged it into a black and white positive on a plate of glass coated with a photographic emulsion. After the black and white positive was developed on the large plate of glass, Mr. Haynes and his people tinted it, supplying the appropriate blues, yellows, pinks, and other colors needed. Finally, he put a translucent pane on the emulsified side of the plate of glass to protect it. The finished picture was then framed and set in place in Madison Museum. The picture confused many people. They would stand before it exclaiming how beautiful a painting it was—the brush strokes were visible in places—but remarking how lifelike the figures seemed! They were quite right, of course, but few knew that such a thing as a combination photograph and painting even existed.

In the early morning the blues and greens of this extraordinary picture were dark and predominant. Toward noon, when the sun's most brilliant light shone upon it, intensifying the lighter hues and muting the darker ones, the whole scene came alive; the river seemed to flow, the men to talk, the pines to wave

Five bull elk in the Madison River

gently in the breeze. Late in the day, when the blues and greens again predominated, all was quiet. On partly cloudy days it would range from full brilliance to a muted splendor.

Jack Haynes' picture was an impressive memorial to the birth of the national park idea. No person who ever came to Madison Museum failed to notice it. It was the first thing he saw as he stepped into the museum, and it was the last thing to catch his attention as he left. And when we had told each park visitor the event it commemorated, he left with a sense of having been at a place significant in the history of his country. He had. Had Yellowstone not been set aside when it was, and had the Yellowstone experiment failed—and there were almost two decades when it hung perilously in the balance, protected almost single-handedly in Congress by Senator Graham Vest of Nebraska—the vast system of national parks which originated in the United States, and are one of its enduring claims to fame in a deteriorating and exploited world, might never have come into being. And millions of people would have been ever so much poorer for this loss.

Madison Museum was built to capture the past. The pictures of early explorers, their maps, their weapons and gear, Billy Owen's bicycle, Langford's saddle, the Indian relics, and the long row of placards along the upper molding around the rooms all fixed dates and people who were important in Yellowstone's history. But it was a recent past, one anchored as much in the early twentieth as in the nineteenth century. And on one occasion that recent past came vividly to life for me.

It was the summer of 1956. I sat in the museum reading Robert Shankland's *Steve Mather of the National Parks,* an account of the National Park Service's struggle for birth and of two men in particular, Mather and Horace Albright, who made it successful. Mather provided the drive and inspiration to get the organization going. Albright had the more thankless task of helping with the endless bureaucratic red tape of getting dreams translated into presentable legislation and legislation into law. But they succeeded by 1917. Two years later, after the Park Service was securely established and functioning, Albright left Washington to become Superintendent of Yellowstone.

I did not need Shankland's testimony to tell me that Mr. Albright had been one of Yellowstone's great superintendents. I had already been told that by Ted Ogsden, who served under Albright during the 1920s. I also had the supporting testimony of Bud Lystrup of Eau Claire, Wisconsin, whose remarkable career as a seasonal ranger-naturalist extended over four decades.

I felt personally acquainted with Mr. Albright because daily he had supervised my morning clean-up routine. He peered down at me out of a portrait which appeared on one of the museum placards representing significant dates in Yellowstone history —Horace Albright, Superintendent of Yellowstone Park, 1919-1929; Director, N.P.S., 1929-33. The most arresting features of that kindly intelligent face were its sensitive but firm mouth and bright probing eyes. It was the face of a man whose personal integrity and quiet strength of character lay deep as bedrock.

That afternoon, as I read on through Shankland's book, I was interrupted by an older gentleman and his wife who were perusing the museum exhibits casually. Nodding toward the placard containing the picture of Horace Albright, he said, "I've weathered a little since then, haven't I?" I nearly fell out of my chair and dropped my book. So totally unprepared was I for this sudden materialization of Horace Albright that I would have been only slightly more surprised had Abraham Lincoln appeared, studied our exhibits, and come up to say that he approved of the national park experiment. Once over the initial shock, I began asking questions so rapidly that Mr. Albright must have thought he would be stuck there for the rest of the week. I spent nearly forty-five minutes talking to the Albrights about their experiences in Yellowstone, about Ted Ogsden, and about Mr. Mather. For me Mr. Albright was living proof that the really big people in any profession always have time for the little people. After a few years I am sure that he forgot that afternoon and the young seasonal with whom he talked. But the memory lives on in me, a bright glow in a quiet summer afternoon years ago.

I remember Madison Museum also for the people with whom I worked. Most were intelligent, friendly, and dependable rangers. But four stand out because they were "unique." When I first went to Madison Junction, the senior seasonal was Jay Rencher, a rugged Idaho farm boy who had gone east and wrested a Ph.D. in soil chemistry from Rutgers despite the fact that he could not spell the commonest English words. (This I first discovered from an entry in our station log: "Repaired flag pole roap today." There were others to follow.) But Jay knew his geology and soil chemistry well, and he was a gifted rhetorician. He was also the most informally dressed seasonal ranger in Yellowstone Park. Although rangers did wear levis for back country duty or special work details, the men in the museums in those days were supposed to be fully uniformed and to apply a little spit and polish. There were regulations about shirts, ties, trousers, blouses, hats, shoes, etc. Most of the naturalists observed them, but Jay carried on his own silent campaign of passive resistance.

Picture a busload of passengers, all of them well dressed, ascending the steps of Madison Museum to hear a talk by the ranger. Jay appears, his shirt dirty, the neck open (I could count on one hand the number of times I saw him wearing a tie), his trousers baggy from lack of pressing. Naturally, he does not wear his Stetson. But Jay is an impressive man. He is perhaps six feet three or four inches tall, and he carries approximately 180 very solid and muscled pounds over a large but well proportioned frame. His skin is weathered but fair; his hair is jet black. The eyes capture his audience; they are dark and intense. Before he has talked for five minutes, the group is spellbound and will be until he breaks off at the climax of the story with a "thank you" which is their cue to applaud—which they do enthusiastically. Some who knew Jay felt his rhetoric was flashy and superficial. That may have been, but the fact remains; the people listened and they got his message.

Those who know me professionally will wonder whether or not I am coming down on the side of a modern Sophist. Not really. In the first place, Jay had done his homework on the history of Yellowstone Park a lot better than many people realized. He had accurate information, not as much as a scholar like Sam Beal, to be sure, but one could hardly expect that. Jay knew the story of the birth of the Yellowstone idea. Plato would not have disapproved. He was not using his rhetorical gifts in a bad cause. He was using them to celebrate unselfishness, the wisdom and far sightedness of those Montanans who decided that the wonders of the Yellowstone region were too great to be the property of a few selfish individuals, that they belonged, instead, to the American people and their guests from all over the world. That is an idea worth celebrating again and again, and Jay told the story in a powerful and convincing manner. Scholarship alone is not enough for such a subject. There must be enthusiasm and a sense of caring, a sense that the story one is telling is so important that it needs to be shared with all who will listen. And the people did listen, carefully, to Jay.

The only two aspects of his job Jay really liked were those museum talks and the campfire programs in the evenings. Here was another opportunity for him to be eloquent. It was also his opportunity to play the accomplished woodsman for his admiring audience. Jay never used the cut wood in the stockade back of the museum. He would come to his campfire carrying a huge armful of lodgepole pine sections six inches thick and five feet long. He stood these on the ground and flailed away at them with devastating strokes from his two-edged ax. In five minutes he could split all the wood. Then he would build those long fresh-cut sections into a large tepee upon which he poured white gasoline. He lit it and in a moment had a small forest fire going. (My campfires were to Jay's as the fire of a match is to a burning tree.) Jay keyed his effects to the progress of his fire. When it was fresh and new, he would radiate enthusiasm and welcome for those in attendance and those just arriving. Coming to his campfire must have seemed to many people like walking into a good friend's parlor at Christmas time. Here was the host, greeting guests as he stood before the roaring fire in his fireplace. As the fire gradually subsided, Jay would get on with the main business of the evening, the talk, and he would be weaving his spell as the coals of his fire were dying some forty-five minutes later. In his way, Jay understood show business. He knew the effects he wanted to get, and he knew how to get them.

Actually, the job of rangering interfered with Jay's first love—trout fishing. When he was not needed in the museum, he was tying flies, building leaders, inspecting his equipment, and mentally planning his next fishing outing. I believe he went fishing every day of the summer—twice on some. Part of the intensity with which he pursued the great browns of the Madison River may have been motivated by his need to feed a wife and five children. But just as much motivation came from his love of fresh air, exercise, and the hunt.

The two summers I worked with him, Jay did not change materially. He divided his time between museum duty, campfire programs, and trout fishing. He was never moody, never contentious. He was an easy man to work near.

Jay would never have understood Dick Townsend, a solidly built balding man with a shiny pink face, long pointed nose, and large expectant eyes which always seemed to say, "You s.o.b. You're thinking about playing a practical joke on me, but don't try because I'm on to your shenanigans." I should say that Jay would never have understood Dick and Martha. Because they had no children, Dick and Martha were a rangering team. She accompanied him on his nature hikes, visited with people in the museum, occasionally dispensed information, and played master of ceremonies at his evening campfire programs. Now, whereas Jay preferred soiled trousers, rolled-up shirt sleeves, and no tie, Dick was the picture of immaculate grooming. He was an ex-Marine with an embedded respect for REGULATIONS. I do not remember ever seeing Dick Townsend on duty without a perfectly ironed shirt, neatly folded tie, sharply creased pants, and highly polished shoes. Dick never told me this, but I always had the feeling that sometime during World War II, in some filthy jungle foxhole, with the sweat and grime and fatigue of combat permeating his body, he had privately vowed to himself that if he ever survived the goddamned war, he would never be dirty again. He was well groomed even when he had levis on. I saw him dirty and unshaven only twice, after two fires he had fought, and he had gone on those more for the fun of it than anything else. He was so conscious of cleanliness and neatness that he would say of his smoking, "This is my one filthy habit; I know it's a filthy habit, but I enjoy it." And he never spilled ashes on the floor.

Aside from his grooming, that which set Dick apart was his use of the English language. It was rarely predictable. For example, one of his more eccentric linguistic habits was his formality in conversation with high level Park Service officials and his informality before large crowds in the evening programs. One would have expected him to do it the other way around. Describing some young grizzlies he had seen playing in the Firehole River, Dick would say to Elt Davis, West District Ranger, "Mr. Davis, I surely wish more of our park visitors could have seen those grizzlies *frolicking* in the water. They would certainly have enjoyed that experience." But, at an evening campfire program, before two or three hundred people (once before nearly a thousand at Old Faithful) he would begin with, "Good evening, folks." It had all the appropriateness of Bob Newhart's great line for Mark

Antony: "Friends, Romans, countrymen! I've got something I wanta tell ya." I used to think that large audiences made him nervous and his folksy tone was his way of calming down and establishing rapport with the crowd. Perhaps "folks" was a better term than "ladies and gentlemen" for the blue-jeaned, blanketed crowds of campers who came to our programs. Dick would never admit nervousness, though. "Shoot, those large crowds don't bother me," he would say in his softest, silkiest tone.

Dick's English was most informal and direct when he expressed himself on a subject close to his heart, quarters, for example. This was his first area of sensitivity. Dick perpetually suspected the Park Service of trying to foist undesirable quarters on him. And number one on his list of undesirable quarters was the converted restroom in which Pat and I had spent our first two summers at Madison Junction.

"Let me tell you something," he would say, breaking off each word and chewing it slowly, "Nobody could ever get me to stay in that dirty little old biffy. No siree, buddy, nobody. I'd tell this Park Service to take their job and shove it before I unpacked in that filthy hole." Which is just about what he did the year they asked him to live in it. He told our immediate supervisor that his trunk was still packed, he had a good home in Belleville, Illinois, and he was ready to go. He absolutely refused to live in that cabin. His insistence won him a trailer.

Dick's English took on a rustic blacksmithian quality whenever he got into his other area of great sensitivity. He could not tolerate impertinence from people breaking Park Service regulations. One Fourth of July when campgrounds were full, Dick found a number of people camping illegally along the Madison River. He moved them on politely with a warning. But one group of Texas tenters went calmly about the business of setting up camp at the very moment Dick was telling them they had to move on. They apparently regarded him as the local boy scout leader registering a complaint about their use of his grounds. Their impassivity raised Dick to the boiling point. "Did you *hear* me? I said it's illegal to camp here! You'll have to move on!"

Indifference by the campers. Dick blazed: "Goddammit! You strike these tents in sixty seconds or I'll *arrest* you! I said move! You sons of bitches! Strike these tents and get your butts out of here—on the double!" Dick was not a man to be trifled with when he was in that kind of mood. He now had the campers' attention, the tents were struck, and a portion of Texas moved on. For days afterward he would get tight-lipped and short of breath as he re-lived the experience up to the climactic "STRIKE THESE TENTS!"

Another of the men who made life interesting at Madison was an unconverted savage who, for reasons that will soon be obvious, I shall call A. B. Origine. Origine had been a savage too long—four years—before he joined the Park Service. He was a tall handsome fellow, and he made an excellent impression in his public contact work. . . when he did it. His trouble was that he still loved to party. He would no sooner finish his work shift in the afternoon than he would head for Old Faithful and his girl friend or friends. And he would leave in such a hurry that he didn't take time to change his clothes. He caused the Old Faithful men trouble because they had to account for the presence and actions of a ranger who did not work out of their station. Rumors reached me that he strolled around the geyser basin, pretty girls hanging from each arm. This was not exactly the image the Park Service wished to project. Origine persisted in popping up in uniform away from Madison Junction until our boss, Dave Condon, Chief Park Naturalist, telephoned for him one afternoon. Dave had a voice that carried about a foot and a half past the telephone receiver.

"STEWART? IS ORIGINE THERE?"

"No, Mr. Condon, he's not."

"WHERE IS HE?"

"He's off duty now, sir."

"WELL, YOU GIVE HIM THIS MESSAGE FROM ME. HE IS NOT TO LEAVE MADISON JUNCTION UNTIL HE GETS OUT OF UNIFORM. GOT THAT? HE'S BEEN DOWN AT OLD FAITHFUL GETTING IN THE BOYS' HAIR THERE. TELL HIM I WANT HIM OUT OF UNIFORM WHEN HE'S OFF DUTY."

"Yes sir, I'll give him the message." I put the phone down, my ear still ringing. I believe I could have heard Dave just as well if he'd shouted from Mammoth which was thirty-five miles away.

Well, Origine got out of uniform, but he couldn't give up partying. And this caused us problems. The museum was supposed to be opened at seven-thirty each day. But Origine had trouble waking up in time to open up. He was getting in about four in the morning, not a good time to start sleeping when you have to be at work by seven-thirty. Even after I warned him that he could get fired for consistently being late, he stayed out and missed again. Dick Townsend's admonitions—"A. B., get your ass out of the sack and get over to that museum! Boy, they'll *fire* you!"—had no permanent effect. We kept telling him he would get canned, but he couldn't give up the parties, and that old adage about not burning the candle on both ends held in his case. At the prompting of the assistant chief naturalist, Origine resigned at the end of the season. It was too bad. He was a likable but immature boy.

Dick Frisbee, in some ways the most gifted of the naturalists I worked with at Madison, was a man of contradictions. He was twenty-nine years old when I first met him, but he looked seventeen. He stood before me, a small wide-eyed boy, it seemed, in a blue and white turtle-neck sweater, and, in the high flat voice we later came to know so well, introduced his girl. Knowledgeable about women and personally resourceful, he still retained an almost child-like need for parental love and affection. He came to us shortly after his father died, a blow he felt keenly. Then he worried constantly about his mother who was living two thousand miles away in Trenton, New Jersey, and who was ill. Perhaps the Townsends, who adopted him during the summers, sensed this need. He wanted us all to know that he was independent and adventurous. But he also wanted us to care about him.

Frisbee despised regulations; he would have felt very much at home with Jay Rencher. His uniform fit him badly—the hat was too big and the jacket too long—and he did not like to wear it. He did not like the routine of station duty—the cleaning, the repetitious talks everyday, the monotony of answering the same questions over and over again. The first time he gave a campfire program, he did battle with Madison's biggest handicap: the lack of electricity. History one could talk about without slides. Geology, his topic, was unthinkable without some kinds of illustrations. Frisbee was very talented artistically. But he had to get the materials. From the old biffy in which he now lived he appropriated the sheet of asbestos behind the stove. This he mounted on two logs; then he used charcoal to draw on the asbestos. For illumination, he mounted two Coleman lamps on stumps, one-half of each shielded by aluminum foil so that they would shed their light on the sheet of asbestos. Frisbee was indifferent to the suggested length of time recommended for talks—forty-five minutes. His idea of an evening program was a talk which exhausted his knowledge of his subject. The first program he gave lasted two and one-half hours, and ten hardy souls stayed to the last. Almost unaware of the gradual diminution of his audience, Frisbee plowed on through the whole history of the formation of the Yellowstone plateau. We never could get him to shorten up too much. He felt he was cheating the people and the Park Service with less than an hour and a half.

Frisbee's problem, of course, was that he had a good grasp of scientific materials but no knowledge at all of basic rhetoric. The kind of talk he wanted to give would have been appropriate before a few graduate students in geology who were studying the Yellowstone plateau. But Frisbee did not accept the idea that he was working in a very different context. The attention span and level of interest in campers was much shorter and far less intense than that of specialists in the field. Frisbee's motives were good, but his sense of audience and willingness to adapt to it were not.

Frisbee was also adventuresome. His first week at Madison he planned a hike on his day off. He was going up Purple Mountain. This was a secondary fire lookout, manned only in periods of extreme fire danger, virtually right at the junction. The trail to the top, an easy one for any person in good health, was about four miles. Dick Townsend told me later that he had been puzzled why Frisbee had studied the topographic map in the museum so carefully. Directions for getting to the trail were simple: one drove up to the old gravel pit, picked up the trail on the far side of it, and started up.

We should have known that Frisbee, an experienced spelunker and hiker, would never have settled for anything so tame as the walk to the summit of Purple Mountain. What he had been studying were the peaks adjacent to it and extending all the way to seven-mile bridge across the Madison River. His plan was to begin at Purple and walk from mountain top to mountain top half the way to the West Entrance. Unfortunately, Yellowstone's lodgepole forest is deceptive. Frisbee got to the top of Purple Mountain, but achieving the summit of its neighbor proved more difficult than he had anticipated. He had to descend farther than he wanted, and in reascending he became confused so that he found himself on other mountains than the ones he wanted to be on. As the day wore on, he got into more and more difficulty.

I was not even aware of Frisbee's plans, but the next morning Martha and Dick Townsend informed me that Frisbee had been out all night and had not returned. Dick had alerted West District Ranger Davis who in turn advised the smoke jumpers in West Yellowstone to stand by. Davis came to Madison, conferred with the Townsends, and was just ready to launch Operation Frisbee when Dick checked one last time at Frisbee's cabin. The little rascal had slipped in, undetected by those creating all the furor over him, and was asleep in his bed. I leave it to your imaginations to guess what Elt Davis told Frisbee. The District Ranger was as volatile as some of Yellowstone's thermal phenomena, and I do not think he was particularly happy about having to come over himself or mobilize a portion of the District's personnel to hunt for a green ranger who didn't stay on trails. It all washed over Frisbee, however, like rain water on granite.

Frisbee had been in real difficulty, he told us later. As night fell, he had had no opportunity to get over the mountains to the highway. Then he wandered into a marsh, and fearing a misstep and an accident, he had stopped walking (this was around midnight) until daylight came and he could see his way clearly again. He had stood in the marsh approximately four hours. When daylight came, he had come over the mountains and returned to his cabin.

Frisbee was the most energetic and creative person we ever had at Madison. In addition to his regular duties, he was doing work for courses at Idaho State College. One summer he secured a special permit to collect flowers as part of a course for Ray Davis, his instructor and a former Yellowstone naturalist. He was constantly busy either collecting specimens or pressing them in a huge press he had obtained. And he always did this work so meticulously. He lettered beautifully and sketched with considerable skill. Those who attended his campfire programs enjoyed his "visuals."

The year after the great earthquake he drew a museum poster telling our visitors where they were, what faulting and sliding had occurred in our area and in the area north of Hebgen Lake. The scale of miles was a precise indicator to any person of normal intelligence. Many who studied the poster never bothered to ask us questions about the earthquake and how to get to the area where the great slide occurred. They had already found this out from Frisbee's poster.

His first summer, 1959, Frisbee stayed in Yellowstone until November doing a post-earthquake study of the hot springs and geysers. With Allan Mebane he was collecting data under the supervision of Chief Park Naturalist Robert McIntyre. But during the construction of a new campground and road system in 1960 and 1961, Madison became dormant. The tedium made us all irritable, and Frisbee eventually rebelled, had a big fight with me and then another with officials at Old Faithful the next year. There were many who were saying that all naturalists wanted to do field work as much as Frisbee did, that he should accept the routine of station life along with the more interesting aspects of the work. The truth is that very few of the naturalists, good and responsible men that all were, would have expended the energy Frisbee would have to collect and organize data on park flora, fauna, or geysers. He finally quit in sheer frustration with a system which he felt cramped him unmercifully. The Park Service felt certain it had separated itself from a malcontent when Frisbee quit. It had; it had also lost a person whose best abilities had rarely been utilized. I wonder if this is the fate of many creative people in our society?

Aside from the naturalists, two other government men, Bill and Larry Wanlass, were vitally important at Madison Junction. I believe the Park Service described them as employees of the sanitation division, which, in plain English, meant that they picked up garbage and cleaned restrooms. But Bill and Larry were no more like the average man's stereotype of the garbage collector than the Superintendent was like an unskilled laborer on the road gangs. Jane Austen would have said they had intelligence in their eyes.

Bill, the older, was a tall gaunt man with flowing white hair and a prophet's manner of speaking. Larry was more easy-going, a rangy, light-footed man of inexhaustible wit and a chuckle in his speech. Retired Teton Valley ranchers, their long experience on the farm had given them confidence that, with the proper tools, they could repair almost anything—engines, trailer jacks, water fountains, broken water lines (after the great earthquake of 1959), and oil stoves. They could do other things well, too. In the years we knew them they sold several color slides (their picture of the Western Tanager appears in the *World Book Encyclopedia*), learned to cut and polish rock and semi-precious stones, collected Indian artifacts, acquired a great deal of information about Arizona history and national monuments, and mastered fly fishing. The universal respect they enjoyed from campers, park officials, Madison naturalists, and their own colleagues was unlike anything I have ever seen.

Pat and I have our own special memories of Bill and Larry. We think of the time Larry fished the mouse out of our oil burner, of the beautiful petrified wood bola tie and the chrysocolla ring Bill made for us, of countless visits in their trailer talking fishing, Yellowstone, education, politics. Our fondest memo-

Bill and Larry Wanlass

ries, however, are of several evenings during the summer of 1957. That year we lived in the trailer in the road camp where Bill and Larry were our closest neighbors. One night, when Pat and I were looking for recreation, and they had nothing special to do, we fished out their horseshoe stakes and, in a narrow alley between the trees right next to the highway, established two pits. Then the shoes began to fly. Because they were so much better than we were, we sided up, Pat with Bill, Larry with me. The games always followed a pattern. In the early part of the evening, before the mosquitoes and the light were too bad, Bill and Pat would win. Larry would throw a ringer using the conventional one-and-a-half turn delivery, but Bill would top his with two. It was disconcerting to see Bill do this because he threw a flipflop shoe; the thing always flopped right against the peg sending up a shower of saucy sparks. Bill would bang that peg time and time again until it began to get dark. When he could no longer see it clearly—indeed, when none of us could see clearly at all—Larry would start to drop them on the pole with stunning regularity, always accompanying his ringers with some gentle needling of "Pancho." Eventually, the matches would end in a draw, Bill and

Pat claiming the daylight hours, Larry and I the dark.

Those who knew Bill and Larry admired them most of all for their basic treatment of each other. Beneath the good natured kidding and occasional needling lay bonds of love and respect that had been forged through decades of work and play together. They used to tell us that after the harvest was in and the cattle rounded up, they would camp out in the woods, in the snows of December, to cut lumber for railroad ties. Often, on sunny mornings, they would awaken to see the shadow of a squirrel on the tent, and they would shoot at it, frequently missing the squirrel but putting holes in their tent through which icy water from the melting snow would drip. Larry would laugh and say, "But we were young then."

Aside from the museum, the most important place for naturalists was the old campfire circle. When I first saw it in 1955, it consisted of one semicircle of logs just outside the northwest camp limit. The person who chose the site must have been timid because it was on a slight decline and consequently barely visible to persons in the campground.

Jay wanted to increase the size of our "amphitheater"—we thought big in those halcyon days—by three rows of seats. This was a job which he and I would do. As I have said previously, Jay was approximately six feet four, 180 pounds of pure muscle developed by years of farming in Idaho. I was 140 pounds of gristle developed by baseball in the neighborhood vacant lot in Kansas City. We, rather Jay, with some interference from me, put in the three rows. We handled logs that were a foot in diameter and about fifteen feet long. I do not know how much they weighed, but I do know that they were too heavy for me to lift. Jay tossed them around like two by fours. How I escaped a hernia or slipped disc I still marvel at today. But we had our amphitheater, and it seated approximately 150 people. Counting the extra fifty who sometimes came and brought their own chairs and camp stools, we had pretty good audiences for programs in which we did all telling and no showing. And there were special compensations for that kind of work. We had the informal intimacy with our audiences which came from working close to our groups. It was something like a nightclub act.

I always began by identifying my audience geographically. "Anyone here from Washington state?" Three hands. "Good for you. Welcome to Yellowstone. Oregon?" Four hands. "So, the Pacific Northwest is represented here tonight. Great states. Beautiful sea scapes and parks, too. Now let's see." Half of my audience would be poised and ready, the half coming from a large state south of Oregon. "Montana?" Several hands—they were locals—and some surprise on the faces of the half not yet called yet. I was just beginning to work on them. "How about Nevada? Utah? Arizona? New Mexico? Wyoming? Colorado? North Dakota? South Dakota? Nebraska? Kansas? Oklahoma?"

And so I went, moving steadily east, picking up states along the way and not missing any. I had always been good at geography, and I had a good memory for portions of the country. And all the while I could hear small children saying to their parents, "But Mom, he *forgot*. . .!" And Mom or Dad would tell them to be quiet because they weren't sure whether or not I was up to something or whether I had indeed, forgot. On to Central and South America, Europe, Asia, Australia and New Zealand. I never forgot to needle the Texans about coming from the second largest state—this after Alaska had been admitted—and I said something special for the people from Wisconsin. Now, I was ready for the grand finale. "Well, I guess we've covered about everyone, haven't we? We haven't? Did I forget someone's state? Oh, yes. Who's here from. . . CALIFORNIA?" By this time they were so wound up that the din was terrific. Californians are travellers; one could depend on half of the audience being from there. It never failed.

After the deafening cheers of the Californians had died down, I would tell them who I was, where I was from, and what I was doing there. Since I was at that time a graduate student in English at the University of Wisconsin, I received a number of queries about how I happened to get into "that kind of summer work." So much has specialization conditioned us, that we think of people as being irrevocably confined to the little professional compartments to which they commit themselves early in life. Since I was an English major, people assumed that I would know little about geology, ornithology, ichthyology, and other natural sciences. Many Americans, particularly, still are not willing to accept the fact that intelligence enables one to become knowledgeable in many disciplines. I was no expert like my colleague Joe Murphy at Mammoth, but I learned to identify and explain the common flowers, bugs, animals, and hot spring formations of the Park.

After warming up with geography, I would precede my talk with announcements about the facilities at Madison, an invitation to the next night's talk, and some good advice about bears. "Most of you have seen those brown and black furry things wandering through the campground and raiding the garbage pits. No, they are *not* teddy's. Yes, they will bite and scratch. Yes, they will come into your tents if properly invited. If you want a bear for company, leave some choice morsels in your tent. Meat, sweets, bread, etc. will do fine. A bear, strolling past a tent and picking up the irresistible aroma of bacon coming from it can no more resist your invitation than a tramp can turn down a steak dinner at Howard Johnson's. You may then find yourselves in the position of one gentleman who told me that until he experienced it he could not believe how much confusion resulted when a bear and five people all tried to get out of a tent at once in the middle of the night."

I also lectured people on portable ice boxes. "Some of you are probably thinking smugly that you don't have to worry about the bears because you have you food in a portable ice box which is odor proof. No bear could possibly smell food in it. You are absolutely right. No bear can *smell* the food in your ice box, but if you think bruin doesn't *know* what's in the long rectangular object on your picnic table, you are badly mistaken. In this park mother bears include portable ice boxes in every cub's ABCs. Now, what does a bear do when he finds one? Usually, he just

Tourists asking for trouble

pries the box open, then proceeds to gorge himself on the goodies he has found. Sometimes, if he isn't too hungry, he will pass up some items and eat others. If you own one of those things, lock it in the trunk of your car. That's the only safe place for it." At which point a number of husbands would suddenly leave the campfire and disappear for about ten minutes.

One night, as I was giving this little spiel, we heard a tremendous roaring and cursing from the campground. Spaced between the curses was a bump-bump-bump. Soon a small black bear appeared in the light made by the campfire; he was racing into the woods with a portable ice box he had swiped from an astonished camper. The camper was in pursuit, but that little bear, despite the fact he had to pull that box along (he had one handle in his mouth), outdistanced the camper. The next day, on our morning nature walk, we found pieces of the ice box scattered through the woods outside the campground. The persons listening to my lecture on bear damage prevention got the point emphatically.

Another of my prefatory speeches involved the traffic problem in Yellowstone: "No doubt many of you have noticed the large numbers of vehicles on our park highways. You might be interested to know that between June 15 and Labor Day over a million people come to Yellowstone Park. Those numbers, coupled with the large numbers of employees, make park highways look like congested city streets at rush hour. In view of these things what must you do? Well, Papa, or Mama, whoever is driving, you must watch the road at all times. And that will be tough because we have more distractions per road mile than one can find almost anywhere in the country. Example: family has just driven into the Park and is now busily scanning the roadside and meadows for wildlife. Before you know it, a pair of bright eyes in the back seat will open up with 'A bear! Daddy, stop, a bear!' Too often Daddy stops in a screech leaving the car behind just two alternatives: to go under or over you. Neither being feasible, he will bash hell out of your back bumper and trunk, and you will lose time making out reports and insurance claims. That is, if you're lucky and don't have to spend some time in the hospital. So promise yourself, that when you are driving, you will not let your eyes wander from the road for deer, elk, buffalo, moose, waterfall, geysers, mountains, or anguished screams from the back seat."

Prefaces over, I could get on with the talk. My subjects over a period of years spanned Yellowstone history—the birth of the national park idea, John Colter's discovery of Yellowstone, stagecoach robberies—and sundry misconceptions about the Park. By the time I had finished, the campfire would be embers. My wife and I would douse it, talk to those who had stayed for post-program conversation, collect our wheelbarrow used for bringing wood to the campfire, and head back to our cottage. I always had a pleasant sense of accomplishment when I finished the day's work at campfire. There we met people from all across this broad land of ours. And distinct as all these Americans were, they were united in their pride in the national parks and gratitude for the men who served in them. In those quiet satisfying moments after a good program, during conversations with those who had come forward to praise or to question, I was proud to be a servant of the people.

☐

The visitor to Madison Museum today will not find Langford's saddle, Billy Owen's bicycle, the remarkable collection of guns once mounted there, the Indian relics, the historical placards along the molding, or Jack Haynes' superb picture window depicting the 1870 campsite of the Washburn party. They have been replaced by gaudy modern exhibits brightly illuminated by spotlights mounted on the interior superstructure of the building. These exhibits tell, in human terms, less than a quarter of the story imparted by the exhibits which once detained visitors to the museum for hours.

Even sadder is the absence of anyone to tell, in living words, the story of the birth of the national park idea. Gone from that place are the Jay Renchers, Dick Townsends, Dick Frisbees, yes —even the Don Stewarts of my era. I re-visited this landmark in my life during the summer of 1973 for a few minutes only—until the echoes of the past in that spiritually empty building drove me from it. I will never enter it again.

14

Euarctos Americanus Campgroundus

IN AUGUST, 1973, when I returned to Yellowstone Park for the first time in ten years, I saw only one bear along the road in three days. In subsequent brief visits, in 1975, 1978, and 1980, the pattern persisted. New management policies, prompted by the large crowds of the 60s and 70s, had at last successfully separated people and bears, neither of which had ever been very good for each other. As the memories crowded back, I began to recall just how bad the mix of people and bears had been.

In the late 1950s at Madison Junction we had many, many bears. And because no protective division personnel were stationed in our area, we had to get help from Old Faithful or West Yellowstone every time some bear started breaking car windows, tearing up tents, or biting people. I suspected Old Faithful of trapping its troublesome bears and releasing them on the bluff high above the Gibbon River near Madison. Eventually, these bears worked their way out to the road and down through the woods, across the river, and into our campground. The situation got so bad during the summer of 1958 that on one occasion I stood at a single spot in our campground and counted six bears in sight. As I walked through the camp—it was not much more than a quarter of a mile square—I counted thirteen. That was too many bears.

When necessary, we removed offending bears by trapping them in a green culvert type affair which had a heavy iron door on one end and bars on the other. The trick was to entice the bear into the trap with a bait tied to the trigger which sprung the door. There were many defects in this kind of trap, two of them in particular. First, we usually trapped the wrong bear. If thirteen bears were in a campground, and one of them was bad, we'd catch the other twelve before old number thirteen would even get close to the trap. Chances usually were that the offending bear had already been trapped and was not enthused about a second experience no matter how rank, how alluring, the bait. Many times campers and naturalists would see the bear we wanted amble up to the trap, sniff at some agonizingly tempting bait (bacon, honey, or foul smelling garbage), and turn away. Sometimes the bear would torture himself like Ulysses passing the sirens. He would put his front feet on the floor of the trap and look way in. He'd stretch and stretch and stretch, then back out, go to the other end, and try to get at the bait through the metal bars. Eventually, he'd go away and we'd catch some naive two-year-old that we didn't want.

The second problem with these traps was that cleaning them and removing bear scent was almost impossible. After some poor, frightened, diarrhetic bear had been in one half a day and all night, all the water in Yellowstone Lake could not completely obliterate the odor of bear. And bears have wonderfully keen noses. The next trappee would detect the previous bear's odor and immediately sense that the can with the juicy morsel was something that was no good for him. About the only thing those traps were consistently useful for was providing campers with lots of good movies of bears playing around them and rangers cursing them.

We had the trap in Madison Campground many times. And we had many, many bears, a few of which stood out from the general population. Veteran campers at Madison would remember them well. Three were senior citizens of long standing: Beatrice, Benjamin, and the "necklace bear." Beatrice was a cantankerous old sow who brought a new batch of cubs in every two or three years. At one time I believe we might have generalized safely that close to half of the permanent bear residents of Madison Campground were Beatrice's offspring. Whether or not she and Benjamin had some sort of permanent love affair going (as far as these things go with bears), we never knew. Anyway, one year she'd be in with new cubs. The next year the cubs would be growing up and getting mean as hell. A year after that she'd be back with another batch of new cubs.

Beatrice rarely bothered campers. However, she gave the male bears rough treatment when she was protecting her cubs. She had a possessive walk. Madison Campground was her turf—at least that's what I think she thought—and we were supposed to step aside when she came through. If we didn't, she gave us the distinct impression that she'd chew the meat off our legs and hand us back the bones. Beatrice and I never had a quarrel. I kept out of her way, and she left the campers alone so I had no reason to trap her. She knew what traps were, anyway, so trapping would never have caught her. But the cubs—that was a different story. Mrs. Taggart told Pat and me of the day when one of Beatrice's cubs got caught in a trap in the road camp. It was a day a lot of people remembered.

You see, Beatrice thought traps were pretty stupid; I got the impression that she thought no self-respecting bear ever would get near one of the filthy things. Like most mama bears, she had rules for the kids, one of which was to stay away from traps. Kids don't always mind, however, and the day the door slammed shut on her cub, Beatrice was all over that trap. She tried to tear it apart six different ways; she walked around it continuously; finally, she just sat by it and huffed.

Now, the rangers didn't want her or her cub so they would

have been glad to release the little trapped cub and call everything square, but Beatrice wouldn't let a soul near the trap. She
was certain that harm was intended her baby, and she was going
to prevent it. So, here were several rangers and assorted help
pondering the problem of one cub in a trap, two in a nearby tree,
and mama keeping strict watch over the trap. It was not exactly
anybody's cup of tea.

The problem was resolved, as problems usually are, by brav-
ery and ingenuity. First, one of the men backed a car up to the
trap. This permitted a man to walk along the roof of the car onto
the top of the trap. Climbing up there with Beatrice on his back
would have been a difficult and bloody feat. Then two hardy souls
took on the responsibility of keeping her at bay long enough for
the man on top to get to the door of the trap, lift it, and release
the cub. This was accomplished swiftly, with temporary cardiac
arrest to several individuals. Comic relief was provided by Beatrice herself who, when the cub jumped out of the trap, gave him
such a whack that he went rolling over and over like a dish down
an incline in the drive. Neither Beatrice nor her cubs visited any
traps again that year.

Like Beatrice, Benjamin was a black black bear. It is necessary to make this distinction because many black bears are that in
species only. They may be light brown, dark brown, reddish
brown, and black. But they are all the same: *Euarctos americanus*. Anyway, Benjamin was black as coal, and in his old age he
got mean. Unlike Beatrice, he *did* molest campers, and he
avoided the trap. But his last summer Benjamin took liberties
which could not be extended to bears even in that most lenient of
campgrounds, Madison. He found a tent with food in it. Benjamin raided it, and the people left. But Benjamin reasoned that
any tent pitched on the site where he had first struck gold, would
also have food in it. The next one didn't. It belonged to a widow
and her son who leaped up in terror when old Benjamin ripped a
whole section of their tent in the middle of the night. The next
night he was back again.

Now a frustrated bear can do a lot of damage. Benjamin

gave every indication that any tent on that spot for the rest of the summer was going to get worked over. Trapping did not succeed. And, when trapping failed with a potentially dangerous bear, the long rifle was called for. The West Yellowstone sub-district ranger came one afternoon and followed Benjamin into the woods. All we heard was one shot echoing down the Madison Canyon. I was always sad about the shooting of a bear. I never got used to it, and I know many good rangers who didn't either. The irony is that man invades the bear's primitive home and corrupts him, then destroys him for not adapting. Too often this has been the sad fate of wildlife in America.

By all means the most personable of the senior bear citizens of Madison Campground was the necklace bear. He was one of the largest black bears I ever saw, weighing probably 350 or 400 pounds. He was a beautiful rich brown, but around his neck was a strip of white fur, hence the name "the necklace bear." He knew all about traps, but we suspected he liked to ride in them. He would come into the campground every summer, mosey from garbage can to garbage can minding his own business like any good bear should. After a few weeks, however, he would begin to feel his oats. He would chew a corner of a tent or start climbing on picnic tables and generally make a nuisance of himself. We never felt that he had a mean streak in him the way Benjamin did; he just got a bit ornery. Anyway, the trap would be brought, this big bear would, in a short space of time, find his way into it, and he would get a long ride up into the Gallatin country in the northwest corner of the Park. A few weeks later, this old timer would be back. He had a homing instinct for our campground. Bill and Larry once said they thought that, over the years, he had been hauled off seven times, and each time he eventually came back to Madison Junction. He must have had deep roots there.

I saw the necklace bear really lose his temper only once. It was about six o'clock one July evening in 1957. He ambled into the southwest corner of the campground and proceeded to open the first garbage can he came to. They were along the campground road and the bears stopped at them the way a postman follows his mail route. This big bear liked to start at the south-west corner and work around. Now I had seen one of the younger bears on that same beat just twenty minutes earlier so I knew brownie would find nothing. He was obviously hungry as he plopped down beside the can and went to work. At that time the garbage cans were set in round concrete forms recessed in the ground. The bears merely lifted the entire lid section off, some-thing resembling a toilet seat, pulled the garbage can out by its wire handle, and then dabbled through it. This saved them the work of standing on their heads while searching through any one can. This night brownie soon discovered that that particular garbage can and Mother Hubbard's cupboard had a lot in com-mon, so, a bit huffy, he proceeded to the next station. Another empty pantry. That improved neither his appetite nor his temper. Brownie was beginning to snort. When he got to the third empty can, he was in a boil. I suspect he was picking up the scent of the bear ahead of him and had begun to figure out why he was get-ting no dinner. The young bear ahead wasn't moving from can to can as fast as big old brownie because, obviously, he was finding some tasty nourishment. It was around can four or five that the big bear caught up with the younger. The old bear made a rush at the little one who had no intention of making a gallant last stand by his garbage can. They raced through the campground until the small bear went for a tree and started up, up, up. Black bears climb very well. With the big brown spurring him on that little black bear went to the very top of one of the tallest lodgepole pines in our campground. The necklace bear went right up, too. Then there was a pause.

Situation. One 150-pound black bear perched atop a lodge-pole pine whose diameter at the point was perhaps four or five inches. Ten feet below, full of indignation and anger at the tres-passer, was the 350 pound necklace bear. That added up to 500 pounds of bear at the lean end of the tree. They both spit at each other; then the brown made a rush. The little black slapped him in the face, knocked loose branches down on him, and generally defended himself with real courage. Brownie backed down.

By this time a real crowd had gathered, perhaps 200 people. It was like ringside at Madison Square Garden, only this was Madison Square Campground, and the contestants were two of nature's own. Naturally, the crowd cheered the underdog, in this case, the top bear. I was supposed to deliver a talk in the amphitheater that evening, and I was taking my wood for the fire when the ruckus started. I felt the compulsion of duty, but I also realized that when culture competes with entertainment for the public's attention, culture might as well forget itself. I doubt that even Johnny Carson could have lured the crowd away from that tree. I didn't try. I just announced a temporary postponement until the issue was resolved.

Meanwhile, the brown, murder in his heart, hovered on his perch just below the little black and caught his breath. Then he made the sudden rush upward again. Involved in the furious biting, slapping, hissing, and spitting, the bears were oblivious to the perilous swaying of the tree which bent the way a metronome staggers when the weight is placed at the very top of the support.

There were more rushes, more fighting, and enough movies and snap-shots taken of that tree to keep Kodak in business a full day before the old bear decided to call off the siege and go look for his supper elsewhere. The little one stayed up awhile longer. But he had gotten the message. I don't think he travelled the necklace bear's route again. Brownie went back to being his peaceful self except when he once again got the urge to travel. Then he would be trapped and carried off for awhile. But he always came back. I think this bear eventually died of old age. It was just as well. He would not have liked the new campground nor the invasion of the protective division. He had had too long and too pleasant an association with the naturalists at Madison.

The campground had its junior citizens, most of them offspring of Beatrice. Two stand out. The first was Buttons, a black two-year-old who had been a campground pet the year before we arrived. Several insisted that it was he who had been caught in the trap. Unfortunately, there were certain campers who liked to feed the cubs on the sly. Buttons was the special pet

of one individual, and by the end of his first year he was thoroughly corrupted. I recognized immediately when I first saw him
that he not only depended upon people to feed him, but
expected them to do so. I spent a good part of the summer of
1955 trying to convince campers that hand feeding even Buttons
could be dangerous business. Some even wanted to give their
children a ride on the bear. (Yes, that story and others of its kind
are really true; they are not Yellowstone mythology. I was an
observer of such attempts.)

Buttons did not confine his activities to the campground. We
knew him also by his antics in the road camp. One day Pat came
to me inquiring what in the world could have happened to the
toilet paper in our outhouse. It was strung all over the ground
and had big teeth marks in it. Well, we could suspect just one
bear, but catching him was another thing. About the fourth roll
we succeeded. Pat thought she heard some thumping around the
outhouse. She went out the door of the cabin and started for the
biffy. Because the door faced away from our cabin, we couldn't
see into it until we got all the way there. On this occasion she
didn't have to go all the way. A little black furry head, its jaws
clamped firmly on the toilet paper, peeped around the outhouse.
We ended his playing by putting a latch on the door, but we often
wondered what degree of hysteria Buttons would have caused
had he surprised some of the temporarily desperate tourists who
occasionally used our private toilet.

When he was not playing with the toilet paper, Buttons was
investigating any laundry hanging out. On many occasions he
peeled my undershirts off the line. Mrs. Taggart had more problems, however. Buttons was fascinated by the way her petticoats
bounced back into the air after he had tugged them nearly to the
ground. He was, of course, playing with the tension in the
clotheslines. Like a kitten chasing a string, he would become
intent on the quarry which, when he released it temporarily,
sprang away thus affording him another opportunity to capture it
and congratulate himself on his prowess as a hunter. Buttons, I
believe, had great imagination for a bear.

Cute cubs and entertaining two-year-olds often grow up, when they have been spoiled by people, into destructive three-year-old bears. This was the unhappy story of Buttons. We were told that early in his third spring he took a number of shingles off the old cabin in the road camp just trying to break in and get an orange. He was trapped and taken up to the Gallatin country. There he went on a destructive rampage, eventually forcing his way into a trailer and doing so much damage that he had to be shot. Buttons' story is a particularly sad one because those who considered themselves his best friends were his worst enemies. They taught him to be a spoiled child, to expect food from man, and then left the unhappy task of controlling an uncontrollable bear to the men of the Park Service. But there were no institutions for bears who became juvenile delinquents—only graves.

Rufus was another bear in the Buttons mold. He was one of the cutest brown cubs I ever saw, and he was liberally spoiled by the same campers who corrupted Buttons. I had sharp words with the offenders over the matter of feeding Rufus, but I could make no arrest without actually seeing them doing it. They were careful to avoid detection. Late in the summer, however, I realized why Rufus liked to sleep under one trailer so much. I had more words with the owner, and I predicted some interesting activity the next summer from the "cute little bear." However, none of us could have anticipated the flowering of Rufus.

It occurred early in the summer of 1959. One of the men who drove a bread truck into the Park daily was a school friend of Frisbee. On the particular morning I remember, Sonny, the driver, considerably distraught because he had to see the Old Faithful sub-district ranger on a speeding charge, was in our museum telling his troubles to Frisbee. Rufus, now a frisky two-year-old, wandered by, but he had no interest in Sonny's problems. His keen little nose was already telling him that the door of the bread truck was open. Inside were fresh cakes, pies, cookies, doughnuts, and bread. No bear can resist a temptation like that, and certainly Rufus, although he had other qualities, was not long on willpower. He was well into breakfast before Sonny, alerted by Frisbee, got wind of what was going on. He raced out of the museum and down to the parking lot where he flailed a broom and threw rocks at Rufus who, though sorely tempted to hold his ground, could not withstand the physical and linguistic assault of the enraged Sonny. It was a black day, indeed, for the truck driver. But it was a significant day for Rufus. He had learned that open vehicles of any kind in that parking lot might contain treasures to appease his bear appetite. Thus began a summer of raiding, the likes of which has not been seen since Quantrill and his men pillaged Kansas. And the next victim of Rufus's new knowledge (he had tasted the forbidden fruit and, like Eve, found it to his liking) was, ironically, Sonny again—the very same day.

Sonny came by the museum that evening to tell Frisbee that he had been generously treated by the sub-district ranger. He had received only a warning; to him it was a reprieve. He would not lose his job. He would not lose the money he desperately needed to go to school. So the day which began with a black cloud hanging over it, a black cloud out of which rain poured when Rufus made his raid, had turned out to be tinted with a little rainbow. Sonny was positively mellow about the Park Service, working in Yellowstone, and life in general.

He was, that is, until Rufus struck again. The little bear, reasoning with that acuteness which bears have about food, smelled the bread truck, again with an open door, and decided to mine the same rich vein he had discovered in the morning. So, Sonny raced out of the museum again and began another assault upon Rufus. There were things which Sonny called this young bear who had victimized him twice, but most of them have nothing to do with species identification; they are terms one would probably find only in *Webster's Third International Dictionary*, and even that comprehensive work does not include all of Sonny's descriptions of Rufus. Well, Sonny never got burned again, but because of those incidents, Rufus began a thorough daily check of the parking lot. For over a month he averaged something like a car per day. And when Rufus got into a car, we had the God-awfullest traffic jams anyone ever saw at Madison Junction. Many a park visitor left that year with the picture everyone wanted—the bear in the car. Rufus is probably in more slides, snapshots, and movies than any other Madison bear in history. He made his fame with incidents like the following.

It was mid-July, sunny and comfortably warm. The parking lot at Madison was about half full. A man from Colorado and I were talking near the backdoor of the museum when we heard a child sing out, "Hey, look! There's a bear in that car." The man to whom I was talking blanched.

"Did you leave your windows rolled down?" I asked. He said he had but that there was only a little popcorn in the front seat. That, I assured him, was quite enough. We were halfway to the parking lot by this time, and sure enough, Rufus was in his car. What to do?

There is a popular misconception of the park ranger as one who, finding valuable tourist property, car seats, for example, in jeopardy, comes to the rescue in a heroic movie-type hand-to-hand combat with the vicious bear which he overpowers and forces from the premises, sustaining only a two-inch gash on the forehead, slashes on the arm, and numerous small bites and scratches. Sorry, folks, tain't so. No ranger I knew ever went hand to hand with a bear; we all had too much common sense to do that. Besides, I was much more practical about such matters. Rufus, I was pretty certain, would do no more than get his dirty footprints on the seat and then leave when he was finished, so I advised the man to stand back and perhaps coax the bear out of the car with food. Well, Rufus was doing no damage, but he wouldn't coax because he was really enjoying that buttered popcorn. He wanted all of it, right to the last kernel.

Meanwhile, the parking lot had nearly filled and the roadway had jammed with spectators. The bear in the car was just the funniest thing you ever saw—it always was, I noticed, to everyone but the person in whose car the bear was. At this moment a blue Falcon pulled into the lot and out of it leaped four exuberant college girls from Michigan. They were enormously pleased and excited about finding a bear in a car. They ran back and forth,

Photo by Ruby Bowles

Rufus in action

taking pictures, giggling uncontrollably, and generally becoming thoroughly intoxicated with the pure comedy of the situation. Rufus, meanwhile, had finished the popcorn and had come to the open window of the victim's car. This gentleman had borne his injuries with remarkable patience, but it was plain that he disliked being the special object of mirth of the girls from Michigan.

"Oh, you're the owner of the car? Tee-hee. Kids, isn't this the greatest? Look how funny he looks just sitting there in the driver's seat!" They weren't really nasty; they just couldn't hide the fact that they thought the poor slob's predicament was the funniest thing since Stunt Day at the university. Rufus paused momentarily, his paws on the window. He looked for all the world like a tired papa waiting on the family to finish surveying yet another museum. But Rufus had other ideas. His nose had told him where dessert was coming from. So rapidly that none of us could react, he leaped from the one car window, hit the asphalt, and bounded directly into the blue Falcon. There he found crackers, cookies, and candy. Rufus settled down to his work, unaware of the poetic justice he had rendered. The four girls suddenly found the bear in the car not funny at all.

"Ranger! Can't you *do* something? Oh! Ugh! He's getting his dirty feet all over my new sweatshirt! Oh, yuk! Can't we do something to get him out of there? This is awful!"

"No, I think the best thing to do is wait him out. When he's eaten all he wants, he'll get out with a minimum of damage. If you frighten or anger him, he might tear up the interior of the car."

"Oh, this is terrible! And we're running late." More wailing and hand wringing.

The man from Colorado found the scene very funny. When Rufus leaped out of his car, he had immediately rolled up his windows, borrowed our broom to sweep out, and settled down to enjoy a joke which up to this point had been all on him. He was a very kind man, I remember. He made no attempt to rub it in. He just sat with a sly smile on his face while the young ladies bewailed the loss of food, the dirtying of clothes, and the rumpling of papers and maps. I just maintained law and order. After all, who was I to steal one of Rufus's big scenes?

Rufus had a glorious summer in 1959, but it was cut short by the great earthquake of August 17. The next year the camp was closed by July 15, and he drifted away. Perhaps he established himself along the road; perhaps he drifted into the wilderness. He had the capabilities for becoming a most respectable and self-supporting wild bear. I certainly hope so. It would be sad to think that he, too, had fallen to the long rifle.

We knew the permanent bear residents of Madison so well that most of us could identify transients as well as the other bears could. But there was one intruder who stirred up the campground and all the black bears frequenting it as no transient ever did. In the first place, he was not a *euarctos americanus*; he was an *ursus horribilis*. There is a great difference. The intruder came one evening in the middle of July, 1959. Pat saw him first. We were driving from the road camp to the campground and had just started to drive around a car ahead of us which was blocking the road. We knew the people in it were looking at a bear, but we had seen too many along the road to care. As we drove around them Pat suddenly exclaimed: "That's a grizzly!"

That's a grizzly!

There were then, by educated guesses, no more than 800 grizzlies in the entire contiguous United States. According to the Craighead brothers, who studied the grizzlies in Yellowstone, approximately 250 resided in the Park at that time. But the average park visitor practically never saw a grizzly. They did not beg along the roads. Although they did come into some campgrounds in the early part of the summer, particularly Canyon, Tower, and Fishing Bridge, they often came at night. So rare was the sight of a grizzly that Pat and I saw one but twice in nine years, and we drove over Park roads always searching for glimpses of them. They do not fear man, but they are shy and avoid him. Madison Campground, according to veteran campers, had not had a grizzly for ten or fifteen years. But there one was at the bridge across the Gibbon River, just yards from the camp. We turned around immediately, returned to the road camp, and alerted Bill and Larry Wanlass. They wouldn't believe it. They left their trailer and followed us through the timber toward the river where we soon spotted the bear. Bill guffawed:

"Aw, just a brown black bear! You get too excited."

Larry was more cautious. We could not see the bear except from the side, and he was partially obscured by the long grass. Bill continued skeptical.

"No, that's no grizzly."

"Bill, Pat and I have seen those things in the interior dumps.

Pat just couldn't make a mistake like that."

"Well, perhaps she didn't get a good enough look. No, that's just . . ." At this point the bear turned and looked back, revealing its long nose and great broad forehead. Bill finished his sentence. ". . . a grizzly!"

Now, there was no question. Our first task was to alert campers. We did not want them to react as casually to this bear as they did to the black bears which were as common as stray dogs in the camp. This we did and soon had a sizable group watching as the bear came back and began fishing along the Gibbon River. Very gently he would slip his paw under the river bank seeking out trout which might be lying there. Unfortunately, he was not finding any fish in the pockets under the banks. However, he was also playing a cat and mouse game with some elk upstream from him. Grizzlies are very fast over a short distance, so their strategy for capturing big game is to attack quickly. If a deer or an elk gets much running room, it will escape the bear. We had watched the elk in the presence of black bears. They were always respectful, but a bit contemptuous. An adult elk can defend itself from all but the largest black bears. As the grizzly moseyed along the river bank seeking to work up close to the elk, they were crossing the river toward him. At first, they were almost lackadaisical; then, all of a sudden they must have picked up his scent and realized that a very different kind of bear was approaching them. They snorted and stormed out of the water just as the grizzly made his move. He was not quick enough and the elk darted into the timber above the river. The grizzly went back to fishing.

For approximately three weeks after this night we kept receiving reports of a huge bear which was coming into the camp at night. Now, this grizzly was not as large as two or three of the big blacks in the camp, but the two species do not mix, and the more aggressive grizzly was obviously driving the others out. For a long while he made no daytime appearance; then he showed up one evening full of wrath. The grizzly started at the east end of the camp and began to terrorize people. Some, not realizing at first that the bear was a grizzly, tried to run him off by throwing rocks, an effective technique with black bears. With grizzlies this can be extremely dangerous. The bear circled the camp, passing between the cottage and the museum and then went for the river. There he chased a young boy fishing who was wisely advised to wade out into the water. He did so and the bear left him to charge three men farther upstream. By this time the camp was in an uproar. Dick Townsend notified the West Yellowstone subdistrict ranger, and he came over in a hurry.

Pat was with me approximately a mile upstream where I was spending a relaxing evening fishing, but as we started back we were met by Jack Hughes, one of the West District rangers, telling us to cross the meadow east of the campground carefully. The bear had been driven from camp and the men were firing over its head to frighten it away. The idea that she was out in the open with a grizzly in the area absolutely terrified Pat. But I grabbed her, and we hurried back to the campground and watched the result. The bear would not leave. It was aroused, and a trap was not available. It would certainly return to the camp that night. It had to be killed, and it was.

Although it was a young grizzly, it sustained six mortal wounds and still remained standing for a brief period before succumbing. All of us felt very bad about the whole incident. I know now that it could have been handled better. The protective division of the Park Service, as a matter of fact, has a terrible record on grizzly management. Grizzlies are too precious to destroy. Yellowstone was created so that our citizens could come come to see a trace of the western wilderness of the nineteenth century. The king of that wilderness was the great grizzly, but so incompatible with man is he that he is near extinction. One can only hope that this marvelous bear, despite the intrusions of man, can maintain an existence in Yellowstone and Glacier Parks, the last two principalities of which he is still king. King over all but the long rifle.

☒

There is a newer campground at Madison now. It was built between 1959 and 1961 as part of the Mission 66 plan. It has paved roads, beautiful sites, bearproof garbage cans, and clean modern restrooms. The protective division has an office there, and it manages the camp efficiently. If a bear appears, one of the rangers skilled in firing darts containing Sucostrin uses his bow and arrow or rifle to put the bear temporarily in paralysis. It is then loaded into a trap and hauled away. There are no more problems of the kind which once plagued us. But there are no bears, either. The new efficiency has taken away forever the color of campground life, a special flavor provided by the antics of *Euarctos Americanus Campgroundus*. Beatrice, Benjamin, the necklace bear, Buttons, and Rufus could never have developed or flourished in the new campground environment. And a damn good thing, say some veteran rangers. But I think campground life is infinitely poorer for their absence. [*]

---

[*]For a provocative and highly critical analysis of game management policies in Yellowstone since its establishment as a park, see Alston Chase's *Playing God in Yellowstone*.

15

Nights on the Gibbon

IN YELLOWSTONE, from the first of July to the middle of August there comes a succession of perfect evenings. Each day, about four-thirty or five, the afternoon heat and wind subside, and the refreshing coolness of evening begins to settle over the mountains, soothing the parched day. Big billowy cumulus clouds melt out of the sky leaving it a pure deep blue. On such evenings I invariably became restless because they demanded that I take my fly rod and go to my favorite haunts along the Gibbon River.

Pat would know I was going fishing. She would have supper ready when I came home from work, and I would eat quickly. Afterwards, with controlled impatience, I would get out my fishing gear. I wanted to be on the river at once; I could hardly bear the precious minutes ticking away unused. Yet, neither could I subdue my pleasure in the preparations themselves. I would shed my uniform and don khaki pants and a cotton flannel shirt. Over the shirt I wore my fishing vest, a pleasantly soiled olive green garment. In its four outside pockets I carried line dressing, leader material, a scale for weighing and measuring fish, a pocket knife, and insect repellent. In two large inside pockets I carried complete leaders and a plastic box containing flies.

I did not have the picturesque felt hat stuffed with assorted flies that more creative and experienced fly fishermen habitually wore. My substitute was a battered rain hat with a few of my favorite flies hooked into the front brim. I rarely used them. The brim was my mantel-piece—a place to retire well-worn flies that had given distinguished service. The place of honor in the front was occupied by a number twelve Little Jack Horner fly that had taken twelve fish. It was chewed down to the shank of the hook, and the grizzly hackle was faded and half-gone; I had been surprised at its effectiveness even in its late phase when it had been most decrepit. A couple of Grasshoppers, a Sofa Pillow, one Royal Coachman, and a Black Gnat plus a barely discernible number fourteen Mosquito completed the group.

The only other article of apparel I wore were my green rubber boots. They were thick soled and well insulated. Good fishing boots fit snugly but softly, not at all like new shoes which resist breaking in and brand the wearer with calluses and blisters. One has only to buy the right sized boot; it will fit comfortably the first day he puts it on. I particularly treasured my boots because I remembered the times I had had to go into Middle Creek bare footed. Like most mountain streams, Middle Creek was rarely deep. But it was paralyzingly cold. Nothing had been so frustrating to me as seeing my fly caught on a log fifteen feet out in two foot water. Because I had so few flies then, I had to wade in after them, experiencing the kind of cold that collapses capillaries and freezes the roots of one's teeth. Fishing boots eliminated my problem. They enabled me to get into streams, cross them, and secure advantageous casting positions—and they protected me from that cold water. A trout fisherman's whole approach to a small stream, particularly one with stretches of shallow water between deep holes, is dictated by his possession of boots. Aside from his rod, line, and fly, they are his most vital equipment.

Assembling my rod was a moment's work, but it involved a small ritual. Before joining the two sections I would sight down

A night on the Gibbon

the top section checking for warp. Then I linked both sections and sighted again. A true professional, seeing warp, gets out his tiny alcohol lamp, heats the tip, and corrects the warp. I did not do this because I was only playing the role. Stringing the barely visible leader tippet through the guides on the rod was the most exasperating piece of work in my preparations. Every trout fisherman, the urge to move toward the stream burning in him, knows the frustration and increased anxiety of letting the thread-like tippet slip from his fingers just as he has painstakingly worked it through all the guides but the last one. I suffered through many such moments. Eventually, however, I would get the tippet through the last guide, pull enough line and leader out to insure against its slipping back and then choose a fly. I always started with a number twelve Jack Horner and changed only if it didn't work. The process of attaching fly and tippet was another painstaking one: I guided the tiny leader through the eye of the hook, looped it four times, fed it back through the first loop, then pulled the whole into a barrel knot. These preparations completed, I hooked the fly to the cork in the handle of my rod, tightened my reel so that the line did not droop, put on mosquito repellent, gathered up my net and creel, and set out through the campground. Even then, in the moment of leaving, the restless-

At one point, it vaults eighty feet over Gibbon Falls

ness of preparing to go would not leave me. I would feel it all through the long walk to the river and right up to the first cast. Then it would suddenly depart, and I would be at peace.

The Gibbon River originates on the central plateau of Yellowstone, north and slightly east of the Norris Geyser Basin. For several miles it wanders through Virginia Meadows, past the Norris Campground, and then in a wide arc around Norris Geyser Basin. As it leaves the thermal area, it rushes rapidly downhill through dense timber into Elk Park, pausing there only long enough to rest then race swiftly downhill again into the much larger Gibbon Meadow. Here, it meanders through broad fields of sedge grass and fallen lodgepole pines. Once it leaves Gibbon Meadow it runs for almost ten miles steadily downhill through the sharply carved canyon it created long before man ever appeared on this planet. At one point, five miles above Madison Junction, it vaults eighty feet over Gibbon Falls, and then boils out from under the Falls until it reaches the last of the meadows only two miles from the junction where, merging with the Firehole River flowing north from Old Faithful, it forms the Madison.

My destination was always this last great meadow on the Gibbon. I would stroll through a campground alive with the pleasing racket of supper pans rattling on open stoves and fires, tent pins being driven, trailer jacks being set, and people talking relaxedly, as they always talk when jobs and responsibility are a thousand miles away and the wilderness is close at hand. Permeating and enriching the whole scene would be the odor of drifting pine smoke curling up from two hundred campfires.

Leaving the camping area, I would drop down the steep incline on which penstemon and blue bells and asters grew. At its base there was a rivulet which flowed through a small meadow and then into the Gibbon. Some thoughtful fisherman years ago had placed large rocks as stepping stones across it. I sought these out and then took the path through the meadow, gulping large masses of crisp sweet air full of the delicate scents of bluebells, lupines, shooting star, and sage. A clump of lodgepole pines stood at one point along the river in this meadow. They were the only survivors of a band of hardy pine cone seeds which had futilely attempted an invasion of the grassland years ago. Cut off from their compatriots which thronged densely on the borders of the meadow, they clung precariously to their tiny foothold.

Beyond the first meadow, lying in two pockets created by three consecutive lateral moraines, were two stagnant pools. The first, the one nearest the east meadow, was rust colored from the algae which grew in it. It was bordered by dense cattails, and a circle of lush green grass which attracted the elk herd which moved through the region periodically and the three old buffalo bulls which did not follow the herds to high country in the summer. Frequently, as I turned around the first moraine and came in sight of the rust pool, I would see the elk; sometimes, one of the bison would be there, a great dark brown hulk framed by the intensely green grass along the border of the pool. Occasionally, I circled south of them, but more often I took the north route through the timber above the second stagnant pool. It attracted

The first pool in the Gibbon Meadows

waterfowl and redwing blackbirds. Mallards were almost always on it. Sometimes Canada geese were there. Infrequently, the great blue heron of our valley appeared. When he saw me coming, he would fly to the river and move upstream, away from me, never letting me approach closer than an eighth of a mile from him. He was like a great grey shadow, restlessly and continuously running ahead of me. Eventually, I would come out on the ridge which divided the second stagnant pool from the great meadow below Terrace Spring.

This is a great sloping bowl, tilting three-quarters of a mile from the road near Terrace Spring down to the river which runs next to dense forest. On its north side it is bounded by the line of mountains which forms the north canyon wall of the Madison Valley. The sentinel of this range, rising 2,000 feet above the meadow, is Purple Mountain, a rounded peak marked in places by fields of purple scree. A line of heavy timber comprises the south and east limits of the meadow, the river channel being the only break in that dense forest. It emerges suddenly from the timber at the point where the south and east boundaries of the meadow meet. The high lateral moraine on which I stood is the meadow's west boundary. It reaches almost to the river, but the stream, evading obstacles with the gentle deftness characteristic of running water, races alongside the moraine then skirts the south end of it.

To the untrained eye and to the inexperienced fisherman going to the stream, the meadow seems an ordinary grassland. Only the fisherman familiar with it knows that, tranquil as it appears, the entire west end is full of wet deep muck. Hot springs flow from the hills above it and, resisting confinement, spread out near the river in a network of channels. The springs make that west portion of the meadow continuously wet and muddy. Pity the man forced to traverse that marsh in rapidly falling darkness! Out of the depths of his subconscious rushes that most sinister of all man's fears—quicksand! The thin line of safety through that portion of the meadow is the fisherman's trail along the banks of the stream. Here the ground is firm; even the river bottom is stable and solid. One can trust that. Only at the east end of the meadow is it safe to leave the margin of the river and traverse the grassland.

A man's love of any piece of water comes with his familiarity with it. In 1959 I could say, after four years of fishing the Gibbon, that I had married it. I knew its physiognomy and its moods as well as I knew my own. And I always followed a pattern in fishing the river here. I would begin by dropping down off the moraine, crossing the little causeway between it and an opposite moraine, and wading into the river some hundred yards below the point where I intended to do serious fishing. Here I occasionally caught one-pounders and smaller fish, but best of all I could test my casting rhythm, take note of any special hatches on the stream, and get a general impression of how the fish were feeding.

The Gibbon River, except in the largest and deepest of its holes, has the texture of an oil painting. Close to shore it runs swiftly under the undercut banks, swirling occasionally around clumps of grassy turf which lean precariously out over the water. Away from the banks its various currents mix and part and mix again, some flirting with the main channel and leaving it only to return. These constantly shifting surface currents reflect the light

So many pleasing choices

with varying intensity. Light and dark, glossy and rippled, the river never presents the same surface on any stretch of water for any length of time.

Like most meandering streams, the Gibbon is deepest at alternate banks as the main channel loops through the meadow. It runs bankfull and murky during the spring thaw. Then, in mid-June it clears and one can see the masses of algae that wave back and forth under the water like mermaid's tresses. And always there is the soft clear song of the river, the music of the water flowing over the long strands of algae, around the banks, past occasional boulders, and through log jams.

As I set myself for the first cast, I was confronted with so many pleasing choices that I scarcely knew where to put the first fly. Should it be along the opposite bank where the stream bed deepened and carved out a dark haven for the larger trout of the river? Or should I test first the pocket directly in front of me? At times I would begin by practicing for accuracy, spotting the fly first to one side then to the other of a clump of algae growing just beneath the surface of the water. Occasionally, a small fish would dart out from these clumps and pursue the fly floating by. If I saw it, and if it was too small, I jerked the fly from it before it could strike and hurt itself. Other times, when the fish were well-fed or particularly wary, they would dart from these strands of algae and follow the fly several yards downstream, their eyeballs right up next to it as they tried to determine whether the strange bug floating past them was a meal or a trap.

The browns, which predominated in this portion of the Gibbon, are great gluttons. I have heard stories from three fishermen, two of them verified by reliable eyewitnesses, of huge browns caught by fishermen who had hooked smaller fish and then found them pursued and swallowed by the great browns they eventually caught. I once found a brown which measured only ten inches—dead, from an attempt to swallow a fish approximately six inches long. It lay on the river bottom, the tail of the fish it had choked on still protruding from its mouth.

After I had warmed up, I followed the river around one big hairpin loop to where it swung north in a great curve through the meadow. From this turn there were about fifty yards of uninteresting water. It was about a foot and a half to two feet deep all the way across, and the clumps of algae in it were small and scattered. Only beneath the undercut banks was there any place for a trout of size to conceal itself, and few did in this stretch because so much better water was just upstream . . . in the sacred hundred yards.

Surveyed from above, the sacred hundred yards and a considerable portion of the river beyond it was like the gently curved back of a nude in a portrait. It began at a point where the river created a small island. The main channel was diverse and deep, but a small portion of the river ran, at a depth of a foot or so, around this tiny chunk of land no more than four or five feet wide and twenty feet long. As I faced the island, working upstream, the deepest water was on the opposite bank. Standing below the island, the sacred hundred before me, I felt richer than Solomon in his giddiest hour. A wealth of undercut banks, large algae clumps, deep holes, and riffles lay ahead, each full of possibilities for trout. Usually, I shot an exploratory cast to the opposite side of the river, hoping that one of the big fish supposed to be there might not see me and be tempted to come out from under the bank and strike my fly. Because the opposite bank was about four feet beyond my accurate casting range, however, I rarely placed a fly well there. One quiet evening, however, I succeeded in nuzzling a fly right up next to the bank, dropping it softly where it could float freely along the edge. Only dry fly fishermen appreciate how much different three or four inches make with big fish. Casts five or six inches from the bank get no response. This one, right at the bank, did. I can only account for it this way. The bank may be undercut as much as a foot and a half. The large fish lie far back in these pockets and may, therefore, have a limited view of the surface of the water. Perhaps the light refracts in such a way that objects next to the edge are visible; those farther out are not. Instinct operates, too. The trout learns in its way that food often drops off the bank into the water. It is more distrustful of objects away from the bank. This night I saw the small bubble a trout lipping the surface makes when it sucks in its food rather than attacks it. I set the hook into an awful weight. I was using playtyl leader tippets that year—I have never used them since—and the fly snapped off immediately. Whether my tippet was old and rotten and a fresh piece of nylon would have enabled me to hold the fish for one rush or not I will never know.

That experience made me wonder, however. Around the evening campfire the topic of the really big fish in the Gibbon often surfaced. Were there some huge browns there, or were the lunkers all in the Firehole and Madison Rivers? We had seen big browns caught in both of those streams, but I never recall a fly fisherman, particularly, coming in with a trophy fish from the Gibbon. I had at least to find out if they were there, so I went one morning about ten o'clock, an unusual hour for me to be fishing, but I chose the time because it had been suggested to me that the big fish might not feed in the evening, or that they might be spooked by fishermen who would more likely be on the stream late in the afternoon or evening. So I was out around ten o'clock working the opposite bank of the Gibbon from the side I usually

The sacred hundred yards

fished. It was difficult to get to because the river did not offer many good fording places—it was usually deep on one side or the other—and it was inconvenient to reach from the road. But I had made the effort and was tiptoeing into the sacred hundred yards, coming up behind a series of deep holes next to deeply undercut banks. The casting was very awkward for a right-handed person. I had to cast mostly over land and let only a small portion of line and leader hit the water and then retrieve it before it dragged. I did this several times without stirring up so much as a minnow. I was just concluding that the big fish of the Gibbon were a myth and preparing to retrieve my fly, which was floating nearly oppo-site me out in the stream, no more than two feet from the bank.

What I saw next was the kind of thing that gives fishermen with weak hearts their immediate passport to the promised land. Out from under the bank, virtually right under my feet, rushed a fish I can only describe as a monster. Remember: I had caught many eighteen inch browns and had had frequent opportunity to see them hovering in the water after being hooked. I had a very clear visual image of the size of such fish. The creature which came out from under the bank stood in relation to the eighteen-inch browns as a modern aircraft carrier does to a small de-stroyer. No. No. This is not a fisherman's story. I do not exaggerate. This was something unlike anything I had ever caught or seen in the Gibbon. My God, this was a big fish. Apparently, it had seen my fly float by and had come out looking for it, exposed, nervous, and moving feverishly as it sought out the fly. This all happened so fast that I didn't even have time to get down in the grass so the fish would not see me. It picked me up and spooked immediately, into the deep recesses of the stream.

Well, could I have held that fish if I had hooked it? I really doubt it. It would have taken the fly down in a hurry, and if it had gotten tangled up in the algae below, I would have had no chance. More than likely, it would have snapped off the leader. My only chance would have been to hold it for one big rush and then work it back to some shallow water where I could watch it dart back and forth across the stream and still keep it from getting tangled up in something. That fish, and a big rainbow I hooked in the Gallatin and another big rainbow which snapped off my fly in the Bechler, were the closest I ever came to catching something that one mounts on the wall. But my question had been answered. There were big browns in the Gibbon. I had seen one no more than ten feet away, and it was no ordinary fish. This one was a *Field and Stream* special.

In a typical Gibbon evening, however, I would be on the opposite side and would only tantalize myself with those deep holes along the opposite bank. Then I would turn to the water ahead. From the main channel on the opposite side to the shallow side on which I stood, the river was a blend of many currents which occasionally swelled above the surface of the water like blood vessels on the back of a human hand. Forming a ridge across these currents was a barely perceptible riffle. Near sunset, when it was still quite light, the fish used to move out along this riffle and watch for food. Because of the texture of the water, it was not easy to distinguish air bubbles breaking on the surface from trout lipping it. I always looked carefully for bubbles appearing repeatedly but at irregular time intervals. These would tell me where particular fish were feeding. Usually, I found two or three big browns working three to six feet from the bank. I would follow the particular current I wanted, drop the fly in it about a foot above the riffle—this would give the fish time enough to see it but not time enough to recognize it as a phony—and wait. It took me three years of fishing to see the tiny bubble which indicated a strike. And I never had much time. A trout has only to close on an artificial fly to discover that it is false. In that second, the fisherman has to react. There is a particular pleasure in hooking a fish with a dry fly. It consists of the perfect cast, the perfect float, the strike, and a quick setting of the hook into something solid. This is like hitting a baseball in the "sweet" part of the bat. And unless you hook a real tiger, the battle is over when you set the hook.

From this riffle I frequently took eighteen-inch browns. In the Gibbon, these were considered excellent fish. They would make a first big rush for cover, usually a moss bed in the middle of the stream. If they got there too quickly and burrowed in, I could not reach them because the water was too deep. If they ran downstream, as many did, I had them because they would burrow into algae in water only two feet deep. I would keep tension, wade down to the fish, and nudge them out of hiding. Then I would play them until netting. I carried a ruler to measure them, after which I would remove the hook gently, right them in the water until they had their strength back, and watch them dart away. The big ones tired quickly if played on considerable tension. Frequently, after I had released them, they would hover in the stream where I could have reached down and patted them while they rested. Some were dazed by the struggle; they would act like birds hypnotized by a snake. Then, suddenly out of shock, they would become aware that they were exposed and unprotected and would dart swiftly into the deep gloom of a large hole or into some distant moss bed.

After I had worked the riffle at the point of the island, I would move upstream, usually casting very close to the edge of the island. I rarely caught any fish at this point. Perhaps they were alerted by the disturbance at the riffle. Sometimes, when I was just playing or practicing, I would cast into the shallow channel of the stream around the island. Once or twice I caught small fish at this point. Then I waded through the river to the mainland again moving along the path next to the river.

If Pat had come with me, I would look up to the top of the moraine above me to see if she were all right. At such moments I realized how thoroughly insulating and absorbing the river was. The Gibbon, because of its cross currents, undercut banks, pockets, and whirlpools, created its own music. Flowing in infinite patterns, like the figure skater on ice, it created a symphony of water sounds. This music was the peaceful rush of life itself. I always felt inescapably and joyfully involved in it. Man in the twentieth century, bullied by the noises of cars, trucks, buses, airplanes, bulldozers, jackhammers, sirens, and shouting humans, needs to be bathed in the soothing sounds of a river in the wilderness. They take him out of an ugly world which he has created into the elemental world from which he emerged but now has almost forgotten. Here he acquires perspective again on his own aspirations and frustrations. I never understood what Wordsworth meant by "hearing the mighty waters roll" until I stood beside the Gibbon and lost myself in the fullness and variety of its music.

Upstream from the riffle at the island lay a very deep pool, so deep that I was unable to see the bottom of it. I believe some whitefish had worked their way upstream from the Madison River and settled in this particular pool. There was always a great deal of activity at it, but these fish were extremely difficult to catch. They have the round sucker mouth and are difficult to hook even when they take a fly. Rainbows frequented this pool, also. I can see them yet, three to four feet above the water, their tails bent under them from the furious effort of the leap and the attempt to throw the hook. For me, one good tussle with a jumping rainbow was worth a whole evening of frustration with whitefish.

Still farther upstream lay an even deeper pool, one difficult to reach and hard to fish. It was fed by the largest of the channels coming off Terrace Spring. I had to leave the path at the river's edge and walk through the muck a short distance to reach a point

For several miles the Gibbon wanders through Virginia Meadows

where it was feasible to ford this channel. And when I got back to the river, I was upon the deep pool and could not get a completely favorable casting angle on it. I believed that very large fish also inhabited this pool. They probably got their food from two sources: insects which fall into the runoff channels of Terrace Spring, are killed immediately by the heat of the water, and are carried down into the great pool in the river; and numerous small fish in the stream. The fish in the pool were among the wariest along the Gibbon. There were many times when a great deal of feeding going on at the surface would almost stop after I began to cast into it.

The second deep pool was the end of the sacred hundred yards for me. There was interesting fishing on upstream, but it was always anticlimactic. Because of this I frequently quit at the second pool, and, if time permitted, paused for awhile and perused the river or the meadow. There was always something to refresh the eye. Perhaps it was the sight of the industrious muskrat swimming quietly along the opposite bank, reasonably certain that I intended no harm to him but cautiously watching to be sure. If the blue heron was still visible, he would be perched on the piece of driftwood in the middle of the stream three hundred yards away, looking for all the world like a broken dead limb of the trunk on which he was standing. Perhaps the bison had moved into the east end of the meadow. The elk might be crossing it, coming out of the woods on the opposite side and preparing to ford the stream, and on occasion, a mule deer or coyote would stroll through taking a long puzzled look at the intruder in their world.

On August 3, 1973, I dropped a fly into the sacred hundred yards of the Gibbon for the first time in ten years. I did so with great apprehension. Twice during the latter 1960s, I had been told, a gasoline truck had overturned near Elk Park and spilled its poison into the river. Fishing since then, said some, had never been the same. I wonder. That afternoon I caught and released four browns and two rainbows, none large but all of respectable size. And fishing on the Gibbon had always been poorest for me in August. Perhaps, I thought, the magic of the sacred hundred still exists. Perhaps this river has conquered even the foulest of man's pollutants. I certainly hope so.

The day itself was cloudy, and a fine rain began to fall in the late afternoon, causing me to leave the stream and return to my car. But it could not wash away my memories of those perfect evenings years ago when darkness would just begin to steal across the meadow. Above, the great dome of heaven would still be bright with the light of the setting sun. In perfect peace I would pause to rest and listen to the feeding trout, the croaking frogs, the splash of the muskrat, and the musical swish of the water weaving its endless surface patterns as it flowed by. At such times I felt as if I stood alone in the open hand of God.

16

Jacobi's Campfire

IN THE LAST two decades the flood of campers pouring into Yellowstone has forced the National Park Service to set strict limits on the amount of time campers can stay in a particular place. Check in and check out times are rigorously observed and enforced. The lax management policies of earlier years have been supplanted by this new efficiency. My wife and I are grateful, however, for an era in which campgrounds were not so well managed. And because it was not adjacent to a store, lodge, hotel, or gas station and hence not so crowded as other camps, Madison Campground was a model of this earlier inefficiency. It was also a very friendly place. Homesteaders came there each year, settled in their favorite spots, and camped most of the summer. Thus Madison Campground was almost a community, a pleasing and interesting mix of old residents and transients.

Our favorites among the old residents were the Jacobi family of Clinton, Iowa. Looking back through the years, I can see the old campground now, in my mind's eye, as plainly as if we were going to Jacobi's campfire tonight. The sun has long since dropped behind Purple Mountain, and I have left the sacramental peace of the Gibbon River and returned to our cabin to take off my fishing gear and put on warmer clothing; the nights in Yellowstone are always cool. By now the campground glows with the light of hundreds of lodgepole pine fragments which burn in irregularly dispersed campsites, themselves little pools of warmth and brightness shutting out the hostile and pervasive darkness of the wilderness. Pat and I pass quietly by Eichman's trailer, slip under the wire circling the campground, and walk past Daughenbaugh's big fire to the road. Then we pass through the trees and along the north bank above the river to Jacobi's campfire.

The fire is blazing in the pit Freddy dug, almost the first chore he performed when the Jacobis arrived back in the Park this summer. It has large rounded boulders circling it, many of them from the river. Freddy chose them in preference to the jagged dusty chunks of unpolished rhyolite which lie all around the campground. Two or three large sections of pine blaze in the pit. The first of these glows underneath, occasional blue flame mixing with the orange and yellow tongues of fire which dart out from beneath it. The odor of pine smoke is thick because the light wind, variable as usual, pushes the smoke first this way, now that, causing an almost constant repetition of the oldest of campfire aphorisms: smoke follows beauty. We are all beautiful this evening.

Fred and Dorothy Fischer are there along with daughter Carol, Freddy's current love interest. Skeets and Mary Emery, their daughter Mary Edith, son-in-law Charles Parks, and their son, little Charles Lee, sit near the Fischers. Arlene bustles about getting chairs and stools, Cathie and Fred are helping, and Al pokes at the fire, a broad grin upon his face. We have come up during a lull, but it is evident that there is extra celebrating tonight. Our good friends are animated by the presence of a grizzled bronze little man who sits between Al and Fred Fischer, his shoulders hunched toward the fire. Jack Horner is back.

There is hardly a person among the regular campers at Madison Junction who does not know Jack Horner. Among other

At Jacobi's campfire

things, he is the finest fly caster any of us have ever seen. A charter member and frequent champion caster of San Francisco's famed Golden Gate Angling and Casting Club, he has quit competing because he no longer has the time or interest to practice with the special equipment which tournament casting requires. Besides, he is a fisherman first and a caster second. He uses his remarkable gifts to pursue the wary trout of the Madison, Gibbon, and Firehole Rivers. Running water is the book that Jack reads best. Although he can show us how to cast—he is, in fact, an excellent teacher, and he has educated half of us who sit at the campfire—he cannot tell us all he sees in a trout stream because his sharp blue eyes have been looking at trout streams for so many years that they see by instinct more than he consciously knows. There is hardly a bubble, a boulder splitting the current of a stream, or an eddy along half-submerged driftwood or undercut bank that does not tell Jack something about the location of trout in any stream. He abjures the wet fly, calling it bait, and takes fish consistently with a dry fly despite the fact that fish feed on the top only about fifteen percent of the time. Last year, the day Jack came in, camp fishermen were complaining that nothing was hitting. Jack said he was going out anyway to get fish for supper. One man, in particular, kept insisting that there was no point in going out. Larry and Bill Wanlass offered a ten to one wager to him that Jack would get a limit. But they could not get him to take the bet. In half an hour Jack was back with four fish, one short of the limit, but enough for his supper.

He has done this for years. He fishes behind us when he is teaching us, and he catches trout in places where we have not even gotten a rise. He fishes banks, riffles, pools, all places where the trout lie, and he brings them to the surface. There is something about the way he sets the fly on the water. It must look to a trout like some irresistibly tantalizing insect fallen by mistake within its reach. I have seen Jack catch fish in all kinds of places in all kinds of weather, even during heavy rain when I could not distinguish the pits made by the raindrops from the circles of trout dimpling the water as they fed.

Those of us who know him are awed by his fishing skill. I think of an afternoon in 1955 when Jack took my stiff, three-piece, $8.50 rod, an HCH line, a $1.50 reel, and a white fly from which the barb had been cut and gave me my first casting lesson. Jack had told me to use the white fly because it would be easy to see. I was to practice casting at targets: a clump of grass on an opposite bank, a lily pad, a rock projecting above the surface of the water, a piece of driftwood, an algae bed. The stream had a hundred targets, and I would not be troubled by fish striking at *that* fly. To demonstrate, Jack let out line and began casting, shooting the back cast high and the forward cast out over the water like a carpet unrolling. It was Heifetz drawing beautiful sounds from a $25.00 violin. He indicated a target along the opposite bank and laid the fly on it with grace and ease. And a fish rose and struck at the fly! Nothing that fish fed on there looked remotely like that ridiculous fly. But Jack had dropped it on the surface in such a perfect imitation of an insect alighting that the fish had come up. No other fisherman in the campground could have done that, and some were among the finest in the country.

Jack is the complete fly fisherman. In his jeep are the sacks, drawers, and boxes which hold the incredible variety of his raw materials. Although his fingers are thick and stubby, they can handle tiny number 16 hooks, thread, and feathers with the dexterity of Rumpelstiltskin spinning the straw into gold. I have seen him read a hatch, go to his truck and reproduce it, then return to the stream the next evening and catch and release fish until weary.

Around the campfire we see another man. By trade he is an elevator mechanic, one of the best in San Francisco. He is undoubtedly the most eccentric of the group. From November until June he works steadily at his job, saving his money for the summer. Abruptly, sometime in June, he decides that it is time to leave 51 Grattan Street and go in search of the high trout streams of Colorado, Wyoming, Montana, and British Columbia. In November he will return to his job, get a thirty-minute tongue lashing from his employer and a final, "Go get your tools you bastard." And he will diligently make money for the company until the next June when peremptorily he will again decide that it is time to seek out the mountain fastnesses.

As intimately as we know him, Jack Horner is something of a mystery. All we have ever learned is that he grew up in New Jersey. I have wondered if he perhaps worked in the dark, dirty, stultifying atmosphere of coal mines. We do know that he served in World War I and then returned to the States, but not to the life he knew before he went overseas. Jack's odyssey took him progressively across the United States until he reached California. In San Francisco he settled and learned his trade. But the fishing. How did he become a fisherman, particularly a dry fly purist?

"One time I took a watch to get it fixed, and I sez to the watchmaker, I sez, what are all those beautiful little things tied to fish hooks you got there? He sez they're flies to catch trout. I sez, 'You can catch fish with those? How do you make them?' And he showed me how to make one pattern and I went home and tied and re-tied that one pattern for a week an a half, till I got it right. And once I learned to tie flies, I started to learn the rest. It took time."

For Jack, the fly, the rod, eventually the cast, and finally the stream were the keys to a quality of life which he sought and achieved. Perhaps locked in his memory are images of the dust, dirt, and dankness of coal mines and a solemn resolution never to be trapped in that life. The Jack Horner we know is uncommonly sensitive to the beauty of mountain streams, to the life that lives in and along them, to the sheer exhilaration of existence in the clean purifying air of the high altitudes.

He is the Marco Polo of our campfire circle—a traveler into strange lands among strange people.

"So I walks up to the one who's peelin' the potatoes—he has a mound in front of 'im like a mole trows up—and I sez to'm, I sez, 'Say mister, that's a lot of potatoes. You expectin' more in your party?' He sez, 'No, we'll eat all these in the morning.' So help me God, there must have been enough potatoes for six people there!"

Fred Fischer interrupts: "But Jack, is that all they had for breakfast?"

"Oh, no. Wait'll yaz hear the rest. They had cases and cases of beer, see. *My God* they had beer! Every morning, when their alarm went off, they'd reach outta their sleeping bags and have a beer for an eye-opener. Then they'd get up, fry all those potatoes, and make their breakfast. They even had beer for a nightcap!"

Al: "Say Jack, did you say those guy were San Franciscans you know?"

"No, I didn't say that! I see enough people from Sanrancisco witout addn' them to the bunch. Sometimes I wish I wouldn't. You see, I have a number of good friends up in British Columbia —very nice people—and last summer one of them gave me a fifth of Scotch, very choice stuff, as a present. Well, I put it on the seat beside me, but I never touched it." At this point Jack gets some ribbing, but it is in good fun. "So, I'm driving along one of the roads and my back tire feels like it's flat, see. I stop the truck, hop out to check, and who comes up behind me but my next door neighbor and his kids. And that Scotch is lyin' on the front seat like I'm tipplin' all along the road. Very embarrassin.' You see, those children think well of me. . ." Jack is quite serious at this point. He has always been fond of children, enjoys their admiration, and is extremely conscious of the example he sets.

Skeets wants to know why Jack never takes a net when he goes fishing. There is a story here, too. Hustling back to camp through the high bush country of British Columbia years ago, in an area crisscrossed by the trails of the big grizzlies, Jack had been whomped in the rear. "My god, I was scared! I almost leaped over one of them bushes. Then I found out the net had caught on a bush and stretched and stretched until it let go and popped me."

"I was so mad I trew the goddamned net in the river! Next day a friend of mine sez, 'Say, Horner, I found this net in the river last night. This your net?' I sez, 'Take that goddamned thing and trow it out of my sight! I never want to see it again!' "

It is the same every year with some innovations. In a more serious vein he tells us about this year's crop of wealthy businessmen and politicians from California who are coming to Yellowstone to fish with him on the Gallatin River. Jack's talk of hobnobbing with the wealthy would probably seem like extravagant boasting to those who do not know him. But we have given directions many times to the Lincoln Continentals and Cadillacs which have come into Madison Campground looking for the little man in his undershirt sitting at the back of his truck making flies, feeding green grapes to the western tanagers, or cooking his supper on his picnic table. In every respect he is an individual. In the best sense of the term, he is "unique."

We never know for sure when Jack will come to Yellowstone. Each summer, *the* June question is, "Is Jack back?" It is on the lips of his friends from California who have preceded him, veteran campers, and the members of Jacobi's campfire circle, his closest friends at Madison. Everyday we look for the jeep. Suddenly, he is there, as he is tonight, and before long we will all feel that last summer is this summer and Jack has been with us all the time.

Of all the people who make up the regular circle at Jacobi's campfire none seems so enigmatic to me as Fred Fischer. I talk with him daily; I fish with him; I pass many an hour by the campfire near him; yet, I do not know Fred at all. And I think that is the way Fred wants it. Fred is a private person. He enjoys his friends, the quiet moments beside the campfire, the pursuit of trout in Yellowstone streams; but he lives a life within himself. It is not that he wishes to hide anything from us. But he has reservoirs of quiet deep within him.

Fred is an engineer but says very little about his work or the people connected with it. And I would be at a complete loss to say what Fred thinks about fundamental issues of living. I do not know whether or not he believes in God. I have no idea who he votes for. I do not know what he thinks of other professions, mine for example. I do not know what kind of people he admires or despises. I do not know how he would define love—of wife, child, or friend. I believe Fred thinks about these things, but they are part of his private meditations which he simply does not care to share with the rest of the world. Perhaps he is still working them out.

Fred is a listener. I have seen his face light up with unrestrained pleasure while Jack Horner, deep in British Columbia, extricates himself from the kind of situation only Jack can get into. I have seen a sudden flash of intensity, like a deep underground river bursting to the surface, erupt through Fred's whole being when he hooks a mighty fish and then loses it as a weak leader snaps.

Conversation with Fred almost always turns on topics of the day. He will talk about the major league pennant races, why Ingemar Johannsen will beat Floyd Patterson, and whether Al Nelson is a better fisherman than Jack. Occasionally, he will talk about rangers, tourists, and our campfire friends, but never derogatorily. Usually, he has on his mind a point of information, neutral in its import. But most of the time, around Jacobi's campfire, Fred is a listener.

Fred's wife, Dorothy, is, like me, a talker. Besides being out-going, she is a pleasant person to look at. She is not a Mrs. America, and she does not think of herself as one. But unlike some women who find putting on jeans an occasion for neglect-ing everything else—neatness, cleanliness, tasteful dress—Dorothy Fischer grooms herself well, even in the wilderness. She is like a well tended garden, a cool and neatly arranged living room. I think she could walk into a church in levis and pass muster. She must look at herself in the mirror of a morning and think seriously about her obligation to the people who will have to look at *her* that day. Perhaps she feels that she owes the world at least a clean face, combed hair, moderate lipstick, clean clothes, and a pleasant disposition. In the vacation lands of the West such people are a blessing.

The Emerys and the Parks who sit next to Dorothy and Fred are a unique family group. They are father, mother, daughter, son-in-law and grandson living amicably together in a trailer. At least, that is how it appears to the rest of us. It is remarkable be-cause of the situation and all its possibilities for friction. One would think life in their trailer would be tense. Perhaps it is at times. But these are socially mature people. They settle their problems privately, not in public. I have thought often about these good friends and their unique family life, and I wonder how they manage to live so well together.

The key to their family life must be the head of the Emery household, Marion Emery if you know him formally, Skeets, if you know him as we do. Skeets is probably in his late forties or early fifties, a wide, powerfully built man with a full head of iron grey hair and frank, open features. Emotionally, he is the rock of this family. He has unquestioned authority, but he never abuses it. He has infinite patience, infinite strength, infinite persistence. He is not ruffled by the trivia of everyday living. As serene as the mountains among which he has always loved to fish, he accepts life as it is given to him, never complaining about suffering nor becoming excessively overcome by immediate joy.

Skeets grew up in Paducah, Kentucky, where he acquired the

fine rich accent of the genteel South. When he was young, he tried his hand at an assortment of vocations. At one time he was a kind of carnival strong man, allowing cars to be driven over him. He told Pat and me, rather matter of factly with just the suggestion of a smile, that the trick was not at all difficult. The only time he ever experienced any discomfiture occurred when a car stopped while still on top of him.

He gave up this line of work for boxing, but after winning a few fights among pugilists of lesser skill, he got popped sharply in the nose once and decided that there was a still better way of earning a living. Eventually, he found it, in the bottle gas business, and after he had made enough money in it to get out, he moved west to Arizona. The Emerys and Parks now live in Tempe, where they operate two garages. But money making, "bidness" as Skeets calls it, is, though necessary, peripheral to the real business of living. Hunting, fishing, camping, talking leisurely around a campfire, watching over his brood—these are the important activities of life for Skeets.

The second man of this family is Charles Park, husband of Mary Edith. His acceptance into the Emery family has been so complete that it is hard to imagine him ever not being part of it. He was their principal assistant in the bottle gas business, at which time be began courting Mary Edith. In any new ventures the family tries, they will depend upon Charles for significant help. But like Fred Fischer, he is a private person. Charles lives for this day. Only a few moments of his past does he ever resurrect. Some have to do with his courtship of Mary Edith, others with the day he hit a softball farther than anyone else in Paducah. The tape-measure home run was a large moment in a past he has chosen largely to forget. He is too content in the present.

Because he is a man of action, Charles's language is simple, forceful, and direct. For example, we learn that he has just been to Mammoth this afternoon. There he stopped in the hotel barbershop for a hair cut, but Charles was not thrilled with the barber's expertise.

"He snipped a little bit up front; then he snipped a little bit on the sides. And it looked god awful. 'That's all,' he says. 'That's all?' *I* say. 'Whaddayou mean that's all? Man, you ain't even begun! You call *this* a hair cut? You oughta be shearin' sheep! I say I want a haircut!'"

"Well, Charles. Then what happened? The barber get mad?"

"Oh, he got mad all right. But I sat there because I wanted a haircut, and he gave me a haircut. A poor job, too. That old rummy couldn't hold a job in town for a minute. And he comes up here and tries to hold me up. I could do a sight better myself and I never been to barber collidge." A moment in the limelight, then Charles drifts out of it. He will listen the rest of the evening.

Mary is wife, mother, and grandmother for this family. She fusses around them like a biddy hen, but she tends to their needs with spontaneous love and unrestrained affection. She is totally involved in the unspectacular but vital essentials of living: doing that which must always be done around the home and creating about her an atmosphere of order and emotional stability that anchors the family. Her family loves her unrestrainedly, sometimes amusedly, but always knowing that without her a vital part of their lives would be missing and irreplaceable. Pat and I think of her as our Yellowstone grandmother. I do not recall ever being ill at ease around Mary. Neither does Pat. And for Pat, who is ill at ease around a great many people, this is the ultimate tribute to the friendly charm and grace of a great southern lady.

Skeets wanted a son, Mary Edith tells us, but when she appeared, he simply accepted the situation and taught her to enjoy many of the activities men enjoy. She can and does fish, hike, play ball, and work with a man's energy and competence. She has, in short, all the freedom and the aptitudes of today's liberated woman. But she is also fond of stylish clothes, a special compliment, of any of the considerations whereby men defer to women. She has complete domestic competence as well as the skills any modern woman needs to assert her independence.

There are a number of things many modern women could learn from Mary Edith. The most important is that she is comfortable being a woman. The men around her have never treated her chauvinistically, either by deferring to her in annoying obsequious ways, or by treating her as a second-class citizen. When we have hiked and fished together, I have noticed that Charles and Skeets assume, as a matter of course, that she will hold her own, which she does, of course. I suspect that in the family businesses she is expected to and does indeed demonstrate the same kind of competence. Yet I have never seen Mary Edith brazenly asserting her "right" to be equal to men. She *is* equal, in every respect, and none of those close to her make a big deal about it.

Charles Lee is the sole heir. A blond, blue-eyed, fair-skinned child, he has every reason to be spoiled but is not. Mixed with the shower of attention and admiration which his parents and grandparents lavish upon him is a leaven of discipline. Consequently, he is a very interesting and very pleasant child to be around. Because he is at the age when jet pilots, firemen, and rangers are the important people of the world, he informs his friends at school that he knows a ranger in Yellowstone who is not just a friend but a "personal" friend.

Already, he is a diplomat. In Mammoth Museum one day he called my attention to a colored drawing of geological strata. He did not really understand it, but he was fascinated by the rainbow of colors. Looking at it, I remarked that it contained red, my favorite color. Immediately, I realized that my five-year-old friend was mulling over a serious problem. Red was *not* his favorite color, but how could he preserve his integrity and still tell me this without injuring my feelings?

"Well, red is my favorite color, too. And blue is my favorite color. And green is my favorite color. But blue is my *most* favorite color."

The Jacobis. Because of them we are here. Mostly, it is because of Arlene. It is she who draws us to the campfire, and we stay because of our affection for the whole family. But who among us can suspect that very soon one will be gone and the rest of the family, now living in Clinton, Iowa, will be scattered from Ohio to California with only memories of these cool nights above the Gibbon River in Madison Campground?

There are five Jacobis: Al, Arlene, Freddy, Cathie, and Carol. Like a number of Homesteaders in Madison Campground, the Jacobis stay for a large portion of the summer. Usually, they leave during July to observe the thirty-day limit on camping. But it is a regulation rarely enforced. Al has to return to Clinton to keep up his dental practice. The family sometimes goes to California during that time. In August Al comes back and the family reassembles. He wants a last bit of fishing and relaxing before resigning himself to the long winter.

Of the three Jacobi children we know Carol least well. Arlene says that Carol has no particular love of camping in the mountains nor of the recreations the great wilderness of the West affords, so she stays in Clinton, watched over by the neighbors. Carol, at this time, is not particularly anxious to go to college. She is graduating from high school and is prepared to marry her high school sweetheart and settle down to a happy life of raising children and keeping house. But Arlene and Al think she should at least experience college before she makes such a momentous decision. Carol has agreed, after a family conference in which she assures them that it will make no difference in her plans, to attend the University of Iowa for one year. But Arlene knows how much the university will change Carol. And it does. She will go four years, take her degree, and marry a chemist. But that is yet to be.

The first Jacobi I met was Cathie. On mother's prompting she came to the museum the first day I worked there to evaluate "the new ranger." She was nine years old at that time, blond, blue-eyed (it seems that all the Yellowstone children I knew had blond hair and blue eyes) and intensely talkative. I knew her only as one of two or three campground children who took special pleasure in visiting with the rangers. When you are that age, lifemanship is primarily a game of knowing on a familiar basis people your immediate friends are awed by. Cathie was two or three jumps ahead of the rest. She talked to me while I swept the floor, cleaned the glass in the display cases, emptied the trash

can, and set the museum in order. Listening to her, I began to recall what it had been like to be a fourth grader. "Old lady _____"
was a tyrant. She kept the whole class after school until "we are
all quiet for one minute." (This done with appropriate mimicking
of the teacher's voice.) How irritating it was to have her say,
"Catherine, I expected more from *you*" just because she was
chewing gum or talking to Billy, or Davie, or Phil or somebody
else. And why was whispering such a crime? And there were the
boy friends on the street who fought with each other over who
walked her to school. Boy friends at this age were not yet
romantic interests. But just what were they? Mostly, they were
boys who thought her very pretty and wanted to hold her hand.

   Then there was the family. Mom and Dad were too bossy.
Brother was a pain in the neck and why did he get to do things
she didn't? Then, she supposed he was a good guy after all. But
her big sister, Carol! A nine-year-old's exclamations followed by
a great silence are pregnant with meaning, but I suspect the nine-
year-old is not exactly sure what that meaning is anymore than
you are.

   Cathie entertained me thoroughly, and she gave her mother
and the rest of the family detailed reports on the new ranger. The
reports must have been favorable because we were included in
the Jacobi's campfire by the end of the summer. Cathie now
divides her time between "museum duty" (other new rangers
come and go and someone must report to the family), riding the
garbage truck with Bill and Larry, swimming in the river near the
campground or in the Firehole some three miles upstream from
the junction, and puttering around their camp. She is a most
interesting child—somewhat spoiled but intellectually advanced
for her years. She seems happy and content with life as it is. But
in the immediate future lies a shattering blow to the present
coherence and stability of her life.

   The blow will strike brother Fred still harder. As we know
him, he is a young teenager confused by what he is and what he
wants to be. He would like, for his father's sake, to be the outstanding athlete his father was. But Freddy lacks the quickness,

dexterity, and aggressiveness which made his father excel. Arlene complains that Al has been too competitive with Freddy, that he not given him the confidence he needs to excel. I do not know.

Freddy does have a physical skill for which his father praises him continuously: the softest fly casting touch of all Jack Horner's Yellowstone pupils. Jack taught Freddy to cast at an age when the rest of us learn to play baseball. It is therefore natural to him, and he has caught many fish, one of them a twenty-four inch, three and one-half pound brown. Al catches more fish than Fred simply because he is on the water more. But Fred is the better caster, and his father is the first to admit it.

For Fred life in Yellowstone has pleasing variety. He is not so tied down as little sister. He fishes, swims, and visits around the campground as he pleases. And he has time for romance. The romantic object is the Fischer's youngest daughter, Carol, a young lady of extremely favorable features and proportions. Like most teenage love affairs, this one waxes hot and cold, seems ever so much more serious to those involved than it is, and eventually runs its course. Both will grow up to marry other persons in remote places and reflect, occasionally, with gentle amusement, on the sunny mellow Yellowstone summers and the intensity of teenage passion. All our lives would be poorer without such memories.

Arlene is the nerve center of the Jacobi family. She directs operations around the Jacobi camp, keeping the men busy with outside chores—gathering and chopping wood, procuring water, cleaning up the camp—and maintaining the interior of their trailer herself. She knows what is going on in every part of the campground. On any given day she can tell you what bears have hit what campsites, what couples have been fighting (she is mother confessor for some of the unhappy wives among the permanent campers), what the government has done now about the camping limit, irresponsible rangers, and which groups of campers were setting off firecrackers last night. She is also a person of great contrasts. In Yellowstone she bustles about in blue jeans like a German *hausfrau*; in Clinton when she is receiving

company, even Yellowstone hoboes like Pat and me, she appears
almost regal in a dress and high heels. She complains about men
who continually want to dominate her, particularly Al, but she
depends on him immensely for decisions in crises. More than any
other member of the family, Arlene is responsible for Jacobi's
campfire. She invites newcomers, creates the informal and relaxed environment around them, and maintains correspondence
with those of us close to the family. She was a Godsend for Pat,
who, naturally reserved, found herself alone except for me, in
Yellowstone. She needed the company of women in those years,
and she never would have met the Emerys or the Fischers without the assistance of Arlene Jacobi.

Arlene has constructed a fairly contented life for herself
around her worries: Al's attempt to dominate her (we sometimes
see it the other way and tease her gently), Carol's early assertion
of independence, Freddy's lack of self-confidence and love affair,
and Cathie's inclination to be younger than she is. There is one
worry she does not want, but it is the most serious one of all: her
mother's illness. Relatives chide her about not doing her share to
help—she is doing more than any of them, as Al continually tells
her—and give her feelings of guilt she cannot repress. It is to be
the principal anxiety for her in the last year of Al's life; too late
she will discover that she has had more urgent and pressing problems right at home. But life is full of shifts and turns like that.

Al Jacobi is a short, balding, blocky man who does everything
with fierce intensity. He makes his living at dentistry in Clinton,
but he makes his life around the campfire and along the quiet
streams of Yellowstone Park. He savors each day of his life, perhaps because he knows, as we do not, that death is now his most
persistent creditor. Outside his family and Yellowstone Park, his
principal interests in life are the Detroit Tigers and Iowa University's athletic teams. These are years when Detroit makes a good
opening run then fades in mid-season before the hated New
York Yankees. But Iowa is in its glory. One great basketball
team has won two Big Ten championships and finished second in
the NCAA tournament, losing only to San Francisco and Bill

Russell. Forrest Evashevski's football teams are putting together two Big Ten titles and subsequent successful trips to the Rose Bowl. Quarterback of one of these teams is Kenny Ploen from Clinton. Michigan is still a problem, but the Hawkeyes have recently beaten Woody Hayes and Ohio State, a triumph Al savors.

In Yellowstone Al has three passions: big brown trout hiding beneath the undercut banks of the streams, weak leaders, and California fishermen (Jack Horner excepted). In his relentless pursuit of the big browns he has been to most of the good spots on the Madison, Firehole, and Gibbon Rivers. On the upper Firehole, he has taken a trophy fish. Like me, however, he knows best and returns most often to the sacred hundred yards of the Gibbon. He has caught more large fish in a short space of time there than anywhere else in Yellowstone.

Weak leaders are a curse to him. The movement of a large trout toward his freely floating fly is a moment of excruciating tension and excitement for Al. Sometimes the anxiety is too great, his joy at fooling a fish into striking too intense, and he sets the hook too hard. Nothing makes him so crestfallen as the limpness in a line which a second before vibrated with energy of a mighty trout. Al has known that feeling many times, as have all fly fishermen, but he goes back to the streams again and again. The challenge is always there, and he always accepts it. He will do this until he dies.

California fishermen he scorns and degrades primarily because they bring their elbow to elbow fishing manners to the much less crowded fly streams of Yellowstone Park. He remembers vividly one morning when he, Fred Fischer, and I had gone down the Madison River to try our luck. After setting our gear in order we divided. Fred went upstream, Al stayed in the middle, and I went downstream. All of us were far enough apart that we could not see one another. I had little luck, so I was moving upstream and was within a hundred yards of Al when I heard him shouting and sputtering like a sizzling firecracker. When I reached Al, he was storming across the river. Two fishermen nearby were moving upstream somewhat chastened. They had waded into the river virtually on top of him, I learned, just as he was working on a big brown, and he had not been thrilled with their company.

"What's the big idea dropping into the stream right on top of me? And there's a man below and one above. Five thousand miles of stream in Yellowstone Park and you gotta drop in right between three men. You must be from California!" The fishermen denied this. "Aw, c'mon! Nobody else but California fishermen would pull a stunt like that! You guys are so used to standing elbow to elbow you think everybody else fishes the same way! Well, in Yellowstone we got more room and better manners!" Al muttered some more and stalked out of the water and up the bank.

He cooled off soon, but he was sure those men had to be from California. We walked along the bank of the river, through the trees, and out to the pull-off where we had parked our car. There, twenty yards in front was the only other car in the area; it had a California license plate. "I knew it! I knew it!" Al was exuberant. He slapped his thigh and kept telling Fred and me all the way back to Madison Junction how he knew those guys had to be from California. That story lasted him through many fishing trips and a number of campfires.

Al's ability to predict behavior was one of his great pleasures in life. Surprising to me was his attention to the speech habits and mannerisms of many of us around him. This came out when Fred Fischer, Al, and I went down the Madison with another man, one who, for the sake of this story, will remain B. A. Loney. Now B. A. had a reputation for gilding the lily. His twelve-inch fish had a way of growing, like Falstaff's assailants in the dark, to fourteen, then seventeen, and even occasionally nineteen inches. When he described the size and number of fish he had caught on any one expedition, we always did some mental deriving of square roots to approximate the truth. This particular day we had no sooner begun fishing than a cold drizzling rain set in. It was clearly not to be a shower. It was going to be an all-day affair, and it would be numbing cold. I never enjoyed fishing in such weather, so I reeled in my line and went back to the car. Soon Al and Fred joined me. But B. A. was still out on the stream. We watched him catch and net one fish.

"That does it," said Al. "Now watch. When Loney gets here, he'll say, 'What's the matter with you fair weather fishermen? I was having a ball!' " We tooted the horn continuously until Loney left the stream and came toward the car. Al was beside himself with anticipation as Loney approached. When he came up, he said, "What's the matter with you fair-weather fishermen? I was having a ball!" Al, Fred, and I nearly choked. We never told Loney why.

For all his aggressiveness, his frequent exasperation with weak leaders, California fishermen, and wary browns, and his occasional roughness of manner, Al Jacobi is one of the most sensitive persons I know. Perhaps his manner is his way of covering situations which might lead to an embarrassing display of feelings. I remember vividly and painfully the morning he came knocking on our door early asking for breakfast. He and I were going fishing on the Firehole, and he was ready. I needled him a bit about waking us up and begging for food, the effect of which was to send him back to his trailer for breakfast. Then Pat told me that since we were going out together, she had invited Al over for breakfast that morning. I was shocked. I had only been kidding, but taking our friendship too much for granted (I have since learned that one never takes love or friendship for granted), I had been the cause of his going back to his trailer. I apologized profusely, but, as I could see, to little avail. Al did not sulk; it was not his nature. But he had been hurt, and he could not dismiss it easily with apologies. It would take awhile to soothe.

There was a happy counterbalance to my thoughtlessness of that morning. On Father's Day we invited the family to our cottage for Sunday dinner. The occasion of the invitation was the day, and Al knew it. We had a very pleasant time, and after dinner he grew sleepy. Before long he had fallen asleep on our bed. Arlene was embarrassed. We told her not to be and to let him sleep. It was the least we could do after my faux-pas of some three weeks previously. And Al slept, comfortably and undisturbed.

The campfire circle is complete. That is, it is *almost* complete. It is the evening of June 24, 1959, my 29th birthday, and these good people and Pat have planned a simple but pleasant birthday surprise for me. But I am not there. I am on the other side of the campground, listening to Frisbee give an illustrated lecture on the geology of the park. I have two reasons for observing. First, as senior seasonal, I must report on his effectiveness at campfire programs. Second, I want to see what Frisbee's ingenuity has wrought. He sketches on the piece of asbestos he took from behind the wood burning stove in the old cabin. The light from two Coleman lanterns, half shielded by pieces of foil, illuminates his drawing board. His information is good, and he has organized it thoroughly. But he goes on and on, for an hour, an hour and fifteen minutes, an hour and thirty minutes. I have seen and heard enough and so slip away through the campground to Jacobi's campfire.

The others greet me warmly, as they always do, but Pat can hardly talk as she fights back the tears. *"Where have you been?"* she whispers intensely. *"Do you know what time it is?"*

"I was just watching Frisbee give his campfire talk. I have to check him out."

"For an hour and a half!"

I look up at the others who are delicately directing their attention elsewhere. "Ah, I think we need to have a brief discussion. We'll be back in a few minutes." All nod approvingly and Pat and I walk back to the cottage.

"Why are you so upset?"

"Why am I *ever* upset? You tell me you're just going to check Frisbee for a few minutes and then come to the campfire. It's your birthday, and we have a nice surprise for you—which you have now spoiled—but where are you? We wait and we wait and you still don't come."

"But I'm just across the campground. What could happen to

Left to right: Pat, Skeets Emery, Mary Emery,
Charles Lee Parks, Mary Edith Parks, Charles Parks

me? Why didn't you come and get me?"

"I *did*. But I looked at everyone sitting there and I didn't see you. So I thought I probably missed you coming back to Jacobi's, but then I get there and everybody says you haven't come. And you're not at the cottage."

"I was standing back in the trees. That's why you missed me."

"But I didn't know that. I thought you might have run into some bear in the dark and gotten fatally injured."

"That's not likely."

"That's what you say. But the bears wander all through this camp at night; you know that. And if you aren't at Jacobi's and you aren't at the campfire and you aren't at the cottage, what am I supposed to think? You may not be scared at night here, but I am. There are wild animals roaming around after dark."

"Is that it, then?"

"No, that's not all. Think how I feel. We have this nice surprise for you. Arlene and Al and Jack and Dorothy and Fred and Skeets and Mary and Charles and Mary Edith are waiting for you. We're going to sing happy birthday and eat some cake Arlene has baked—just for *you*—but you go off to watch Frisbee, *for an hour and a half!* What were you thinking? It's your birthday. You knew that we'd do something nice for you. And I feel so humiliated, like the mother of a child who doesn't have enough sense to come home when he's supposed to. I'm so confused I can't tell whether or not I'm mostly mad at you for being irresponsible or sick with worry that you might be lying in the campground somewhere bleeding to death after a bear has chewed you up."

More tears as she lets the tension and the anger of evening work its way out of her system. Her anger, I realize once again, is rooted in her fear. She can never be fully relaxed in this wild setting unless she is with me or together with me and our friends around Jacobi's campfire. She does not need the added anxiety caused by my thoughtlessness.

"I'm sorry. I should have been more alert. You know I don't want to upset you."

"Oh, I know. But Don Stewart, there are times when you can be so damn dense! I wonder how you ever grew up!"

"Luck, pure unadulterated luck. Runs in the family."

We laugh softly, and I hold her close to me, feeling the fragile softness of her hair and cheek against mine. Then we work our way back to the campfire where the delayed birthday celebration takes place, to the satisfaction of all, including the prodigal but forgiven celebrant. Then we lapse into our comfortable evening routine. Jack is off on another story—this one about the back country of the Big Hole; Fred, Skeets, and Charles listen and smile broadly. Dorothy, Arlene, and Mary serve coffee and cookies to supplement the diminishing cake. Carol and Freddy look a bit moony and Cathie needles them. Al and I are arguing about Floyd Patterson. I say he is a good fighter; Al will have none of it. Pat divides her attention between a conversation with Mary Edith, Jack's narrative, and Al and me. "Brown eyes" sees more and talks less than I do. She will give me a full report of the whole evening back at the cottage when we go to sleep.

It is a typical summer night in Yellowstone. The faintest breeze blows. Bushels of stars are scattered across the heavens like sparkling grains of sugar spilled on a black tile floor. We hear a faint yipping of coyotes on the bluff above us. They are barking at the moon. Nearer a solitary owl hoots once, twice. And the

Gibbon River below us swishes softly and musically toward its junction with the Firehole. The hurly burly of the cities is far away. Activity there seems irrelevant for those of us gathered around Jacobi's campfire tonight.

Jacobi's campfires ended abruptly on July 1, 1959. For three weeks Al had complained of lack of breath, of fear of heart trouble. We asked him if he had gone to Mammoth to the hospital for a checkup. He replied vaguely. Later we had reason to suspect that he had and had been told to go to lower elevation and have more extensive checkups. It is quite possible he knew how serious his condition really was and wished not to alarm Arlene and the family. We will never know for sure. On the morning of the second Arlene came to tell us that they were breaking camp because Al was having another spell, and they feared for his health. Fred Fischer agreed to drive the trailer down out of the Park. At first their plan was to go out the South Entrance, but that was altered at the last minute in favor of going north past Mammoth and the hospital if it were needed.

I do not know why now but as I shook Al's hand as they were ready to depart, I knew, as I'm sure he did—his eyes were full of tears which he could barely restrain—that this was the end of everything between us. Why we all sensed it and feared it, I do not know. We could have been acknowledging the end of the Jacobis' annual treks to Yellowstone, but I felt it was more than this. I felt imminent tragedy. They left. Between Mammoth and Norris Al suffered two massive heart attacks that left him barely alive when he reached Mammoth Hospital. There he lingered one week. The Emerys and Parks moved to Mammoth Campground to help Arlene and take care of the children. Pat and I went several times during the week, but we were at Madison the morning of the ninth when Al died.

It is difficult to describe now the reactions of this complex family to whom we were so close. Freddy was the most visibly shaken and hurt, but Cathie did not reveal her feelings. She seemed stunned and bewildered by the swiftness with which this death had come to them. Arlene told Pat and me the loss meant for her agonizing hours of self-appraisal. But I cannot really speak at all for the family or the other members of Jacobi's campfire because each person who was close to Al carries within him his own special memories. I can only speak for myself. Al Jacobi was a very special person for me for reasons I have only recently understood. He was, in a way, a Yellowstone father for me, an older man with whom I felt perfectly comfortable and who shared two of my keenest interests: big-time college athletics and the outdoor recreations of Yellowstone Park. I understood in deeply emotional ways his competitive intensity, his excitement at the things he loved to do, and his sensitivity. A great void came into my life when he died, and it has never been filled since. And his passing destroyed the *raison d'etre* of Jacobi's campfire. For Pat and me, Yellowstone was never the same afterwards.

Al is buried in Clinton Memorial Cemetery high above the town and the Father of Waters which flows past it. But the Mississippi was never his river. The Gibbon was. Although I do not believe in an afterlife, I would like to—for Al's sake. For him I would wish a world full of fat brown trout hiding beneath the undercut banks of softly flowing mountain streams, weak leaders, and California fishermen. Al would be happy in such a place.

17

Earthquake!

AT 11:37 P.M. on August 17, 1959, Pat and I were sleeping soundly, having gone to bed earlier than usual to catch up on our rest. The Townsends and Larry and Bill Wanlass were settled comfortably in their trailers over in the old road camp beneath National Park Mountain. The campfires had gone out in our campground, and most of our campers were well into a peaceful night's rest. Only Frisbee was still awake. He had been reading by Coleman lantern in the museum until the last minute when he had stopped to enter in the station log his reports of two earth tremors. The first shook the museum. The second brought two plaster Indian busts off glass display cases, shattering them on the stone floor. Now he sat alert, staring out into the dark.

"At 11:37 P.M. M.S.T. a sudden displacement of rock occurred along a fault ten miles beneath the earth's surface at 44° 50′ N. Latitude and 111° 05′ W. Longitude."[1] Pat and I awoke when our cabin began to vibrate slightly. We sat up in bed, alert and puzzled. My first thought was that some confused camper was backing a truck into us. But as the vibrations increased in force I feared the Russians had, at last, pushed the button. Only when the cabin began to tremble violently and rock did I shout out to Pat, "It's an earthquake!"

She, looking out our windows into the bright moonlit night, kept crying out, "It's a wind; it's a wind!" And so it seemed. The tall lodgepole pines near us were swaying violently as if battered by the force of hurricane winds. We clung to each other to prevent being thrown from bed. Dishes rattled in our cupboards and then, as the force of the tremors increased, were thrown from them onto the floor. I stared at a corner in our ceiling which kept rocking back and forth violently. It seemed as if our cottage would suddenly disintegrate and come crashing down upon our heads. Outside we could hear the crash of rock all down the Madison Valley and see the great billowing clouds of dust which rose from these slides and filled the clear night air. The moon, so sharply defined before, became partially obscured by the haze.

When that first great tremor ceased, I leaped out of bed and raced into our kitchen. I was sure we would have no water, and we didn't. It would be morning before Bill and Larry were to discover the main break. The three-inch water line which supplied our cottage and the public restrooms of the campground was attached to a stone bridge across the Gibbon River, and two elbow joints, at the point where the line left the bridge and dropped into the ground and at the point in the ground where it levelled out again, had been stripped by the movement of the bridge. Water poured from these ruptures.

We dressed quickly and went out into the night where the campground was in turmoil. Most of the campers in trailers had thought at first that a bear was rocking their trailers. But the swift onset of the severe tremors quickly dispelled that presumption. Many trailers were thrown off their jacks; their interiors were a shambles. Tenters had been violently tossed and bumped as they slept on the ground or on cots. For a few moments we feared that the Townsends and Larry and Bill had been killed by rock falling from a now disintegrated pinnacle of National Park Mountain. But they came across the river just as we were setting out to look

The road was completely blocked by fallen rock.

for them.

When they arrived at the museum, we conferred immediately about necessary steps to secure the safety of the campers. We were certain that road damage was heavy and that slides might exist in some places. Our suppositions were quite correct. Up the Firehole Canyon, only two or three miles from the Junction, the road was completely blocked by fallen rock. On the road to the West Entrance huge boulders lay, one of them approximately seven feet tall and wide enough to block an entire lane. These rocks had splintered off Mount Jackson and come bounding down upon the road. More did not reach the highway because they were checked by a thin barrier of trees at the base of the mountain. Days later we were to look upon the old lichen covered boulders in the Madison River with new eyes. At Gibbon

Falls the earthquake had brought down a hillside of rock and debris and separated approximately a hundred feet of rock retaining wall from the road, sending it tumbling into the river 150 feet below.

But we could not know about these things only a few minutes after the first great shock. Our first decision was to close the campground and permit no one to leave, a decision which, in the light of circumstances, proved to be a good one. We explained to the campers that they were in the open, hence quite safe from the danger of falling rock. We did not know the condition of the roads and would not until morning when it would be much safer to travel. And, as Frisbee pointed out, strong aftershocks often accompanied a major earthquake. He was quite right. Between midnight and nine-thirty the next evening we were to have five additional shocks only slightly less intense than the first one.

People in the campground were in all stages of emotion, from humor to terror. Veteran Madison campers were jovial about the event. They, like Larry Wanlass, would not have missed a minute of the experience. We had had a ringside seat at a major event in the geological history of the region, and fortunately, had not been hurt. We were only inconvenienced. Just how inconvenienced we were shortly to find out. Larry and Bill had counted something like 267 camps in Madison that night. That meant, assuming between three and four people at each camp, nearly 1,000 people in our campground. And now, because of the break in the water line, our two large restrooms would have to be closed. The only available ones were two small dry toilets at the back of the campground! One thousand people using two small dry toilets? They queued up the next day like World Series fans on opening day.

The terrorized ones stayed up all night, screaming with each new tremor. With fearful impatience they waited for daylight and information about how to leave. One tenter spent part of the night carving out a cryptic message on the dirt floor of his tent: GOODBYE EARTHQUAKE! Madison campers, of course, would like to have joined the streams of people pouring out the south

To the east, Montana Highway 287 had ceased to exist.

and east entrances to the Park, persons who, fearing all sorts of things like the Park blowing up in one huge volcano, had unwisely headed out at night. Had our campers known all that was taking place to the west of them, they would have been grateful for the haven Madison afforded because down the Madison Valley outside the Park terror and tragedy were running hand in hand.[2]

The initial shock at 11:37 P.M. had caused a massive landslide above Rock Creek Campground in the Gallatin National Forest. Loose schist and gneiss which had been weathering for centuries had piled up on that hillside behind a cracked dolomite ridge which the first tremor had broken. The schist and gneiss then poured through the rent in the dolomite ridge with devastating suddenness. To those awakened by the earthquake, the roar of the landslide must have seemed like the end of the earth.

Earthquake: Main Slide, Rock Creek Campground

So swiftly had that great flood of rock rolled down the mountain-
side that some great boulders rode the top of it all the way across
the valley. Some geologists thought it might have been over in
just thirty seconds. When the dust settled, eighty million tons of
rock in a mass a mile long and three hundred feet deep lay across
the Madison Valley blocking the river. Earthquake Lake, called
by the *Salt Lake Tribune*, in one of its less lucid moments, the
new "artificial" lake in the Madison Valley, was forming and rising rapidly. Before the Corps of Army Engineers were to cut a
channel through the slide, the lake would be nearly three hundred feet deep. The engineers had two serious problems: as the
lake backed up, it threatened persons trapped in the valley,
roads, property, and Hebgen Dam. However, if the water broke

over the slide and began eroding it too rapidly, it might rush down and spill out over the lower Madison Valley from the end of the canyon to Ennis and north to Three Forks. Working swiftly and purposefully in those first days and weeks after the disaster, the engineers cut a channel in the slide and then prevented too swift erosion through it by dumping granite boulders into the stream bed.

In addition to the giant slide and Earthquake Lake, this portion of the Madison Valley experienced still other astonishing effects of the earthquake. The slide blocked the west end of the canyon thus closing that as a possible escape route for 200 persons trapped between it and Hebgen Dam. To the east Montana Highway 287 had ceased to exist. Portions of the road had been horribly bent and broken or had sloughed off into Hebgen Lake. Even more spectacular were the effects on Hebgen Lake itself. The tremor had produced vertical faulting, displacement in some areas along the Hebgen and Red Canyon scarps reaching eighteen feet. The north and west end of the lake had dropped, producing an effect on the lake's surface similar to that of water sloshing in a bucket. But when the bucket is seven miles long, the sloshing becomes tidal waves twenty feet high. Four times they rolled across the lake smashing into Hebgen Dam with thunderous force. The dam cracked—but held. Had it given way and released the waters of the reservoir into the Madison Valley at that point, total tragedy would have resulted. There would have been no time to save either permanent residents or the 200 campers in the valley. Because of the crack, however, people in the valley all the way to Ennis were instructed to evacuate their homes as soon as possible.

Back at Madison Junction we had no knowledge of these catastrophic events. We had felt all the violence and force of the tremor, and although we were at the most direct point along what the *Tribune* was to call five days later the "little-traveled deep interior of Yellowstone Park," we were only inconvenienced. Our phones were disrupted so our first word from the outside came from District Ranger Davis who had threaded his way through the boulders on the West Entrance Road. At great peril to himself, considering the severity of later shocks that night, he had come to see what condition things were in at Madison. He concurred in our decision to keep all persons in the campground. For him the earthquake was the beginning of a thirty-six-hour race from one point to another in his district (which stretched from West Yellowstone to Old Faithful) which terminated when, from exhaustion, he fell asleep driving his car and wrecked it.

Many of us remember well the second great shock at 12:56 A.M. We stood in the parking lot, then in front of Madison Museum, talking with Mr. Davis. We had a premonitory warning at 12:54, then the tremor at 12:56. Somebody said, "Here she comes again," and she came, with almost as much intensity as the great tremor of 11:37 P.M. I grabbed a guardrail post in the lot; Pat held onto the district ranger's patrol car. There were people flying this way and that in the dimly moonlit area. Because we were alert at that time, we were much more aware of the dry rattle of rock falling from National Park Mountain, the dust clouds rising down the valley, the swaying of the trees, and most of all, that unbelievable shaking of "terra firma." Man has an unacknowledged confidence in the solidity of the earth. Why else, when disembarking from a boat, or even an airplane, do we say we are glad to be back on good solid ground? However, when that good solid ground begins to vibrate and shake, one suddenly realizes that there is nothing to grab hold of. That which has been solid and permanent has become as unstable as a body of water. The experience has a deep effect upon one's psyche. I would not say that it produces fear. It is more a sense of fundamental things being out of joint, of the universe being slightly ajar.[3] However, as we experienced more and more tremors, we began to study them dispassionately. By morning, when the next to last of the great tremors occurred, a number of us had become sufficiently accustomed to them to stand our ground and ride them just as we would waves under a surfboard.

That first night Pat and I eventually went back to bed. Fris-

Earthquake boulder on West Entrance Road
(Martha Townsend beside boulder)

bee, the Townsends, and the Wanlass brothers roamed through the campground talking with campers who had suddenly developed a fierce desire to be anywhere but in Yellowstone Park. But they stayed with us, wisely accepting our decision to wait for daylight and some way of evacuating safely. The district ranger was checking the roads and finding what we had suspected: the roads north and south were blocked and the West road, because of the ever present danger of falling rock off Mt. Jackson, was too dangerous. He would run that gauntlet himself; he was unwilling to permit a stream of cars, trucks, and trailers to follow him.

Morning broke over a restless campground. But we finally had a plan. The old Mesa Road around the Firehole Canyon was open. It had deep ruts, it was narrow, but if graded, it might be passable. Elt Davis called for a grader from Old Faithful, and by eleven o'clock it had cut down the deep ruts and cleared enough of the worst boulders from the road that house trailers could traverse it. When the word came through that the road was open, the campground mobilized immediately. When we took down the barrier, there began a migration from Madison campground, the likes of which I had never seen. For hours the column of cars, trailers, trucks, campers, and microbuses flowed steadily out of the camp, across the bridge, and up the road in the forest. When the sun dropped over Madison Campground on August 18, only eighteen camps were left; these were the Homesteaders, still sufficiently attached to the old camp that they would not be frightened away. But on Wednesday, the Superintendent ordered complete evacuation of the campground. Thursday, August 20, during what was normally the week of peak summer traffic, I sat in Madison Museum looking upon untravelled roads and an empty campground. It was a phenomenon which had never occurred to the junction in all its long and fascinating history. And it would continue past Labor Day. In effect, Madison Junction was closed for the season.

From the very beginning of our earthquake ordeal, we were concerned about communications. We could reach no place except Old Faithful. And we could not find out from anyone there how extensive the earthquake was. However, the night of the eighteenth, through Old Faithful, we were finally able to talk to our immediate supervisor, Dave Beal. From him we first learned of the terrible tragedy down the Madison Valley outside the Park. The essence of Dave's message to us was that as long as the possibility of danger for any park visitors existed at Madison Junction, we were to remain there. But there were scarcely any people at Madison, and they could be moved quickly. The more we thought about what Dave said, the more perplexed we became. This was, in all my experiences with Dave Beal, the only silly thing I ever heard him say.

With the road closed and the campground evacuating, Madison Junction became a good place for reading. The only work we had to do was sit and wait for the phone to ring. Bill and Larry were busy trying to repair the water line. Besides the stripped joints near the bridge, they suspected breaks in a number of other places. We did need drinking water immediately, however, and they had found a still active spring, used in the past, some two miles down the West Entrance road. They advised us to boil the water, of course.

It is only in the kind of predicament in which we found ourselves then that we began to realize how vital water is to a human being. Food we can do without or improvise for long periods of time. Water, however, is a daily necessity. One needs it to drink, to cook with, to wash, to do a hundred things in one's daily life. Unfortunately, one potential source of clear cold water was unavailable to us. The water table had been so jarred by the earthquake that the Gibbon River had turned a muddy brown. I had never seen it so ugly. More disappointing was the fact that fishing in it was out of the question. It did not begin to clear, we learned from Frisbee the next year, until a month after the earthquake. When I returned to Madison Junction in 1960, I returned to a Gibbon so changed in its subtle bottom contours that I had to learn the stream all over. The big holes were still there. But so many ridges with which I had become familiar, all sorts of little pockets and undulations in the stream bed, were radically altered. It was like looking at the face of a loved one after plastic surgery. The face is still the loved one's face. But it has lines, marks, and other changes which make it different from the face you knew before.

The evening of the eighteenth, Dick, Martha, and Frisbee walked up the Firehole Canyon to see for themselves the extent of slides there. They did not go too far because the ground seemed to be still vibrating. Dick described the experience: "You know how an old drunk will put one foot in front of the other, feeling around for the ground? Well, we started staggering around like a bunch of drunks. I'd put my foot out and start rockin'. I tell you, that whole canyon is still jiggling!" Now Dick Townsend has his eccentricities, but one is them is not embroidering the truth. If he said that canyon jiggled, I believed that canyon jiggled. Possibly the rocks there transmitted the minor shock waves which were occurring frequently but could only be felt in the canyon and not at the museum. Whatever the cause, a jiggling canyon had been an eerie experience for the Townsends and Frisbee, and they had returned to the museum.

By then we all were becoming positively jovial. We had begun to accept conditions as they were; in fact, the whole adventure seemed like a lark. Then we turned on the news. This was our first of two experiences with news media, and it permanently altered our attitudes toward "crises" which they broadcast. We were the top story of the day. "Terror in Montana," Lowell Thomas began. Well, there was terror west of us, but he seemed inclined to include the whole area affected by the earthquake. Varying his tone from controlled hysteria to pulpit ecstasy, he described the violence of the tremors and the destruction which followed in their wake. Somehow, listening to him was much more frightening than experiencing the earthquake itself. Pat said she wasn't really nervous until she heard that newscast. Martha Townsend was similarly affected. Dick and I were both wishing that news reporting, at least by some commentators, was less show business and more reporting.

Back in St. Joseph, Missouri, Pat's family, especially Grandma Lawnick, was in a state of agitation. Grandma was sure, despite all the protestations of the others, that we were buried under that landslide. Pat's brother tried to point out to her that it was forty miles downstream from us, but Grandma would not be made easy. They all wanted reassurance by hearing us. My parents had reasoned that we were safe, but as Mom later admitted, when they saw the newspaper pictures and listened to the reports, they were glad we had called home when we did to tell them all was well. Calling home was not the easiest thing to do that first twenty-four hours. The Bozeman and Livingston exchanges north of the Park were scarcely equipped to handle 6,000 long distance telephone calls all piling on top of one another. Our good friends, the Bunces, in Madison, Wisconsin, tried futilely and frantically to get through and gave it up as a bad job. Eventually, we were able to call them. It was easier getting out than getting in. The waiting line was shorter.

After the news broadcast on the eighteenth there was an adjustment in living quarters. Although Bill and Larry decided to return to their trailer in the old road camp, Martha and Dick and Frisbee had decided they were too close to the face of National Park Mountain. They adopted the museum as their home away from home at Madison, and thus began a ritual which lasted for a few days and provided us some of the most humorous moments we experienced during the aftermath of the earthquake. As evening settled over our area, the migrants would come to the museum with their lanterns and sleeping bags. Pat and I would then go down and the five of us would discuss our situation.

Martha: "Dick, I don't see why you don't tell Dave Beal we're leaving now. Your job is in Belleville, Illinois, not here. And there are no people here now and who knows what could happen if we had another quake. I just think we ought to pack and go home. Your job. . . ."

Dick: "Martha, will you please *shut up?*"

Martha: "I can't Dickie. This quake makes me so nervous that I just have to get it out of my system."

Dick: "Yes, I understand that, but must you get it out nine hundred ninety-nine thousand, nine hundred ninety-nine times?"

Frisbee would then cheer us up with his knowledge of post-earthquake phenomena. He would tell us of the likelihood of more severe tremors as the movement along the fault which had caused this one produced the possibility of movement along other fault lines in the Park. As we began to learn about the great slide in the Madison Canyon, Frisbee speculated about the possibility of a similar thing happening at Madison Junction. We had discovered boulders among the trees on the northwest side of the road. After getting us all tuned to a fairly high pitch of anxiety, Frisbee would then suggest that none of this would probably happen (which it didn't), but the anxiety had been created and we thought about it constantly.

By the nineteenth our routine had set in. We just kept our regular work schedules at the station and sat around ready to answer any calls. But it was strange to see no people, no cars, no campers. Madison had died. The rest of us rapidly became bored, but Dick Townsend soon found recreation to occupy his time. The minor tremors continued to make Martha jumpy, so when he sat behind the big desk in the museum, Martha sitting on it, Dick would jiggle his leg against the desk causing it to wob-

ble slightly. Martha would say, "Here she comes again." We had
said that so much and had felt so many tremors, it was quite feasible any wobble would be another one. After several "here she
comes" in close succession, however, Martha became suspicious.
She gave Dick a long hard stare and asked him whether those
were all tremors she was feeling. Detected, Dick rolled his eyes a
bit and smiled a smile which reached from one high cheekbone
to the other. Martha looked like she wanted to clout him.

The rest of the Park, as we discovered from our occasional
telephone conversations with Old Faithful, was buzzing with activity. I learned from our earthquake experience that people in
official capacities, in crises of any kind, once they have determined they are perfectly safe and not likely to sustain injury, immediately set up a flurry of activity so as to call to the attention of
all around them the fact that they have been in a crisis. At Mammoth, for example, Superintendent Lon Garrison had moved
Park Headquarters from the stone buildings into tents. The
official reason given for this move was that it took personnel out
of places where danger of falling rock existed. Actually, it was
just some executive grandstanding for newsmen and photog-
raphers. Subsequent pictures of the "earthquake era" show the
Superintendent and his staff outside their temporary headquarters. Now it took us no time at all to figure that the distance
from the epicenter of the quake (eight miles north of West
Yellowstone) to Madison Junction was considerably shorter than
the distance from the epicenter to Mammoth. In fact, it was quite
obvious that the most intense shock waves emanating from the
epicenter had struck our station and Norris. One of our
colleagues in Mammoth thought the evacuation there a bit of
nonsense and sneaked back into the buildings to get his work
done. But it was not nonsense; it was excellent publicity.

Our friends at Old Faithful were as considerate as they had
time to be. They appreciated our predicament, but they were
having a jolly good time checking up on all the new geysers and
watching the old ones, so they did not have time for us. George
Marler, the most knowledgeable man in the world on the geyser

basins of the upper Firehole, reported eruptions of 298 hot springs, 160 of them having no eruptive history before the earthquake. Big geysers in all basins had erupted: Grand, Giantess, Beehive, Fountain, Morning, Great Fountain. Never before had the whole galaxy of Yellowstone's most glittering stars performed so closely upon one another. For the general public there was the comforting news that Old Faithful seemed least affected of all. However, in the days and months that passed there was bad news for the faithful among geyser watchers. Grand, the most beautiful geyser of all, was thought to have been permanently and adversely affected. Fortunately, six months after the earthquake, Grand began to revive. But it would be years before it eventually re-established the frequency of eruptions which characterized it during the summer of 1959. While the Old Faithful naturalists checked the sudden explosion of geyser activity, however, and while the Superintendent played Boy Scout in his tent at Mammoth, we, who wanted some attention from our superiors, sat isolated and perplexed.

One never realizes how meaningful work is in one's life until he is without it. At Madison Junction Frisbee, Townsend, and I went through the daily routine of opening and closing the museum, cleaning, answering occasional telephone calls, and sitting. Where we would normally have been giving our lectures, nature walks, road and park information, and campfire talks to hundreds of people, we now had no one but ourselves to talk to. Empty road, empty campground, empty museum.

Occasional park officials passed by. Elt Davis was on the run until he wrecked his car. Joe Frazier, the West Yellowstone subdistrict ranger, made occasional forays into our area. Larry and Bill were around, of course, checking on equipment and trying to detect other breaks in the water lines. A telephone company helicopter dropped down briefly into the meadow at the junction. The bears, who had cleared the campground in a wild stampede the night of the earthquake, began to drift back—but to nothing. And there is nothing so mournful as a campground bear, full of expectation, going up to a garbage can and finding it empty. They were slowly coming to grips with a reality they did not understand but had to cope with. Where there is no food, there is soon no bear. One of our local bears, however, was working himself up to a high pitch of excitement. He had been walking up the road in the Firehole Canyon the night of the earthquake, and trees and rock had fallen around and over him, trapping him in a pocket under the debris. Workmen who later dug him out said that the bear, once free, ran up over the ridge next to the road and into the timber as if someone had burned his back end with a hot branding iron. Speculation was that he probably did not stop running until night fell.

In our quiet moments we read books, worked around the museum, and checked the area. The most noticeable effects of the earthquake, in the immediate vicinity of the museum, were fissures approximately two feet deep in the meadow by the Madison River. The Gibbon, of course, continued muddy. The Firehole River had a rockier bottom, and its ground water table apparently had been less disturbed than that of the Gibbon, so it began to clear somewhat. But the junction of the two streams was visibly altered. Whereas before two clear mountain streams melted in a long smooth riffle, now a brown mass of water impinged upon partially clear water. The Madison River, formed by this junction of the Firehole and Gibbon, was discolored also. A portion of the road along the Madison had slumped and seemed ready at any moment to slide down into it leaving but one lane for traffic. Park Service trucks and cars coming upon it veered nervously into the one safe lane.

The Park Service eventually began to realize that a ridiculous situation prevailed at Madison—three men tied up doing nothing but answer the phone. Dick Townsend and Frisbee were pulled off the station and taken to Old Faithful. Fortunately, one day off came for Frisbee before he left, and he took all our cameras to Gibbon Falls and the Firehole Canyon to get pictures of the damage. Officially, none of us were to go into these areas because of the danger of additional tremors and falling rock. One road crew man had been hurt at Mammoth when he and his group had gone up the road to clear Kingman Pass on the morning of the eighteenth. The Superintendent had promptly declared all slide areas out of bounds and decided to wait for things to settle down before starting road clearing again. But Frisbee was adventuresome, and all of us wanted pictures of the rocks and slides. And he got them.

From Frisbee we got a graphic picture of the extensive damage to the road and the retaining wall at Gibbon Falls and the extent of the rock slides in the Firehole Canyon. Then Pat and the Townsends walked down the West Entrance Road to the huge boulders which lay on it. Slowly, as we comprehended the scope of the damage near us, we realized what might have happened had the earthquake occurred at 11:37 A.M. rather than 11:37 P.M. First, the principal loss of life would not have been at Rock Creek Campground in the Gallatin National Forest where twenty-six of the twenty-eight earthquake fatalities occurred. Most of those campers would have departed. The great slide would have been deadly to cars passing through the canyon then, of course. And there might have been many. Montana 287 was the primary route leading from Yellowstone to Virginia City, which many park visitors stopped to see going from or coming to Yellowstone. And what would have been the situation along the north shore of Hebgen Lake? Because large portions of the road simply dropped off into it at a place where it was quite deep, it would have been sink or swim for any persons caught in cars on that road at that time. But the greatest disaster area outside Yellowstone would have been Hebgen Lake itself. Who could have come to the rescue of small boats while they were being swamped by the massive seiches which rolled back and forth across the lake in those first few hours? Many persons would certainly have drowned.

And inside Yellowstone Park? Only one who has seen the bumper-to-bumper summer traffic could begin to speculate on the damage and loss of life. Rocks rolling off Mt. Jackson would have ripped through cars on the West Entrance Road, carrying some into the river, smashing others into pulp. Other cars would have been forced off the road into the Firehole Canyon by rock slides there. Gibbon Falls would have been a holocaust of smashed cars and bodies. Madison Junction would have become a massive first aid station. And how many would have died? Impossible to guess—perhaps 250, perhaps 500. It would have been the most grisly experience of our lives. Only then did we realize what a blessing the timing of the earthquake was. For a few, it meant death or loss of property. For the 18,000 in Yellowstone that night, it meant a good fright and an experience, but no disaster. Such is the occasional luck of portions of the human race.

Our isolation was rendered official when the Superintendent sealed off Madison Junction. Visitors were not permitted to travel roads on the entire western side of the Park. The rock slide at Mammoth effectively blocked the road south from there, but Park Service vehicles could use the Bunsen Peak Road when they needed to. A barricade was set up at Canyon to block people from coming over the Norris cutoff and down into our area. And there were barricades north of Old Faithful right below Riverside Geyser. A man was placed on duty constantly at the Old Faithful barricade to see that no unauthorized personnel went beyond the barrier. The general public accepted this state of affairs. But there were busy minds slowly waking up to the fact that no reports on the effects of the earthquake on Yellowstone's west side were available. A news scoop was hanging like a ripe plum from a tree for whoever would be bold enough to pluck it. Clarence Durham of Ft. Smith, Arkansas, and Dickinson Mulholland of Billings, Montana, were bold enough.

The morning of August 20 they crossed the barricade at Canyon on a motorcycle and raced across the Norris cutoff. Ahead of them lay the startling pictures at Gibbon Falls, the Firehole Canyon, and the West Entrance Road.

When they roared through Madison Junction that morning, they caught me completely by surprise. Dick Townsend heard them too late to stop them as they went up the Firehole Canyon. But I went back to the road junction to stop them on their return trip. Fortunately, Joe Frazier came in from West Yellowstone at that time, and I told him what had happened. Joe is a big burly man with a short temper, especially for people who take a cavalier attitude toward Park Service regulations. We blocked the road and waited. Soon, the motorcyclists came back. Joe chewed them out, arrested them, and escorted them to Old Faithful where their film was confiscated. But that was only the beginning. They knew they had pictures and a story. The *Salt Lake Tribune* wanted it desperately. And the paper eventually got it and reported it in the very best traditions of sensational journalism.

> Whole forests of trees split like matchsticks, huge boulders spilled in every direction and roads crushed into gravel. This vivid picture of destruction caused by Monday's earthquake was described by two camera enthusiasts who 'walked and rode' a motorcycle through the entire quake-damaged area Thursday.
>
> They are the first civilians known to have visited the little-traveled 'interior' area. . . .
>
> They filmed a huge cavein (*sic*) near Fire Hole (*sic*) river, got pictures of damage wreaked at Virginia Cascades and North (*sic*—they mean Norris) Junction and at Gibbon Falls.

There was damage all right, but "whole forests into matchsticks"? And "roads crushed into gravel"? One also got the impression that like Stanley, these men penetrated a dark continent and lived to return and tell their story. When I remarked to Otto Brown, then Chief Ranger, that I felt the newspaper had exaggerated the amount of damage which actually existed in the Park, he replied, in one of the bitterest condemnations of journalism I have ever heard, "Don, I learned long ago, that in journalism there is no truth, no honesty, no integrity." I wondered many times afterwards, just what experiences had made the Chief Ranger, a cool and rational man, condemn the press so thoroughly. Perhaps it was too full and too frequent a diet of stories like this one about the earthquake.

The newspaper sensationalism carried on into the blurb accompanying Durham and Mulholland's pictures which appeared in the paper on Saturday, the twenty-second.

> First pictures to come out of little-traveled deep interior area of Yellowstone Park. . . . Far inside Yellowstone National Park: Deep, jagged slashes in the road mark the far-reaching trail of a rumbling quake. . . . Two young men rode their motorcycle deep into the interior of Yellowstone Park this week and scooped the nation.

The last caption revealed the *Tribune*'s real objective. I'm not sure the rest of the nation really cared that much, but competing papers in the Rocky Mountain area might have. How desperately the *Tribune* wanted this story may be inferred from the way in which it reported the apprehension and arrest of the two cyclists, an event with which I had some familiarity.

> The cameras and film, only known to have been used by non-government personnel in this particular area of the park, were promptly seized by Yellowstone Park Rangers and just as promptly ordered returned by Elmer F. Bennett, Under Secretary of Interior.
> Mr. Bennett, who was in Salt Lake City to make a speech, ordered the cameras and film returned to the pair as soon as he heard of the seizure.
> Rangers who confiscated the materials contended the action was taken merely to assure appearance of the two before the U. S. Commissioner at Mammoth Hot Springs Friday at 11 A.M. to answer charges of running a barricade and violating traffic signs.

Exactly. And they got $25 fines. Bennett's intervention really annoyed us. He was helping his old newspaper get a scoop, even if it meant letting those turkeys who shouldn't have come into our area in the first place, get off with light fines. I wish their confiscated film had been "lost."

When the Townsends and Frisbee left for Old Faithful, only Pat and I, Larry and Bill remained. Since the Wanlass brothers stayed in their trailer in the road camp, however, Pat and I had the sensation of being completely alone at Madison Junction. For both of us, reared among the noises of the city, the silence of the wilderness was deafening. I had heard it in the back country, and I both loved and feared it. But Pat was afraid.

Our isolation did not last long. Into the vacated campground moved some of the seediest neighbors we have ever had. They were members of a crew of wood cutters. Bill and Larry told us privately to keep everything under lock and key. This group had the reputation of stealing everything from small household items to large pieces of construction equipment. They also had the reputation of being poachers. Whether or not these rumors were true, we never found out. They stayed away from us, doing their job of clearing trees for the new campground, and we did not encourage their company. One night we heard a shot ring out through the valley. I did not go prospecting, however, because tracing the location of the shot would have been impossible. Even if I could have apprehended these men poaching, I had no weapon, and one unarmed man against a group of armed poachers fourteen miles from the nearest assistance is not in a position to do much arresting. I did not want to be listed as mysteriously disappeared and never found. And there are so many places in Yellowstone Park where a man can disappear and never be heard from again.

The practical problems created by the earthquake were all solvable except one: finding adequate drinking water. Bill and Larry's spring never appealed to Pat me. The water from it was murky and had to be boiled; we could never tell how much animal contamination it contained. A larger problem was that we simply lacked the equipment to hold the amount of water we needed for our purposes. We had a gallon thermos and this, with a glass jug which formerly held distilled water, was sufficient to hold our supply of drinking water. But we needed buckets and other utensils for wash water. We could go to Old Faithful to shower and wash clothes, but it was a nuisance to do so. Eventually, we worked out a solution to our laundry problem which should have been obvious to us from the first. We had, within a mile, a source of ample hot water: Terrace Spring. Normally, use of the Park's natural features is not permitted although campers had long bathed in a little pool above Terrace Spring. They dammed up its small runoff channel when they wanted a hot bath and succeeded in lowering the temperature to exactly the right level. We had heard some very funny stories of accidental midnight rendezvous between naked campers, park patrols, buffalo, and bears near the little pool. But Pat and I were not concerned about baths. We just wanted to do our laundry. We set our wash tub down alongside one of the spring's run-off channels and proceeded to dip out all the water we needed. We had a scrub board and an old fashioned plunger for squishing clothes up and down and all around. So, on a clear, sunny morning, we stood alone at Terrace Spring dipping out hot water, washing and scrubbing clothes, dumping the dirty water on the ground, and chuckling to ourselves about the curious ways emergencies can be met by those alert enough to take advantage of nature's abundance.

While we worked, a plane passed over and circled, apparently trying to discern whether or not unauthorized personnel had got into the closed area of the Park. The newspaper story had caused Park officials to clamp an even tighter security lid on Madison Junction and the roads radiating all directions from us. Apparently, whoever was in the plane recognized Pat and me. We went on washing, rinsing, and finishing our housework. We left, with a grateful thanks to our friendly hot spring, useful to us in a way we had never dreamed of in the more stable summers of the past.

The last, and in some ways, most memorable of our earthquake experiences occurred the night of August 28 when we went to Old Faithful for food and water. Actually, we went there, as much as anything else, just to hear the sound of human voices, to see activity and some kind of routine prevailing. We got our water and food, visited awhile with the men in the Old Faithful station, and then started back. We were stopped at the Riverside barrier by Harold Beals, who had been instructed to let no one past that roadblock without a note from Lee Robinson, the sub-district ranger of Old Faithful. We explained, Harold continued to refuse, but nobody got mad. I finally suggested to Pat that we go back and get a note from Lee, which we did. After all, Harold was just doing his job.

We gave him the note, he let us pass, and we went, past Biscuit Basin, past Midway, past Fountain Paint Pots, and onto the Fountain Flats. The moon was up that night, casting a silver sheen over the plain. There was no wind; the night was cloudless. As we drove over that ghostly-lit open grassland, Pat and I became aware that we were probably the only persons on the roads in the whole west side of Yellowstone Park. Distances are insignificant in such an experience. The sense that you are alone is everything. I am sure that Neil Armstrong and Buzz Aldrin on the moon's surface felt no more isolated than we did speeding along that plain of burnished silver that night. Even today I can feel the softness of the moonlight, the unending openness of the flats, and the motion of our solitary car, a tiny pinprick of light moving slowly across a seemingly vast uninhabited planet.

The earthquake closed the summer of 1959 for us. More significantly, it marked the end of an era. The life we had known at Madison Junction was disappearing. The government mess hall, the bunkhouse, our first cabin there, the coal shed—all vestiges of the old road camp would be moved or destroyed within the next year. Our comfortable cottage near the museum would survive, a few years, as a storage office for the protective division of the Park Service; then it, too, would be removed. Eventually, the museum, unattended, would be the only structure left of our era at Madison Junction. Life in the old campground would flicker momentarily during the first half of 1960, then cease. The saws had already begun to buzz in the area northwest of the campground cutting out trees for the new campground and the new road. The Gibbon River, violently shaken by the earthquake, was changed, its subtle bottom contours radically altered. And the ashes of Jacobi's last campfire were already cold, never again to be revived. For Pat and me, although we could not know it just then, this was the end of five golden summers.

Notes

[1]William A. Fischer, *Yellowstone's Living Geology* (Yellowstone Park, 1960), p. 1. Originally calculated at 7.1 on the Richter scale, recent recalculations have put the 1959 earthquake at 7.5. Alston Chase, in *Playing God in Yellowstone* remarks: "Known in Montana as 'the night the mountain fell,' this was the Hebgen Lake earthquake, at 7.5 on the Richter scale the severest ever recorded in the Rocky Mountains and the second strongest in the history of North America. More destructive than two hundred atomic bombs, it brought new attention to the geology of Yellowstone." (273)

[2]Actually, these fears, which seemed irrational to us then, have more foundation in fact than we knew. The Park is now believed to be the product of a geologically recent caldera of such magnitude that its power exceeded the combined nuclear arsenals of the Soviet Union and the United States.

[3]Charles Darwin made the same observations on a great Chilean earthquake in his February 20, 1835, entry of *The Voyage of the Beagle*. "A bad earthquake at once destroys our oldest associations: the earth, the very emblem of solidity, has moved beneath our feet like a thin crust over a fluid;—one second of time has created in the mind a strange idea of insecurity, which hours of reflection would not have produced."

Part III

18

Change

ON THE SURFACE of things, the summer of 1960 at Madison Junction was just like all the previous summers we had spent there. The museum was unchanged, we returned to our cottage on the edge of the campground, and life went on as usual. But a curtain was coming down. Mission 66 was at last coming to Madison with a host of deleterious consequences. The woods across the road from us were alive with activity. A new road, a new campground, a new government area complete with modern apartments was being chopped out of what had been for years a pleasant and unobtrusive woodland at the base of the mountains along the Madison and Gibbon River valleys. The Townsends were excited about the coming modernity. I was sick at heart at the desecration of an area and the impending loss of a quality of life which made the Yellowstone experience unique for us.

Perhaps because of all that, I find 1960 the hardest summer to remember of all we spent in Yellowstone. We went, relieved and more relaxed than we had been in years because I had passed my prelims at Wisconsin and only the writing of my dissertation now stood between me and the Ph.D., my necessary union ticket to the kind of life I wanted in the academic world.

We were visited at the end of June by John and Faye Scandrett, good friends from our graduate school days in Wisconsin. John was the best combination cellist, physicist, tennis player, all around handyman I have ever known. He and Faye had been in the West, and they were on their way to East Lansing where John had taken a job at Michigan State. Their daughter, Claire, was with them. Claire, now a professional flutist who got her training at Juilliard, was then just a cute, curious, and excitable four-year-old. Each morning she came to the bathroom to watch me shave. I would lather up, get my face covered with soap, and then turn around and give her a swish across the face with shaving soap. She thought this the most exciting and funny thing in her morning, and she would run squealing with joy to her parents. I had to do it every morning they were there.

John also poked around our fitfully burning wood stove and discovered what I had never even looked for: the ash bin which was so choked that it was a wonder we could get any draft at all. He cleaned it out and the stove began to burn wood and heat up as if it were new. That, of course, was an elementary job for John. A more typical spare time occupation for him was, for example, replacing the headlights in his used Sunbeam automobile, a job we found him in the middle of once when we visited them at Bloomington, Indiana, where John had gone after leaving East Lansing. John always liked exotic cars.

As I remember the Scandrett's visit now, I recall that we introduced them to many aspects of our life in Yellowstone. John and I played three innings of wiffle ball, and for two, as I have said earlier, I had him helpless before a gently breaking slider. He was throwing me fastballs, and the pitching distance in our improvised diamond by the side of the cottage was so small that I felt he was releasing the ball about four feet in front of me. I am sure hitters who have stood in against Sandy Koufax or Nolan Ryan when those pitchers were in their prime have felt the same way. The ball gets to you so fast. But I had good reflexes then. I nailed one of those pitches and should have had a home run, but the damn ball hit some branches and I had to take a ground rule double.

We all went fishing one afternoon on the Gallatin, and John and I had a very peculiar experience. Since he was left handed, and I am right, we worked opposite sides of the river and were moving pretty well together. At one point, however, I hooked a small rainbow in the middle of a riffle in the middle of the stream, so John asked me if I minded if he cast there, too. I told him that I didn't mind at all, that we might be into a good hole, and sure enough, he hooked a fish . . . but it was a whitefish! I cast again and hooked another rainbow. John cast into the riffle again and got another whitefish. We did that four times in a row! I am still at a loss to explain why the rainbows were hitting my fly and the whitefish his because we were using the same kind of fly, the same size hook, and were casting into the riffle at the identical place. It defies reason.

The Scandretts also came to one evening program. Friends later told us that John had said, "I was with him *all* day, and he TmeU had no time to prepare that talk." John was referring to a talk I gave about John Colter, the discoverer of Yellowstone. I had given the talk before, and I reviewed it mentally during the day, at quiet productive moments. John's presence did not distract me, but he evidently thought I required some time to go "into my study" and get my head together. For some kinds of subjects that would be necessary, but if one is giving a talk on a subject about which you know as much as you should and for which you have enthusiasm, such preparation is not necessary.

We wished the Scandretts goodbye about the first of July and began the countdown to closing. On July 15 the old Madison Campground closed for good, and the events which occurred between that closing and the opening of the new campground would provide material for a Hollywood comedy . . . or a tragedy, depending on your perspective.

Before the construction became a real problem, however, we had another experience which was novel for us and a bit frightening. July, 1960, was not a typical Yellowstone July. The daily maximum temperature went over 90° on several occasions at our station and at West Yellowstone. A daytime high of 80° is much more normal. We were suffering some from the heat and the fact that nighttime temperatures, which had always been so predictably near freezing or at least down to 40° were staying above 50°. I loved the cool nights and the heavy blankets. They meant good rest and refreshment. Now we had much too much bedding and we slept too warm, and, as a result, fitfully.

The more obvious and unpleasant effect of the sustained drought and hot weather was a steady drying out of the timber and an increasing fire danger. In mid-July the inevitable happened. Fires began breaking out all over the Park. One by one they exploded, three or four hundred acres each, and in no time three were going. All park personnel were on standby if needed to fight the fires. Frisbee was more ready than anyone at our station. Once the campground had closed, our duty had become tedious and boring. He craved action. But he was not called, and we continued to mark time anxiously.

One morning the last week of July two men from the West District sub-station came to the museum to make a call. They were temporarily away from their base but keeping tabs on all the fires and reporting in so that their people could reach them quickly if needed. They also wanted to talk with us about one incident which had already occurred near us. A fire had started up along the Gibbon River just two miles north of us, but it was contained by smoke jumpers and one anonymous but public-spirited Californian who, familiar with forest fires, had stopped his car, taken a shovel from his trunk, and waded the Gibbon River. When he reached the fire, he began shovelling dirt back on it and making a containing ring around it. The smoke jumpers really had mostly mop-up work to do. The anonymous Californian had done the important work of containment. But the fire so close made us very jumpy.

We hoped for rain but got none, just one storm from which came a single spectacular bolt of lightning but no moisture. On

that hot July morning, with fires all over the Park and everyone
on the alert, the two men from the West sub-district made their
call and then stood on the stone porch of Madison Museum, visiting with us about the general state of affairs. In a moment a
white puff of smoke suddenly and explosively billowed up on the
plateau just south of our museum. Within ten minutes Sheridan
and Pelican Cone both sighted it, and the Fire Dispatcher began
organizing men to contain it. For the first time in my Yellowstone
experience, I was sitting right on top of a forest fire and recognizing the fact that I probably would have to go fight it. I did not
like the prospect. Frisbee was jubilant. He was ready to go in an
instant.

Unfortunately, those in charge of fighting the fire in our area
were not the best managerial types. There are those who, in any
kind of crisis, become hysterically self-important, flinging orders
here and there, rushing into action with plans only half-formed,
executing at the scene of the action with a certain reckless aban-
don and lack of purpose that messes up a whole operation. I
cannot say that the fire above our valley was handled with purpose and intelligence. All I remember is a great flurry of activity,
smoke jumpers being called out, fire fighters being rushed into
action, food being requisitioned (on one day the food turned out
to be cheese sandwiches—for hot, dry, thirsty men who had been
working hard all day—the ground was strewn with those rejected
cheese sandwiches).

There were some cool heads, though. Lee Robinson, Old
Faithful's sub-district ranger, got his men organized and functioning purposefully, and the smoke jumpers knew how to go
about their work with dispatch. Bud Lystrup came up from Old
Faithful to run the base-camp out of our now deserted campground. Bud was a veteran of many fires, and he went about his
task in a calm and orderly manner, one sharply contrasting with
the general hysteria which prevailed.

Frisbee had gone right away, and reports later came in that
he was very effective in working spots in front of the main line of
the fire. A good hot forest fire will set up some wicked convection

currents, and burning material will occasionally carry a quarter of a mile in front of the main fire line and greatly complicate things. One has to be either brave or quite mad to go out ahead of the fire and contain such places. Frisbee had no fear.

My own experience, however, was convincing me that too large a number of knaves and fools were involved in the project. I was taken up with a group, and my understanding was that we would be dropped behind the fire line and would work up to it. But the idiot who took us let us out at a different place and told us to walk east in front of the fire to contain it. That did not seem too bright to me, but I went anyway and soon was greeted by one of the most frightening things I have ever seen: a fire crowning out in the tops of trees and coming straight for me. In addition, we were in dense timber and very easily could have become confused about our directions and walked further in front of it. I retreated quickly with another man with whom I fought my way past some extremely dense thickets of small trees—one was so compact that one literally could not get through it—and eventually worked around to the back of the fire. There we began some cleanup work and the process, much more intelligent it seemed to me, of letting the afternoon wind die down so that we could go after the fire on the ground that evening.

We did a lot of digging and shovelling and cutting of timber that evening, to no very great overall purpose that I could see, and then went back to base camp. I stayed there for the duration of the fire, alternately attending to station duty and helping out some in the base camp. The whole business struck me as silly because far too many people were involved in fighting the fire. Both Frisbee and Townsend enjoyed themselves tremendously. They got hot and tired and dirty, but they had wanted combat with Mother Nature, and she had obliged. Because we were so close to it and could get such a mass of people on it quickly, our fire was contained before too long, and the crew disbanded. But the weather stayed dry.

August came and with it considerably cooler weather, but there was no break in the drought. Most of the fires in the Park had been fought and controlled, but everyday the fire danger report was exceedingly high. The timber was still one large mass of kindling waiting for something to set it off.

During this time I remembered some of the stories told to me about fires in the western mountains. Some had been huge conflagrations which covered thousands of acres and burned for weeks. One of Yellowstone's district rangers told us of a fire in Glacier Park that was, if I remember correctly, fourteen miles long and about a mile wide. It had been a bear to contain. A forest ranger (there is a distinction here most people do not know: park rangers, such as those in Yellowstone, are employed by the National Park Service, Department of the Interior; forest rangers are employed by the National Forest Service, Department of Agriculture) told me of the time when he and his companions were trapped in Idaho by a fire coming down a ridge and so they had taken the only resort available to them: refuse in a creek at the bottom of a ravine where they literally had their noses to the water as the fire jumped over them and raced up the ridge. The danger in fires is not being burned to death: it is asphyxiation. A forest fire is a ravenous devourer of oxygen. They had gone to the lowest point, where some oxygen might remain, and put their noses to the ground. They were saved from suffocation and, of course, benefited from the inrush of new air into the vacuum created by the fire which passed over them. An even more remarkable story was told to me by this man who was trapped on the side of another ridge on a different occasion and despaired of saving his life. The fire, he said, was racing down the ridge, and he had no time to get to the bottom of the ravine. Then, an abrupt change of the wind occurred, throwing the smoke and carbon dioxide of the fire right back on it. A fire deprived of oxygen by its own force, dies. It was, he said, the most beautiful natural put-out he had ever seen.

Our weather and our timber stayed dry, so we bit our fingernails and marked the days as they passed in August. Looking back on those years in the light of new management policies, one sees the folly of our concern. Fires have been a regularly occurring phenomenon in forests of the west for centuries.[1] They serve very useful purposes: clearing out ground debris and too densely packed stands of trees thus making more growing room for other kinds of plants and surviving trees; destroying insect infestations such as the pine bark beetle which is disfiguring a number of lodgepole pines in the southern portions of the Park now. Today the Park Service controls only those fires which pose a threat to property or the lives of those in the Park. But we were still in a pre-enlightenment period in 1960.[2] And so we waited each day, and watched.

Then, on the anniversary of the great earthquake of the year before, August 17, the skies turned leaden. Early in the morning, snow began to fall, softly at first and then more and more rapidly. As the hours passed it came in a rush—three inches at our station, five inches at Old Faithful, eight inches at Canyon. The entire tinder box character of the Park's forests changed in one day. The tourists cursed the bad weather. They had waited all summer to come to Yellowstone; they did not appreciate weather which was worse than some got in December. But I put on my warm clothes and exulted in Madison Museum. The snow was so deliciously wet. It soaked everything an inch or two deep. What had been dry wood became soggy, damp, unusable timber. I was sorry

---

[1] In *Playing God in Yellowstone* Alston Chase discusses the extent to which various Indian tribes (including those in and around the Yellowstone plateau) had profoundly and beneficially modified their physical environment by controlled burning of forests. See pp. 94-97.

[2] In view of the awful fires which ravaged so large a portion of Yellowstone in the summer of 1988, one might now easily question Park Service policy in this matter. Actually, the policy is still sound, in years when normal weather prevails. Because of the terrible drought of 1988, however, the Park Service officials should have discarded the policy temporarily and controlled every fire that appeared as quickly as possible. But they did not, and the result has been destruction of Yellowstone forests on a scale that in our worst nightmares, none of us could ever have imagined.

for the tourists. But I was not unhappy to see the fire danger of 1960 end so suddenly and so dramatically. Les Gunzel, then Chief Fire Dispatcher, said that the snow, coupled with the coming cool weather and the inevitable Fall rains, had ended the fire season.

Pat and I missed the activity of the old campground. We also missed Mrs. Taggart and the government road camp which had once provided some life and activity on the other side of the river. We missed our summer friends whose presence meant so much to us in the late 50s. And we could not forget Al Jacobi, dead less than a year, but whose absence was a terrible loss to us and to his family. In many ways I would have to say that 1960 was a somber summer. Too many connections from previous years had been broken.

On one rainy off duty day, Dick Townsend came to the cottage to tell us that a tourist had reported an accident about two or three miles up toward Norris. He had to remain in the station and had no way of checking out the report. We had to do these things ourselves because at that time no protective division personnel were assigned to the Madison area. I did not take the report too seriously, however, because we frequently got accident reports which turned out to be false or greatly exaggerated, usually only mechanical failures. But we had a job to do, so Pat and I drove up toward Norris just to check out the report. What we found was startling, to say the least.

It was raining lightly, and the road was slick. At one very sharp turn along the Gibbon River were the tracks of a car which had skidded and gone down over an embankment. There was a pull-out right next to the curve, so we stopped there and went back to the spot where the car tracks went over the edge. We saw below us a red Volvo with a tremendous dent in its roof, sitting with one back wheel in the river, and three people, a woman and two teenage children, huddled beside it. And cars on the road were going by this scene, just thirty yards away, steadily, and *no one was making any effort to come to the assistance of these people!*

I could not fathom it. In the West there is a tradition of helping one another out, and one frequently saw, in Yellowstone, acts of kindness extended by strangers to others in distress. But this behavior truly dumbfounded me.

Pat and I went down to the river's edge and approached the three who were huddled there. I spoke to the woman. "Excuse me, but you appear to have had an accident. Would you like to come in out of the rain? I'm the ranger stationed at Madison Junction, and I'll be happy to assist you."

They were coherent but really in shock. Why else would anyone sit in the rain beside a car after a wreck? The children were in better shape than their mother—it was a miracle that no one was hurt because the car had rolled once and got that awful dent from a huge boulder which it had struck—and they began telling us what had happened. The children's mother had lost control of the car on the curve; it was much slicker than she thought it was, and they had gone over the embankment before they realized what was happening.

They locked their car, and we took them to our cottage at Madison where they could dry off and get some lunch. We fixed some soup and sandwiches, and that seemed to get them all a bit more settled. They were moving from Michigan to California, and their father/husband was already there, but they would have to call him. We took them to West Yellowstone for that, and Pat and I were relieved to note, from a distance, that the lady's husband asked the right question first. He wanted to know if they were unhurt and generally all right. Property could come later. That question brought a flood of tears from his wife, mostly relief, then some calming, and after that the wrecker, the insurance man, and a train trip from West Yellowstone to California.

All in all, it was a bad experience for that family, but it was one of our better moments. Pat always has had a special feel for the emotions of people in difficult circumstances, and she had good instincts about the things which would be most reassuring and calming to them.

Car wrecks were, of course, something we were always conscious of in Yellowstone. Although the speed limit on Park roads is 45, people abuse it or they are distracted by some sight and do strange things or they get drunk and then all kinds of trouble happen. I was fortunate in not being in the protective division most of those years and thus having to investigate accidents, especially one at Canyon in the late 50s which may have been the worst accident in park history. Nothing in the situation suggested that such a thing could happen, but what car accident ever catches those involved prepared? The only vehicle involved was a small panel truck holding a bunch of boy scouts in the back, in the open, and three girls, park employees, who had hitched a ride on their day off. The truck was going through the Canyon Area about thirty-five miles an hour when it swerved and left the road for reasons I do not know to this day. It hit a tree and kids were tossed carelessly out of it like rag dolls. There were thirteen passengers in or on this vehicle, and only the driver escaped serious injury. Three died, one girl was critically injured and escaped death only because of the presence of an unidentified doctor who administered first aid for hours until the park ambulance got to the scene and took the injured to the hospital. One ranger said he had seen nothing to equal it since he had been in World War II.

We had a certain number of fatalities from kids driving while intoxicated. The pattern was rather familiar. They would be cautious going through areas where there were many curves, but when they came to a wide open straight stretch, they would push the accelerator to the floorboard to see what the car would do and, as expected, lose control and roll it. I suspect that in the more than twenty years since I have worked in Yellowstone, there have been incidents like this every year. Young headstrong kids cannot learn that alcohol and driving do not mix. Why would they? Television commercials tell them, continuously, how to enjoy themselves and relax after a day's hard work or exertion: by drinking. And they believe what they see and hear. Until they die.

19

Our Situation Deteriorates

MUSEUM DUTY and night programs were pretty generally fouled up by the closing of Madison Campground. A temporary camp was established near West Gate, and in 1961 we took our act there. We were even given an electrical outlet, a screen, and a selection of slides so that we could pep up our talks. I still think we learned more from the talks we had to give without slides, but it is true that when telling people about geological formations, birds, flowers, park animals, and geysers, slides help tremendously. The Park Service in Yellowstone has a fine collection.

The experience at West Gate was not very good, however, because the campers there were nothing at all like the community we had at Madison. They were strictly transients, looking for a place to bed down one night and then move on, and their interest in programs was not very great. So the whole experience was, at best, a partial success.

Museum duty was better as long as the roads were still open, because we had steady traffic into the museum and we had our daily talks to give. The busses still stopped, and their crowds gathered. Frisbee did a great service by preparing a sketch of our location in relation to the great slide in the Madison Canyon because many people wanted to go into the earthquake area to see what had happened there. But Frisbee was also restless. He was tired of the monotony of station duty; he wanted to do field work, so he spent his off hours tramping the area and projecting where we might put some good nature trails. Had I known then what I know now, I would have recommended to the Chief Naturalist that Frisbee and Townsend both be transferred, which both were, eventually, to another station where they would be more needed. I could handle the duty at Madison on an 8—5 basis, and I could have offered programs at West Gate two or three times a week. The other days could have been covered by men at Old Faithful.

One of the reasons we did not get these matters worked out, I now believe, was that our administrative structure was changing. Dave Condon, the Chief Naturalist, and Dave Beal, his first assistant, both excellent men, responsible for the development of the fine core of naturalists with whom I worked, had not got along with the new Superintendent. Eventually, they were "promoted" to assignments in other NPS areas, and Yellowstone was divided into separate districts through which we had to requisition our materials. It was a sensible system for the protective division, but it made no sense for the naturalists because we were few and all of our needs had been very adequately taken care of by Dave Condon, Dave Beal, and a third man in the Mammoth Office. We would check in there, requisition our Coleman lamps, bedding, gasoline, and other needs, and get on to our stations. But the new system required us to get this stuff through our districts, and we quickly discovered that in the districts the protective division had permanent men year around while the naturalists were supervised by a veteran seasonal who usually didn't get back each year until the protective division had gotten all the good quarters. Dick Townsend noted, pointedly, that we were moving into a period in which the chiefs were beginning to outnumber the Indians, and that kind of situation inevitably contributes to the growth of an inflexible and stupid bureaucracy.

There is nothing worse than a short-sight bureaucrat, of course (just ask the Russians who have dealt with them for centuries), and I discovered that pointedly when dealing with the Bureau of Public Roads during the period when the new campground was being built. The incidents which follow occurred during the summer of 1961, and they characterize the closed and short-sighted bureaucratic mind at its very worst.

Situation: I had done my usual morning chores: putting up the flag, unlocking the museum, sweeping the floors, and cleaning the glass on the exhibit cases. This work usually took around half an hour, and we did it in the cool morning hours before many visitors came into the museum. I had paid no attention to the traffic while I was doing this chore. About 9:30 Pat came in to ask me how many people had been through the museum that morning. I looked at my counter: only five. That would be all for the day, she said. I asked her how she came to that remarkable conclusion.

"They've opened the new road and closed the old one."

"What? They haven't put the signs up yet! The parking lot isn't even paved! Who the hell made that decision?"

"I don't know. I'm just telling you what I saw on the way down here."

I was livid. The old roads at the Junction, from Norris, from West Gate, and from Old Faithful passed right in front of the museum and its parking lot. No one had any trouble finding our place. And those who wanted to stop and get a drink of water or go to the nearest campground restroom, had little difficulty locating those either. But the new road went *behind* the museum, under a slight ridge and through a cut which effectively made it impossible to see our building. Furthermore, since there would be no access to the parking lot, no one could even get into our place. Someone had abruptly shut down our whole operation without consulting us.

I was really steaming, and I went out looking for the responsible parties. I found the man in charge: the chief official of the Bureau of Public Roads, hereafter referred to as the BPR man, and began to ask him some questions in a hurry. Although I was a hot tempered kid when little, I had, over the years, learned my father's self-control and congenial disposition and was not used to making waves. But this action was so mindless that it short circuited all of my usual self-control. I can see the guy yet: probably in his early forties, curly black hair, the look of efficient stupidity which characterizes builders whose satisfaction in the completion of a project makes them unable to see that project in a larger context. Our BPR man was very happy at getting his road open close to his deadline. He even told me so. This is what I told him.

"Well, I appreciate your desire to meet construction deadlines, but I've got some other concerns you might like to think about. Three of us are working in that museum, and as things now stand, the general public we are paid to serve can't even get to us! What do I tell my boss, the Chief Naturalist—that I've got three men sitting in an inaccessible museum whittling and whistling while the public goes buzzing by on this wonderful new slab of asphalt you've opened? Why can't you leave the old road open until people can get to the museum by the new one? And, by the way, how long will it be until you get some signs up and that parking lot paved?"

"I think about a week and a half on the parking lot."

"A week and a half? Are you out of your gourd? A week and a half? I'm supposed to tell my men that we sit here for 10 or 11 days with nothing to do? Give me a better answer."

"Well, we want to begin to remove signs of the old road, and we can't have people driving on it now that the new road is open."

"Oh, to hell with your new road! What is this park? A giant trafficway or a place for people to view and appreciate a variety of natural wonders? You talk like a goddamned city engineer. We have a job of interpretation to do. Why didn't you consult with me before you decided to close the old road? I could have saved you some grief right now by pointing out our problems!"

I might as well have been talking to a chunk of rhyolite. The dim-wit was determined that his new road should stay open, that the old road would be closed, and that the parking lot behind the museum would be paved in a week and a half. I think now that had I not raised a big fuss they would have taken their own sweet time getting the parking lot paved, but they at least discovered that something besides new roads had priority at Madison Junction, and they had better figure a way to get the public into the museum. I did make one point with this BPR guy: he would tell me before they did anything else of significance in the area. And he did, and the second thing they did was even more stupid than the first.

Curly Locks showed up at the museum early one morning to tell me that they were going to take out the old bridge over the Gibbon River. It was no longer needed since they now had the new road and bridge.

"Okay, I appreciate knowing that, but there's a problem."

"What's the problem?"

"A water line is attached to that bridge. It serves our drinking fountain and the public restrooms down the path. If you knock down that bridge, we have no drinking fountain and no restroom. On hot, dusty afternoons, people on bus parties, particularly, look forward to a pit stop and a drink of water."

"Oh, they're going to take care of those problems in the new museum."

"What new museum? A replacement for this one? (I knew at the time that a considerable argument was going on over the preserving of Madison Museum. A man from the Western Office of Design and Construction had come to check out our building, and he asked me how I felt about it. I told him unequivocally that I thought ours was a beautiful building, functional in that it served the purpose for which it was intended and aesthetic because it blended so beautifully into the landscape. It was a perfect structure in the national park setting. BPR didn't know I knew these things.)

"Oh, the new museum they're going to build up at the edge

of the parking lot."

I thought I would go along with that fantasy for a bit.

"How soon will this museum be built?"

"In about three years, I think."

"What? THREE YEARS? Are you nuts? For *three* years we are supposed to tell people that there is no drinking fountain, no restroom at this station? That's the silliest thing I ever heard."

He heard no more. He had done his duty. He had informed me. So, the next day there was the steam shovel with the wrecking ball hanging from its crane. The pounding began, and chunk by massive chunk, the old bridge came down. But I knew trouble was coming, soon.

A few days later, when our parking lot was completed and vehicles once again had access to our station, a bus party arrived. "Ranger, could you tell me where the water fountain is? Ranger, which way to the restroom?"

"I'm sorry, but we have no water fountain or restroom here."

For a moment these people looked at me, blankly, uncomprehendingly, as if I had said something like "We don't use money here." The full import of my message came to those in greatest discomfort first.

"What? Did you say no restroom or water fountain here? You did? That's outrageous? Why not?"

Briefly, I told them the story of Curly Locks and his wrecking ball. That made them even more livid. "Who did you say's responsible for this idiocy? The what bureau? By God, some heads are going to roll! I have connections." And much more muttering.

Park visitors travelling in their own cars were no happier. A few days earlier, one woman driven by desperation had had her daughter drive around a barrier and down the old road as they hunted for our museum and restroom. They stopped me as I walked to work, and I gave them the bad news. The old woman just threw up her hands and cried for mercy.

The situation was not going to remain static very long, I predicted. In *two weeks* angry bus passengers had written angry letters to their congressmen who had sent those angry letters to the Department of the Interior which passed them to the National Park Service which promptly told the Yellowstone Park Service to do something about the problem. Which they did by digging dry toilets along the path to the old previously functioning restroom. The water fountain problem had no solution.

Eventually, the Park Service created a picnic area behind the museum, and it built modern restrooms connected into the present water system. The old museum, as I have indicated, remains, but gutted of the interior features which once made it so attractive.

Yellowstone's own bureaucrats, not to be outdone by those of the federal government, had their own moments of lunacy during the period of new construction. The apartments were built, and we were to be very grateful for this great improvement in quarters. I'll have more to say about them in a moment, but I first I have to report one incident which happened about a week after we moved into the new apartments. They were surrounded by asphalt, of course, for parking and traffic. I longed for the dirt roads of the old camp, the smell of wet earth and pine trees soaked by rain, the scurrying of the chipmunks and ground squirrels under and around the cottage. The small creatures of the forest cannot burrow into asphalt. But the district's maintenance people had a very protective instinct about it. Ray Baker, one of the protective division's patrolmen, was washing his car on a Sunday afternoon when the district maintenance foreman came wheeling into the parking area at high speed.

"Hey you! Stop that! Stop washing that car!"

Ray looked up at him in a rather puzzled way. "Why?" He thought perhaps the water was being rationed for purposes of which we had not been informed.

"You'll get that asphalt all wet!"

Ray didn't think he had heard the man correctly. "What?"

"I said you'll get that new asphalt all wet!"

Ray was a school principal, hence no dummy, but he was also a politic man. With a puzzled but charmingly pleasing look on his

face, he said to the district foreman: "But ____, what are you going to do when it rains?"

Ray never told me the man's answer, but I would love to
have seen his face at that moment. I still think Ray had to stop
washing his car. I suppose one could reason that he should never
drive a new car because he might wear it out, if one were inclined
to this kind of logic. Let's see: don't walk on the concrete—you'll
wear out the sidewalk. Don't open a book and read it; use will
cause deterioration of the pages. Don't put on new clothes; you
might get dirt on them, and they would have to be cleaned. Well,
you get the point. People who protect asphalt parking lots get
locked into a frame of mind which makes them say and do nutty
things.

Even the bureaucrats of business fumbled the ball on this
project. We were supposed to be thrilled at the advent of modern
conveniences in our hitherto rustic and primitive Yellowstone
quarters. We were getting running water, electrical power, and
thermostatically controlled heat. We got the running water all
right. That part of the job was well done. But Montana Power
had evidently done very little thinking about the nature of the
Yellowstone forest. It was right before their eyes: acres and acres
of *fallen* lodgepole pines. These trees grow in bunches, crowd
each other out, die, and fall . . . onto freshly constructed power
lines. The slightest wind or storm created repeated power failures in those first months.

Imagine the delight Pat and I took in going to West Yellowstone, buying perishables and ice cream and frozen foods. We
were going to eat in Yellowstone like we did in civilization. No
more Coleman stove; no more ice chest; no more wood chopping
and erratic heat from pot-bellied wood stoves. So, we filled the
refrigerator and prepared to live like kings. But then a gentle
breeze blew so many trees on the power lines that they were out
for twelve hours. Bring back the Coleman stove; save what you
can in the ice chest; eat as much of the frozen stuff as possible
and kiss the rest goodbye. And that wonderful thermostatically
controlled heat? Our oil burning stoves filled with oil which,

when ignited, caused awful roaring fires. We could never adjust them to regulate anything. And when the power failed, we couldn't even *use* them. I remember well the agony of freezing to death in those wonderful new quarters and remembering in detail, the warmth radiating from a wood stove, properly stoked, which would not be stopped by rain or lightning or trees on power lines. The old days seemed infinitely better. I never wrote a letter to Montana Power expressing my gratitude for bringing to us all the good things of life.

Before leaving the subject of bureaucrats, I should not omit one person who, while he worked for the government, never got trapped into the kind of tunnel vision which some of his colleagues did. He was a fine man, dedicated to his work, and thorough but sensible in seeing that it was done well. His name, the spelling of which I can only approximate, was Hans Schieffler, and he was a graduate of the Berlin Polytechnic Institute. He left Germany during the 1930s because of the increasingly intolerable political situation and came to America. When I knew him he was employed by the National Park Service in the Western Office of Design and Construction.

Hans was the principal architectural engineer in building the present Madison Amphitheater. I know because I watched him supervise the work as I stood at the back door of the museum. He had chosen a gently sloping hillside for the seats, and the screen was to be placed at the bottom of the hill. Through a series of weights and pulleys, an immensely heavy metal screen could be lowered after each evening program so that those coming for the next program would file into the amphitheater and have, before them, a view of the Madison Valley, the historic campsite at the junction of the Firehole and Gibbon Rivers, and the elk which frequently grazed in that area. The screen would be raised only when the slide show was ready to be presented. In practice, the concept worked perfectly. I know because I gave some programs in that amphitheater, and it was aesthetically as pleasing a place in which I have ever lectured.

Hans was particularly concerned about the grade down the

hill. He wanted it to be sufficient so that one row could see comfortably over the heads of another, but he didn't want it too steep.

"Vee should do zis mit shoffels, men vorking mit shoffels," he would say, as he sighed and went back to pacing up and down with the man running the grader which was determining the slope. Hans made that poor fellow move the dirt back and forth, back and forth, over and over again, until he could get something approximating the grade he wanted. The man on the grader would say to me, in moments when he was eating lunch or drying off from the exertion, "You know, that feller wants me to grade this thing down to the half inch, but you can't do that with a machine." No, I thought, you can't. You should do ziss mit shoffels, men vorking mit shoffels.

Hans had been trained in the old school. He told me that when he graduated he was, like most young people, full of enthusiasm for the career ahead of him and anxious to begin, immediately, creating immortal works. His first assignment, if I remember what he told me correctly, was to assist in building the beautiful gardens along the Danube near Budapest, and his expectations were soaring.

"The first day; I never forget that day. The architect in charge (he named a man who I am sure is famous among architects but whose name did not mean a lot to me) told me to pick up trash and trow it over a vall. A vall, mind you! A janitor could do zat vork. I vas furious! Why, I say to myself, am I on zis job to throw trash over a vall?"

But Hans was also disciplined. He spent the day doing just what he had been told to do: throw the trash he picked up over a wall. The next day he got a better assignment. The reason, he told me, was that the architect in charge wanted to see whether or not he was disciplined enough to do the laborious and cruddy work which goes with any project. All young architects want to do the glamorous jobs; few take on the tedious ones.

The summer of 1961 was, in many ways, personally uneventful for Pat and me because we were in the apartments which were acceptable (except when the power failed), I was no longer fishing as much as I used to, and we were not doing much travelling or hiking on our days off. There was a good reason for this. Pat was pregnant with our long delayed first child, and I was treating her like a queen. She rather liked being spoiled; it was a nice trade-off for the discomfort of pregnancy, and she liked the modern conveniences to a point. After years of roughing it, it was nice to have electric lights, a stove which cooked food quickly and without gasoline odors, a shower and bath, and the amenities of civilized life. I still missed the privacy of the cottage. But we had a nice arrangement that year. We were on the end of the string of apartments, and the couple next to us were just married, so they took one of the bedrooms and we took the other.

I should explain. These apartments, with all their modern conveniences, had been designed by an idiot who viewed people as chess pieces, not as human beings. The government people pointed out to us how intelligent and flexible the design of these quarters was. At the east end of the complex there were our living room, kitchen, and bathroom. Two bedrooms were placed between our living room-kitchen-bathroom section and that of the adjacent apartment. The theory was this: if a couple without children lived in one of the apartments, they could sleep on the hideabed in their living room and the couple next to them, with say two children, would get both bedrooms. Or the arrangement could provide for each apartment getting one of the bedrooms. Fine. Flexible use of space . . . for animals in fancy pens.

Were there problems? You're damned right. You see, one of the doors to our bedroom, if opened, led directly into the living room of the next apartment. Suppose my wife and I wanted to go to sleep and the occupants of the next apartment were having a party. Could you sleep with conversation going on ten feet from your bedroom door? Could you make love, knowing that every creak of the bed, every endearing expression you said, might be food for the ears of the people just outside the door?

That is why I concluded that the idiot who designed the apartments had the sensitivity of a clod of dirt. He or she was interested in efficiency and flexibility, not in quarters which were both physically and emotionally comfortable for human beings. Our first year we managed, however, because of the young couple next door. They went to bed when we did, so we were both in opposite bedrooms at the same time. But 1962 was just plain grim. A family with children moved in and denied us both bedrooms. We had a seven-month old baby whose crib we had to place in a recessed portion of the wall and for whom Pat had to design a special curtain to act as a partition from the rest of the room. Further exacerbating our difficulties was one of the children of the family next door who cried incessantly, right next to our living room. Ellen did not sleep well all summer.

To make matters still worse, the senior seasonal at our station (there had been a great shuffle of people and one of the Old Faithful veterans who outranked me had replaced Dick Townsend) assigned me all evening hours so that I was not home when I was most needed. He thought he was doing me a favor. I should have had guts enough to say, "Wait a minute. The shifts we had in previous years were just fine. Don't mess around with them." But I was a sheep for some strange reason which now escapes me, and I said nothing. Pat was miserable spending all her evenings alone with a restless and upset child. Things got very tense.

We did not fully realize how disoriented Ellen had been (remember, this was a seven-month-old child) until we returned to Illinois in the fall. We had moved from Madison, Wisconsin, when I finished my degree in late June, spent four days in Urbana, and then headed west. Ellen had never lived in Illinois, but the moment we returned to a house which contained a rug she recognized, a sofa and rocking chair and other items of furniture with which she was familiar, she gave a little cry of delight, wiggled so that I would put her down, and began crawling all over the little university-owned house in which we were living. She was psychologically back home, out of an environment which had disoriented and troubled her. I think she would have been very comfortable and contented in the old cottage. There we had an extra bedroom, and we would have had room for her crib. We would also have been spared the continual crying of the children of the ranger who had taken both bedrooms in the apartment complex. I do not remember the year with any great affection.

There were other things about 1962 which were upsetting. It was cold all summer; we never did get a warming up and a real mountain summer. I noticed the contrast because it was so stark with the previous year. In 1961, when Pat was pregnant, we had one of the bedrooms, the weather was normal, and our lives, even in the apartments, had been pretty tranquil.

My sister and her husband had visited us that summer, pulling a trailer which was nerve-racking and a chore, but they enjoyed the vacation once they got into the campground, and the kids—they had two of their three with them—could get out and run around and play. My nephew was particularly restless and needed room to run and let off steam. He had that, and their visit was pleasant. It even had some amusing moments.

I was so used to going fishing there that I paid little attention to some aspects of our environment which caught my brother-in-law's attention immediately. For example, I was taking him through the woods toward the Gibbon River for a morning's fishing one day, and he seemed very uneasy and a bit frightened. Then he said to me, "You don't suppose those buffalo are around here, do you?" He was referring to three old buffalo bulls which no longer followed the herds to high country in the summer. They grazed and sunned themselves around Madison Junction and lived a pretty contented life. We accepted them. Whenever I went fishing on the Gibbon I was alert to their presence and gave them a wide berth; I am not stupid around wild animals. They don't like to be crowded, especially buffalo, and I was always very courteous about respecting their wishes. The buffalo and I got along just fine. But my brother-in-law had seen them, and he was as jumpy as a nervous squirrel.

Imagine his pulse rate, then, as we came out of the woods along the top of a small glacial moraine and one of the old bulls just fifty yards away stood up and began watching us nervously.

My brother-in-law was anxious to put a lot of distance between himself and the buffalo in a very short time. I told him to stay cool and not worry. We walked casually away from the buffalo, and he sat down again and went on resting.

In 1962 I didn't have much time to worry about buffalo or fishing. We spent most of our time adjusting to the rotten schedule, the weather, and our new child. My sister and her husband came back again that summer, but it turned into a very bad experience for them. They were pulling a tiny house trailer and this time had three small kids in tow. Worse yet, it rained most of the time they were there. Have you ever been far from home, in a fifteen foot trailer with nothing to do and three restless kids to entertain? That is no vacation. That is a sustained headache and stomach ulcer. In fact, the night they came in, Don, my brother-in-law, was not in too good shape. He had a migraine headache which was dividing his mind. I mean that quite literally. He looked, visually, as if someone were doing brain surgery on him without anesthesia. Neither the weather nor the mountains could provide him the relief which he had experienced the previous summer when we took several days to fish leisurely, enjoy the summer sunshine of the mountains, and get a change of pace. In 1961 he had told me that his productivity would double if he had those months in the mountains in the summer away from his job. I know now what he meant but did not then.

I should not have been surprised that the summer of 1962 turned out to be such a trial for us. There were too many stresses in our previously routine and tranquil life. The problems began with what should have been one of the happiest moments in our lives: the birth of our first child. She was a doll (still is), and we should have done nothing but toss her around with unrestrained affection and absorb her into our routine without missing a beat. But I was too cautious. We never had a lot of money, but Pat quit work six weeks before Ellen was born, depriving us of needed income and her of something to occupy her. That was a mistake. I think now she should have gone on working as long as she was not too uncomfortable. Then, after the baby was born, I tried to take on the role of breadwinner while Pat stayed home taking care of the child. But that was confining and drove her nuts. And I wasn't earning enough money to make ends meet so we had to borrow from my parents. Very stupid all that. Very stupid. Just one example of 20/20 hindsight. So we had too many stress points —adapting to a new baby and dealing with a shortage of money —and I was job hunting, a search which eventually ended when I accepted a position at the University of Illinois.

At the time the thought of going to a good Big Ten school was exhilarating because I would literally be moving from the student to the teacher without changing the kind of environment in which I had been living. But it is one thing to accept a job at a place like Illinois and quite another to stick it out, get tenure and promotions in some regular order, especially when powerful people in the department have one perception of what English teachers should do and you have quite another.

Illinois was a lot of lessons for me, and it was geographically barren, a situation made even more depressing by the fact that Dutch elm disease had terribly denuded the campus. This made even more apparent the essential flatness of the terrain around Champaign-Urbana. I was born among the small but pronounced hills of Kansas City and lived in the hills at Lawrence, Kansas, and Madison, Wisconsin. Summers, of course, I was spending in the mountains of the West. Why I did not notice the flatness when I went to Illinois I will never understand. Had I known that I would have to give up the western trips and spend entire years in Illinois, I would have been even more desolate than I became. But that is part of another chapter in another book which I may never write.

The fact is, we had made our decision for Illinois. I was already late getting out west that Summer, and had first to move to the university-owned house in Urbana before we could go west. The mover came and we headed south, struggling with a clutch which had almost gone out in our 1954 Chevrolet. It was so bad that I had to have it fixed in Champaign which made us still one more day late going west. Pat's mother came from St. Joe to help us in Urbana, and we unpacked there briefly, loaded the car for the trip west, and got moving. It was not fun.

We dropped Pat's mother off in St. Joseph, but we had the long haul in a car made much smaller by the baby crib in the back seat, the need for periodic stopping to give Ellen her formula, the washing up of bottles at night in motels when Pat was already so tired that she was spaced out. She needed the rest, too, because she had helped me type my thesis, a 350-page effort of average quality in an era in which carbon paper was still in. We had no xerox machines, no liquid paper, no home computers/word processors. Instead, we had mechanical, not electric, typewriters. The effort nearly disabled us.

When we eventually arrived in Yellowstone, to be met and congratulated on the degree and the new baby by our friends there, we were so drained and so strung out that we could not appreciate the experience. There was no joy in it for us. But it was good to be back in the mountains, except that we now had a new anxiety: we were miles from competent doctors and this worried us, particularly with Ellen who was only seven months old. And the cold weather . . . and the rotten work schedule . . . and the apartments in which we had insufficient space and Ellen was unsettled.

If you have noticed a contrast between my enthusiasm in describing the golden years and the later ones, you are correct. This was not a good year. And things were not to get any better in 1963.

20

Goodbye
To Yellowstone

I SHOULD have known from the first day I arrived that 1963 was to be my last summer in Yellowstone. I discovered that the world I had known and loved was in disarray. Eight years at Madison Junction were over. The new dispensation—a new chief naturalist, a new assistant chief naturalist, the delegating of authority in each district to a senior seasonal naturalist—were all part of a plan that was disrupting my experience of the previous years. And at that time I wasn't very flexible. In 1963 some changes for the better were actually occurring. West District actually had a permanent man as senior naturalist: Chuck McCurdy. He was—is still, I am quite sure—a very decent, compassionate, and capable man, but in that year he was tossed into a den of wolves. He was new to the Park, and the protective division men who had preceded him took full advantage of that fact.

I was to be stationed at Old Faithful. I liked the Old Faithful area very much—it had been my location during that wonderful first summer of 1951—but in 1951 I was a single male undergraduate college student. In 1963 I was a college professor with a wife and a small baby, and after years of the tranquillity of Madison Junction, minus the summer of 1962, I suddenly found myself assigned to a living area that was about two miles from the station. The rangers and the concessionaires both housed their people in this remote back area of Old Faithful, a place not too far from the sewage treatment plant, a fact the significance of which was not lost on us, and to my amazement and horror, I discovered that I was to be put into the trailer Pat and I had had in 1957. It had been barely tolerable for us then. Now, we had no place in it for the baby, and the oil burning heater, which had never been very good, gave off asphyxiating fumes and leaked oil steadily. Pat was in despair. Our old cottage at Madison, particularly the one near the museum, would have been wonderful. No matter that it lacked electricity. We would have had room for ourselves and the baby, I would have been nearby, our friends in the old campground would have been around to help spoil Ellen and perhaps give us some baby-sitting relief. I can think of all kinds of reasons why that situation would have been better.

But that was all past, and we were thrown into a new living situation in grossly inadequate quarters, and our only consolation was that our nearest neighbors were the Lewises and the Marlers, both of the men veteran seasonals that I liked. But I had to take the car to work, something that had never been necessary before, and something that was very bad for Pat because of the sense of isolation it gave her, something she certainly didn't need then, and we had no space and that with a small child. At least the apartments at Madison had been new and clean and roomy. It was a demotion in quarters that was ill-timed and most unfortunate. I took one look at the trailer, the leaky oil-burner, and the situation, and said to Pat, who was both desperate and grim: "This will not do. If I can't work out something better, we will leave. I will resign."

Those were terrible thoughts for me then; I was reluctant to give up the Yellowstone experience, but emotionally it was turning into a nightmare, and just at a time when we needed some-

thing else very badly. Illinois was no picnic; it was barren, emotionally, geographically, and socially for us, and we needed that
comfort, peace, and tranquillity that Yellowstone had given us in
years past. None of that was now available. I went to see Chuck
McCurdy and told him bluntly that my quarters were simply un-
acceptable and that I would have to get better quarters or leave.
This was unfair to Chuck; he was having plenty of problems just
making the adjustment himself, and he certainly didn't need veteran seasonals pressuring him, but I had never before been a
bastard about anything, and this occasion was the limit. I had to
have a change.

I got a change. The old trailer was hauled away, and we were
given a tolerably larger one, but it was still very confining for a
mother and small kid. We needed one of the portable houses
that others had. Bill Lewis had one; so did George Marler, but
they had large families and seniority at Old Faithful. I didn't
mind that. What I really resented was the fact that a protective
division man had one of them, and whereas I had twelve years in
the Park, he had five, and he had no children. How did he get
that place when I, who should have outranked him, got only a
crummy trailer?

My sense of personal injustice didn't last very long. I became
aware of what they had done to Joe Murphy, and that was even
more outrageous. Here was a naturalist—an authority on eagles,
and one of the finest men and biologists that I had the privilege
of working with in Yellowstone—and he got a trailer and a *tent* in
which three of his kids had to spend the summer. A goddamned
tent while this protective division man with far less need sat
comfortable in his house. And all because the protective division
got there first and glommed off all the good quarters for their
people before Chuck McCurdy and the naturalists realized what
was happening.

This new dispensation took its toll, however. At the end of
1963 the Park Service lost two good naturalists: Joe Murphy and
Don Stewart. I know that Joe, who is a professor of biology at
Brigham Young, left as reluctantly as I did, but you cannot treat

people the way we were treated and keep them. Actions of this kind melted most of the fine naturalist division of which I was a part in the late fifties, and I don't think Yellowstone has ever recovered. It was a terrible shame. The taxpayers lost something, too. They lost people who were knowledgeable and competent in all areas of the Park. Yellowstone was well served through the 1950s. After that. . . .

So we settled into life in the quarters area. Pat had Ellen in the trailer while I went off to do battle with the public and the geyser. Pat's life was exceedingly boring. Mine was a bit too exciting. Old Faithful (Ellen called the geyser "whooshy-whoosh" when she saw it) never was anything like Madison Junction. Although we had occasional spurts of activity at Madison, perhaps as many as 1,000 visitors in a single day, they came in mid-morning and early afternoon. By four o'clock, the museum was usually pretty quiet, and I could read about Yellowstone personalities and history, or watch the chipmunks and squirrels chase each other or even stare eyeball to eyeball with our periodic weasel as he crossed the ledge in front of the big picture window looking out upon the Madison Valley. It was a supremely good life.

At Old Faithful everything was in motion. For the person who is about to see a geyser for the first time in his life, the moment is a big one, and he wants to know "just when it will go off." One Old Faithful naturalist once published an article in the *Saturday Evening Post* on some twenty different ways you could ask about a forthcoming eruption of Old Faithful. Our schedules were keyed to it. When you came on duty, the first thing you checked was the approximate time of the next eruption. Old Faithful naturalists had the guessing game on it down pretty well. In the earlier decades of the century they had observed the eruptions and timed the intervals between them, arriving at an average interval of around 63-67 minutes. It varied some from season to season. But their guesses were often far off the mark until Harry Woodward started timing the eruptions in 1938. He discovered a correlation between the length of an eruption and the interval. In general the rule was, with some exceptions and refinements, short eruption (about two minutes), short interval, say about 45 or 50 minutes; long eruption (four minutes or so), long interval, about 75 minutes. We could get pretty close that way. The man on the desk had the responsibility for timing the eruption and making the prediction on the next one. He also had the job of coping with a three-deep pile of people and their questions about everything from the next eruption to the location of the bathroom. The man who left the desk went out to give a talk at the cone of the geyser. He would try to anticipate the eruption so that the talk would take about ten minutes before the geyser began to play.

Giving a talk at the cone of Old Faithful was not as easy as it looked. A small microphone was located in a small stone obelisk about fifty yards from the orifice of the geyser. The speakers were located in the trees about 75 yards from the mike. The first thing the novice at Old Faithful discovered was that his voice came back about half a second late. If you have ever tried to keep going while a delayed echo is coming back at you, you know what I mean. I have seen some otherwise stout and brave men become absolutely tongue-tied by the difficulty of speaking in that situation. I adapted quickly. I simply screened out all the background noise, including my own voice, and talked into the microphone as if I were having a conversation with a person standing next to me. After some practice and thought about the kind of talk I wanted to give, I developed a very good routine. But Lystrup, who was our senior seasonal that year, wrote in his report that I had given the best talk he had ever heard at the cone of Old Faithful, and he mentioned the amount of information I had worked in, not only about Old Faithful but about geysers in general and the basins of the Firehole. I was proud of that because it was the culmination of several years of experience in practical rhetoric.

After eruptions, we would take a party of people for a walk over the geyser hill, stopping at times to point out specific geysers and pools as well as various hot spring phenomena and formations. I consider myself fortunate not to have been the unlucky man who had one small boy in his party—this occurred some years later—whose glasses became fogged and who fell into a hot pool right before his parents' eyes, struggled very briefly, and sank out of sight. A few bones were all that were ever recovered.

The sheer horror of such a tragedy—always possible on geyser hill because some people did not hold their children closely and the small ones did not realize the danger of open pools whose temperature was 180 degrees Farenheit, still dumbfounds me today. As a matter of fact, I tried to forestall exactly such events by giving a brief lecture on the dangers of open pools before I took the party with me. Often I saw parents take the hands of restless children and grip them tightly, explaining to them that on *this* occasion, they were going to be held in check whether they liked it or not. You don't get second chances in places like geyser basins.

Museum duty was very wearing. People crowded around the desk three-deep. They wanted to buy publications; they wanted information on things to see and roads to take; they wanted fishing regulations; they wanted information about specific geysers or formations; they wanted to know something about campgrounds and accommodations.

Once in awhile, however, we had some entertaining moments. The best one I remember involved a tall man who strode purposefully into the museum and asked me, "Where is the bubbler?"

"Straight through that door and halfway into the arbor back there."

"Thanks."

When he came back, I said to him, "Where do you live in Wisconsin?"

"Milwaukee." He had hardly uttered the word when an expression of growing astonishment began to come over his face. He had suddenly realized the absurdity of a complete stranger in a remote corner of Wyoming asking him where he lived in Wisconsin. He looked down at his shirt.

"How did you know I was from Wisconsin? I'm not wearing

any clothing with Wisconsin logos. Did you see me drive up?"

"No."

"Okay. How did you know I was from Wisconsin?"

"Your speech gave you away."

"My accent?"

"No. One word."

"Yeah? What's that?"

"Bubbler. I know of very few people, outside of some New Yorkers or your neighbors in northern Illinois who call public drinking fountains 'bubblers.' "

"You're kidding! What do you call them?"

"Oh, water fountains, drinking fountains, something like that."

"And we're the only ones who call them bubblers?"

"Almost. Most of the time, a 'bubbler' user will be from Wisconsin." That was the English teacher turned ranger. Couldn't resist the opportunity.

While I was at Old Faithful I had my first close experience of the division between the protective division and the naturalists. I had seen it surface when I was at Lake in 1952, in the snide comments Steve made about the naturalists. There was no one at Old Faithful like that, but still you noticed a difference. The protective division, because they patrolled the roads, did the law enforcement work on crazy cooks who occasionally disturbed the peace and quiet of the Old Faithful night, dropped in on illegal parties along the Firehole, etc. developed a certain machismo. They were the *men* of the Park Service. Naturalists, who sold books and told the dudes where to see what, and led the parties around geyser basins, were just posey pickers, overgrown Boy Scouts on a holiday in the mountains. It was a perception they couldn't shake, and a most unfortunate one. The real *men* of the Park Service were those naturalists. They presented the Park Service's image to the public; they were, as a group, better educated than their counterparts in the protective division; and they were more efficient at fighting forest fires when they had to than the others.

To give the protective division its due, however, I will admit that they had nasty work to do on occasion, and from what I hear and read in recent months, their work has gotten worse. In my youth, savages would occasionally have unscheduled parties along the river and booze it up a bit. If they were caught, they had to put out the fire and pay a fine for building it and littering in an unapproved area. Since then we have seen the rise of illegal drug use in our culture and the attendant violence that has gone with it. I can visualize a ranger dropping in on a party now and getting shot because the partyers are OD'd on God knows what. I don't like the idea of thugs in Yellowstone. Let them wander the streets of our major cities, their more natural environment, where both they and law enforcement personnel have some understanding of the rules of the game between them.

I remember an amusing story from the old days told by Ray Baker. He was patrolling at night, and as he passed Midway Geyser Basin, he heard voices and splashes. That meant that some savages were swimming in the Firehole River where the runoff from Excelsior Geyser poured so much boiling water into the river that it was positively comfortable. I do not remember there being any law against people doing that, but we discouraged it because night swimming in streams is not the safest thing to do. People have accidents and get drowned without their companions realizing it before it is too late. Ray was going to stop and suggest to the young people that they ought to come out of the water, but a more persuasive argument presented itself to him immediately. He turned the patrol car's spotlight directly on the swimmers splashing in the water. There were some squeals of surprise and embarrassment, the "Oh ranger, you caught us, didn't you?" type. The savages regarded such encounters as a kind of game. Ray then moved the light slowly over the water and up the far side of the bank, eventually bringing the beam right onto a large grizzly bear sitting at the edge of the river and evidently trying to figure out what was going on. Ray said he never saw savages come out of the Firehole as fast as that group did.

When I joined the Old Faithful naturalists, it was with a

sense that I was going to be tested with the Park's professionals. At that time Old Faithful had three men, Sam Beal, Bud Lystrup, and Ted Parkinson, each of whom had over twenty summers experience in the Park. George Marler had once been a seasonal, but he was now the Park's geologist, spending most of his time at Old Faithful checking the geysers and hot springs. He knew more about the hot spring phenomena of the Upper Firehole River than any person alive. Bill Lewis and Joe Murphy were in their second decade of service, so that gave us a staff of veteran seasonals who were knowledgeable and alert. I do not remember my other colleagues there now—there were others because Old Faithful was a big station, but faces and names slip away over the years.

As I said, I took my turn at the desk and on geyser hill without difficulty and was soon holding my own very well. But we had the evening programs, too. My topic was "Misconceptions about Yellowstone," and it was a good presentation. Sam was our resident historian, so he took care of the birth of the national park idea, Indians, and other subjects of historical interest; Bill Lewis liked to do the geysers; Murphy took care of biology and birds. I don't remember how we distributed the rest of our work.

We had a good slide collection at Old Faithful, and I appropriated what I needed from it for my talk. Actually, there were many misconceptions about the Park: about its size, its wildlife, and its geysers, especially Old Faithful. How many times I remember people coming to me after the talk, especially Europeans, and saying that they had had the same perception of Yellowstone that our New York visitor to East Gate had: that of a large city park. Two English ladies told me how exhausting it had been for them to travel all day and still be in Wyoming and then to come upon a park of such magnitude. Others were intrigued by the little number I used to do with chipmunks. I would show them a golden-mantled ground squirrel and say, "Now, I know all of you know what that is."

"Yeah. Chipmunk."

"What?"

Epilogue

THIRTY YEARS have passed since Pat and I sat among our friends around Jacobi's campfire in the cool summer evenings in Yellowstone Park. Some of those chairs, Al's, Jack Horner's, and Fred Fischer's, would now be empty. But resting here, on a hot and sultry Kansas summer night, I close my eyes and see Madison Campground, as it was then. We are all sitting around the campfire which flickers unevenly, as light gusts of wind fan it. Fred Fischer draws on his pipe and pokes quietly at the logs smoldering in the pit. Mary Edith has just excused herself, gotten up, and taken Charles Lee off to bed. Arlene, Mary, and Dorothy converse casually over cake and coffee. Cathie sits by her mother, listening intently to the conversation of the women. Freddy is with Carol, both of them half lost in a romantic haze. Al, Charles, Skeets, Pat, and I are listening to another of Jack Horner's stories. He is back again, this time with an account of a flash flood and a night rescue in British Columbia. Jack stands on the roof of his inundated truck swinging his lantern so the rancher who has come rowing his boat to save him can find him. Then he pauses, and a temporary lull settles over the campfire. We are all one people again, contented with a fellowship so deep we cannot express it. Jack smiles quietly and speaks to himself, so softly that only Pat and I, who sit on either side of him, can hear—"So nice . . . so nice to be back among such good friends again."

.............Please Cut Along This Line.............

Wilderness Adventure Books
320 Garden Lane P. O. Box 968
Fowlerville, MI 48836

Please send me:

_____ copies of *MY YELLOWSTONE YEARS* at $12.95

(Postage and sales tax will be paid by the publisher.)

Send check or money order—no cash or C.O.D.

Mr./Mrs./Ms. _____

Street _____

City _____ State/Province _____ ZIP _____